QUALITATIVE RESEARCH SKILLS
FOR SOCIAL WORK

D1478712

For beautiful Otis Leon

Qualitative Research Skills for Social Work
Theory and Practice

MALCOLM CAREY
University of Manchester, UK

ASHGATE

Published by
Ashgate Publishing Limited
Wey Court East
Union Road
Farnham
Surrey, GU9 7PT
England

Ashgate Publishing Company
Suite 420
101 Cherry Street
Burlington
VT 05401-4405
USA

www.ashgate.com

British Library Cataloguing in Publication Data
Carey, Malcolm.
  Qualitative research skills for social work : theory and practice.
  1. Social service—Research—Methodology. 2. Qualitative research.
  I. Title
  361.3'0721–dc23

Library of Congress Cataloging-in-Publication Data
Carey, Malcolm.
  Qualitative research skills for social work : theory and practice / by Malcolm Carey.
      p. cm.
  Includes bibliographical references and index.
  ISBN 978-1-4094-4931-7 (hardback : alk. paper) — ISBN 978-1-4094-4932-4 (ebook)
  1. Social service—Research—Methodology. 2. Qualitative research. I. Title.
  HV11.C317 2012
  361.3072–dc23

2012002372

ISBN 9781409449317 (pbk)
ISBN 9781409449324 (ebk)

Printed and bound in Great Britain by the
MPG Books Group, UK.

Contents

List of Figures and Tables

Figures

Tables

Part 1

Foundations of Qualitative Social Work Research

This book offers an accessible and easy-to-use guide for those undertaking research for small qualitative projects in social work or social care. This might include research undertaken for a dissertation, a Master's degree or larger thesis, or perhaps a small project or evaluative study that links to the role of a specific social work, social care or voluntary organisation. The book may also assist a practising social worker, volunteer or employee based in the third or independent sector who is undertaking qualitative research that relates to aspects of their longer-term interests, casework or general practice.

The book is divided into three sections encompassing, first, the foundations and guiding principles of qualitative social work research, second, its core methods, techniques and methodologies, and, finally, the writing up and dissemination of any findings. This first section looks specifically at indispensable skills, concepts, notions and principles that underpin all forms of research: such as the research process we follow when undertaking a project or what we mean by and what form a methodology may take. Other core principles, including research ethics and the theoretical and philosophical perspectives of qualitative social work research, are also detailed.

1 Introducing Qualitative Social Work Research

Introduction

It is not uncommon for many students and practitioners to feel uncomfortable or even distressed about the prospect of undertaking social research. This is hardly surprising. The reputation of research as a difficult and perhaps mechanical or even tedious set of rituals that are linked to 'scientific' or 'objective' routines and tasks hardly appears inviting. Possibly eventual efforts may also lead to the production of remote, dry, even aloof and impenetrable, reports, books or academic papers. Whilst such stereotypes or even myths may sometimes hold seeds of truth they are far from representative of many researchers and their 'outputs'. Although often challenging, most forms of qualitative social research are also accessible as well as rewarding, relevant and perhaps enlightening. Typically, a research project also allows the instigator to choose their topic of study, to quickly gain expertise, permit control of the majority of the processes followed and, within social work unlike some other disciplines, apply their findings; often to benefit vulnerable groups or communities with whom social workers ply their trade.

Many of the core skills involved in qualitative research are also likely to have already been developed – if not mastered – by many students or practitioners. For example, a typical essay will demand related tasks such as collecting, processing and analysing information. Social work practitioners undertake interviews as part of any assessment or write reports for 'funding panels' or as part of court proceedings. We are therefore at least reasonably prepared for many of the tasks and roles held within the seemingly privileged domain of the professional researcher. Just as importantly perhaps, qualitative research is learnt just as much through direct experience as through study. It can also help promote our imagination and sense of creativity or curiosity and urge to know more. Qualitative social work research can however also be labour intensive and demanding. Whilst true, this book hopes to save the reader time and energy by providing a clear guide on how to focus your study, plan ahead, apply research methods and techniques and develop a theoretical and philosophical framework for a study, and finally how to write up and disseminate any findings.

What is social work?

Before we begin to discuss research in more detail we need to first explore what we mean by 'social work'? Social work is recognised as somewhat difficult to clearly define as the role is broad and encompasses numerous roles and competing responsibilities and tasks. One reason among others for this lack of clarity remains that it is not physically restricted to a confined space such as a classroom or a hospital ward and instead tends to be dispersed as an almost 'invisible trade' within and among a variety of institutions and community settings (Pithouse, 1987). In contrast to teaching in schools, say, social work's core 'business' also entails contact with a broad range of social groups (according to age, ability or gender, etc.) although many of its roles and tasks are class- (Jones, 1983) and gender-specific (Dominelli, 2002), just one of many attributes that distinguishes social work from other welfare professions. Unlike medicine (diagnosis and treatment of symptoms) or teaching (learning) there is also not one universal role that neatly encompasses the social work task: from foster care and adoption to child or adult protection and the provision of domiciliary or residential care to older or disabled people or advice and counselling to people with HIV, among many more examples, there remains a wide range of disparate activities involved within social work that are difficult to neatly categorise or control.

As a result of this eclectic range of largely 'invisible' tasks and roles social work has tended to draw upon a wide variety of theories, models of intervention and skills. This is reflected in the International Association of Schools of Social Work and International Federation of Social Workers (2001) wide-ranging and universal definition of social work practice:

> The social work profession promotes social change, problem-solving in human relationships and the empowerment and liberation of people to enhance well-being. Utilising theories of human behaviour and social systems, social work intervenes at the points where people interact with their environments. Principles of human rights and social justice are fundamental to social work.

Although helpful, this definition is not complete. For example, it understates the social control-related aspects of social work practice, which often sit uncomfortably alongside any social care and support roles. Also there is no recognition of the bureaucracy or regulation which again remains a central part of the social work task (e.g. Jones, 2001, among many others). In essence, as well as being eclectic social work is also a challenging and often unpredictable role that nevertheless accommodates numerous tensions and rewards alongside ethical and political doubts and certainties. It is also now an increasingly diverse organisational pursuit, no longer confined to discrete statutory organisations such as the Social Service Departments of yesteryear (Jones, 1983; Pithouse, 1987). Instead, it remains a more fragmented activity that is spread across a wider range of institutions and 'providers' of 'social care' services: from the multidisciplinary centre in the community to the hospital, and the private foster care company to the 'call centre'.

Qualitative research in context

Research is not merely about gathering information or describing facts in detail and, in social work especially, should also not be too detached from practical and professional life. As Denzin (1970: 323) notes, qualitative social research seeks to also explore and understand its subject matter or people from the perspective of those we are seeking to study and from where they are currently located. We might look at a person's background, where they live, study or work, and perhaps also their relationships, status, ethnicity, gender and role within, say, an organisation, before making judgements, assumptions or drawing conclusions. Ragin (1994: 83–5) adds that qualitative social research often gives voice to marginalised people, including 'the poor, sexual minorities, racial and ethnic minorities, immigrant groups, and so on', a point echoed throughout by Humphries (2008) for social work related research. Yet it can also seek to interpret historically or culturally significant phenomena, including by speaking to minority groups affected by riots, homelessness, discrimination, social policy or service provision. Ragin (1994: 84) adds that qualitative research also often seeks to advance theory, such as by providing 'new information about a broad pattern that holds across many cases ... especially rich raw material for advancing theoretical ideas', or by analysing 'the commonalities that exist across cases [within literature or interviews, etc.]'.

Qualitative research also involves purposeful investigations, searches or processes that collect and evaluate information in order to gain knowledge and understanding. It typically accommodates the identification of a research problem or query and leads to subsequent planning and the use of skills, methods and theory to systematically investigate a social problem or answer a research question. In contrast to quantitative research that may instead prioritise the collection of large-scale objective 'facts', scientific rigour, generalisation, explanation and prediction, qualitative social research will tend to privilege meaning and understanding. This will usually follow the reading of related literature and contact with a small to moderate sized number of research participants. More specifically, as Marvasti (2004: 7) suggests, qualitative research 'provides detailed description and analysis of the quality, or the substance, of the human experience'. Importantly, as with the best and most effective forms of social work practice, it may also seek to promote care and sensitivity to the topic or people under investigation and, ideally at least, look for rich and meaningful textual and/or personal interactions from which greater knowledge and understanding may prosper.

Brewer (2003: 238) offers two practical examples of how qualitative research is distinct:

> Qualitative research might explore how an individual who voted for the Green Party in the United Kingdom sees themselves as a member of a minority group dealing with environmental issues rather than, say, exploring overall voting trends over time for the Green Party and other minority parties within Britain's two-party system … if someone [also] wanted to explore what being vegetarian means to someone, the focus would be on the social meaning around organic food use and animal welfare and so on.

Qualitative social research may also:

- be 'subjective' regarding the researcher's concern or empathy 'with the perspectives of the research subjects';
- attempt to bring the researcher *emotionally* closer to participants, such as through gaining a better understanding of their attitudes or experiences;
- remain flexible, especially with the researcher's capacity to adapt to circumstances and changes through the research journey or process (for example, stop or alter our questions or style during an interview if a participant becomes upset);
- seek to capture the World *in action*, such as how events unfold.

Finally, a notable attribute of qualitative research is the researcher's tendency to revise and reflect upon the research process or journey as it unfolds. In contrast to more 'scientific' quantitative approaches that aim to follow a precise or linear series of research tasks or stages over time, there is typically a movement back and forth between or within research stages through qualitative investigations. For example we may alter our research problem or topic following further reading or revise our questions asked of participants as a response to our findings or interviewees' responses. This movement back and forth during the stages of research is generally known as 'iteration' or iterative processes (i.e., to move back and forth).

Despite important differences, the distinction between quantitative and qualitative social research can be exaggerated or over simplified. For example, it is not unusual for some students or researchers to assume that one method is good and legitimate and another serves little purpose or is inappropriate. Such prejudicial reputations can overstate the distinction between each approach and, as with much else within the social and human sciences, the reality is far more complex and less certain. For example, most forms of qualitative social research draw from cultural tendencies and processes which were pioneered within quantitative research, and which largely remain within each. This might include the planning that takes place prior to a research project beginning, or the focus and research objectives set that provide a core foundation on which to build any study. Although there are practical, political and ethical distinctions between both types of methodology, there are also numerous similarities. There is also the possibility that both approaches can be used in one project: for example, a questionnaire (quantitative) used alongside unstructured interviews (qualitative) in order to evaluate the impact of intense support provided for a relative with dementia upon young carers. Such 'mixed methodology' or 'multi-strategy research' is recognised as having both benefits (e.g. collects richer information and strengthens a project) and drawbacks (e.g. typically prioritises one approach and may confuse the objectives of a project), yet is becoming increasingly popular within social work including in view of greater political pressures for so-called 'legitimate' or 'evidence-based' research.

Crotty (1998: 14–17) highlights that quantitative approaches dominated all types of social research up until the 1960s. Since then, qualitative methods and techniques have expanded and significantly increased in number and variety. Brewer (2003: 239) nevertheless insists that due to 'governments, civil servants, policy makers and other users of research' demand for 'hard facts', and also the 'status and authority [given] to numbers', qualitative findings are often considered less legitimate or may be dismissed as anecdotal. Humphries (2008: 4–7) indicates that any such prejudice has been evident with much government policy relating to social work: most prominent with the New Labour government's priority given to evidence-based research and 'best practice'. Within the evidenced-based remit, qualitative research is identified as offering less legitimate forms of 'evidence' to guide practice. Indeed, practitioner casenotes stand above qualitative research of all persuasion within a medically determined 'hierarchy of evidence' held within the evidenced-based discourse (Aveyard, 2010: 62). Nevertheless, such government and health or social care viewpoints have been criticised as promoting conservative agendas, including the promotion of behavioural psychology or the justification of the rationing of welfare services (Webb, 2001). Despite often unfounded governmental or managerial scepticism, qualitative social research continues to flourish as a legitimate professional activity within academia and welfare support services, and there now remains extensive choice to the budding researcher regarding which qualitative methods or methodologies to apply in practice. Most of the different available approaches are explored within this book.

Qualitative social work research

Perhaps surprisingly within its contested role, social work has in the past tended to sometimes neglect the positive role that research may play in supporting its core functions. Whether due to a lack of resources or support, or owing to an implicit assumption that social work should be practice-led and non-theoretical, research may be ignored in favour of more pragmatic 'street level' principles and perspectives. Whittaker (2009: ix–x) nevertheless reiterates newer policy-led initiatives that seek to encourage greater 'research mindedness' within social work when he advocates 'an approach which is practical in focus but which integrates the best of research findings and theoretical knowledge so we can be as effective as possible in our practice'. In the UK there is also now a requirement that in order to qualify social work students should be aware of how to apply knowledge critically to practice, reflect and self-evaluate, develop understanding of social research skills and methodologies and understand research-based concepts and be able to use them critically in practice (QAA, 2008). Clearly, any past era of practically applying social work without at least some understanding of research skills and knowledge is now coming to an end. Whether this ideal is fortified with the ample availability of resources provided by governments to other sectors of welfare such as health care remains to be seen.

Qualitative social work research draws significantly from qualitative social research, methods and theory. However, more specifically it also seeks to explore and address concerns or topics that bridge knowledge, meaning, tangible experience, emotions and reflexive understanding to the applied practice of social work. So, for example, a qualitative social work research project might evaluate the capacity of a voluntary organisation to fulfil its mission statement, or the different ways that practitioners in a social work department undertake assessments and what this organisational or cultural process means to them. We may instead critically explore relevant literature (policy documents, government websites, academic papers, etc.) so to evaluate the impact of social care legislation on service users or carers, or draw from sociological and psychological theory to understand the impact of the ageing process upon a particular group of service users diagnosed with early stage dementia. We might instead seek to understand the role and identity of volunteers in a local charity that supports people seeking political asylum or the effect of discrimination, exclusion and poverty on a group of disabled men who attend a local day-centre. In essence, as in types of practice and service provision, the topics and interests that encompass qualitative social work research are varied, often unpredictable and rarely ever easily confined to clearly labelled compartments.

Qualitative social work research may also look to comprehend or improve professional practice, evaluate services or seek to better explain 'social problems'. It may in some ways also seek to draw attention to discrimination, inequality or social injustice. To achieve any of these aims, social work research has traditionally drawn from a mixture of theories and disciplines that help to better accommodate its diverse interests: including social policy, social anthropology, law, psychology, philosophy, sociology, as well as social research studies.

Reasons for doing qualitative social work research

Alongside personal interest or simple curiosity there may be occasions when a person has little choice, as a research element remains a compulsory part of a taught course. Nevertheless, other benefits are likely to prevail from engagement with qualitative research and these may include that such research can:

- offer a more detailed understanding of social 'problems' or issues, the person-centred needs of service users or the impact(s) of social work interventions;
- increase capacity to use our imagination by stimulating thought and new ideas;
- help us better understand the context and circumstances in which we practice;
- offer an opportunity to gain new insight into themes such as those relating to policy, legislation and political, economic or cultural dynamics – for example, issues related to class, gender, power relations or the educational needs of service users, etc. – which impinge upon aspects of practice;
- broaden our understanding of the complexity of service user, carer or wider family related needs;
- help us to provide better advice, guidance and awareness of other forms of support to people in need following knowledge and skills gained.

Humphries (2008: 3) also stresses the wider philosophical benefits often gained by researchers in social work, including those that may again benefit service users:

Research within social work may also seek to ask wider ontological (in philosophy, the nature of being or existence) questions that link to the experiences or attitudes of research participants, or a particular theme under investigation. Such questions may seek to unravel the ethical or moral dimensions of a form of social work intervention, or seek to ask difficult questions about why a particular 'service user' group has not received necessary support.

Through current or eventual practice one of the distinguishing aspects of social work research remains its many forms of application. That is, since they hold statutory or legal powers, and are in regular contact with communities and service users or carers, social workers are often quickly able to apply their research findings in direct practice; a privilege that does not always remain in many other disciplines. Potentially at least, social work interventions can also have a positive impact upon service users, informal carers or in work with colleagues or other professional groups and people.

Practical examples of qualitative social work research

Alongside a high number of qualitative social work projects within social work there also remains a wide variety of different approaches. This reflects both the interests of researchers and also the possible research methods to apply. Below are three good examples of qualitative social work research, each of which is either literature-based, ethnographic or draws from the increasingly popular participative research perspective.

Sarah Banks (1998) undertook a critical literature-based survey (see chapters four and five) to investigate the ethical implications of a UK-based code of ethics for social work; at the time recently developed by the British Association of Social Work (BASW). Banks carefully read and interpreted the code but also contextualised its content in relation to important changes that were taking place within the social work profession (and which still continue). For example, Banks highlights the tensions that persist between the fragmentation and commercialisation of the social work role and the emphasis placed upon standardised procedures attached to this role. These changes contrast sharply with BASWs call for a standard professional code of ethics, tension which is increased further by the emergence of calls for greater service user participation in decision-making processes. Although highlighting contradictions between the increased role of the market and a professional code, as well as other inconsistencies, Banks nevertheless concludes her research by calling for a 'new radicalism' within social work that stresses practitioners 'own personal or political commitment and individual moral responsibility as opposed to an externally imposed code of professional ethics'.

In a more 'hands on' or ethnographic study (see chapter twelve) Andrew Pithouse (1987) spent a year amongst two social work teams providing child-care support in South Wales. Pithouse shadowed social work staff in their role and also provided minor administrative support whilst keeping a diary of his observations and insights. His use of participation observation drawn from the social anthropological tradition of ethnography – in which the researcher lives among groups being studied – led to new and more detailed insights into how social work teams operate and engage with one another and a local community. For example, among much else he notes the tensions that can persist between 'clients' and practitioners as well as the family-like team support networks that held the hard-pressed employees close together. Pithouse (ibid.: 65) for example highlights the support articulated by one of the team managers alongside the view that the real work remains outside the confines of the local authority office:

> I always make sure I'm available during the day for the team. They can come in with any query and I'm here. In the evening I catch up with the admin – it's the one way I can work…you see the real work's out there in the field – that's where the real issues are. The social workers are out there and the pressure's on them – not me – but I'm here all of the time for them.

Finally, Elizabeth Whitmore (2001) evaluated a voluntary drop-in centre for 'high risk' street-involved adolescents within a major Canadian city. Importantly, Whitmore involved the youths directly in the research project, which lasted for several months. She was particularly keen to discover how the centre should develop and improve from the perspective of service users themselves. Whitmore lead the research project up until the youths grew in confidence and then gradually began to take over. The research included training, team building exercises, meetings and outings. Whitmore wrote up the final report, yet all of the researchers provided a contribution through 'brainstorming' meetings. The youth researchers also contributed to the dissemination of the findings, such as by presenting at conferences, annual general meetings, and elsewhere. The recommendations in the final report have since led to the centre and its manager altering the service and its management approach.

These case examples – of which there are many more in textbooks, online sites or journals such as *Qualitative Social Work* or the *British Journal of Social Work* – highlight the diversity, rigour, validity *in application*, richness and sincerity of much qualitative research within social work.

Core skills for qualitative social work research

As implied earlier, perhaps surprisingly many of the core skills required for research-related activities will already be familiar to us. Whether as a student who has written essays, given presentations to an audience or who has been based in a practice placement setting – or as a practitioner who has completed assessments, court reports, reviews of services or spent considerable time with service user groups – a myriad of often adept skills will have formed or even been mastered. If we don't already possess the most important competencies already then they are all within reach through reading, guidance and practice over time.

Qualitative social work research will call upon a broad range of skills but we can decipher proficiencies that remain especially significant. For example, curiosity or intrigue regarding a specific topic of interest or social issue will help induce a researcher's drive to sustain a project. As we can gather from Whitmore's (2001) participative research with youths in Canada discussed earlier, types of 'hands on' and intense qualitative projects will require commitment, persistence, resilience and energy from the researcher, for which interest, if not passion, are likely to be of great assistance. In this sense, emotional intelligence – as the French anthropologist Claude Levi Strauss (1966) concurred – may be just as, if not more important than knowledge to the researcher in the field.

Just as significant remain traits such as patience and honesty, such as when interviewing or talking informally to participants, and an approachable or warm disposition that includes empathy and tolerance for disadvantaged or so-called 'hard to reach' groups. Shaw (2005) notes that social workers more often spend considerable time with people who are socially disadvantaged or marginalised. This can throw up numerous problems, such as a struggle to earn trust or gain access as well as develop a capacity to communicate with so-called 'difficult' people with whom culturally or socially we may not have a great deal in common. This can equally be noted of a hard-pressed social worker recently returned from a court hearing or a nurse who has faced a difficult week on the wards. Projecting respect, sensitivity, tolerance and empathy – although ideal traits – will nevertheless further support a researcher in such circumstances, as will the questioning of any previously held prejudicial and stereotypical views possibly held about minority or excluded groups. This type of reflexive stance, in which the researcher challenges their opinions throughout the research journey, can be an especially useful resource. Reinharz (1983) has also argued that ethically it is important, yet not always easy, for qualitative researchers to ensure that participants are also interested in the focus of any research project, and also that it has relevance to their life. Again, engagement and empathy will help to support this principle.

Since qualitative social work research retains aspirations to understand or analyse social problems or issues, these skills require a disposition that seeks to forage and gather facts and information and then look carefully 'beneath the surface' at hidden values, habits, experiences, beliefs or trends. That is, we should never take anything for granted and much qualitative research within social work is about investigation and evaluation as well as the capacity of the researcher to be innovative and enterprising so as to gain new insights into a social group or problem. Alongside prejudice or stubbornness, conservatism is unlikely to help the qualitative social work researcher not only come to terms with a problem, issue or group under investigation, but will also make our task that much more difficult through a lack of understanding. Finally, researchers will nearly always need to present their findings and complete a report or dissertation. You may also wish to present any conclusions to an audience. Although each requirement calls upon obvious proficiencies such as communication, writing or confidence, such competencies or traits tend to improve over time for all of us. As is noted in the final chapter, beginning to write up findings at an early stage and continuing throughout a project is always a good habit to develop for most qualitative social work projects.

Scope and organisation of this book

This book can be used in isolation but may be of more benefit if used in conjunction with some of the recommended reading listed at the end of each chapter. This is because qualitative research has generated numerous textbooks and other publications to assist and support the budding researcher. In addition, most stages of the research journey, or specific research methods, now have one or more books dedicated to each (for example, Gillham's (2005) Research Interviewing – the Range of Techniques or Krueger and Casey's (2000) Focus Groups: A Practical Guide for Applied Research). Such publications are likely to offer more specific detail relating to the methodology or theory that fits with your interests or approach, and this material may supplement the core and succinct knowledge provided within the content of this book.

This book is divided into three sections. In exploring the foundations of qualitative social work research, the first section looks at core underlying themes, values and knowledge that impact upon all forms of qualitative research in social work. This includes the research process or journey, ethics, the use of different theories within research and how each might link to any topic of study. The first section also details how to undertake a thorough literature review and the different methodologies that may be used, all of which remain a key stage in all forms of qualitative research. How to undertake purely literature-based research is also detailed. Finally, the first section discusses the philosophy of qualitative social work research, which includes the ways in which research process and findings link to theory, knowledge production and how this links to our understanding of the nature of being (or 'ontology').

The second section is more practical and instead looks at some of the many types of qualitative research methods that can be used in social work. These include the most popular method of the interview, as well as less common yet still established approaches such as the use of grounded theory , focus groups or case studies. In addition, less familiar methods and methodology such as life histories, biographical research, narrative and discourse analysis, participation and internet research are also detailed.

The final section looks at the significance and different forms of analysis which in qualitative social work research typically runs throughout the research process and begins from an early stage. This section of the book also details the writing up of any final report or dissertation and concludes with a discussion of how to disseminate your findings, not least in terms of how it might impact upon your practice.

Conclusion

This chapter has introduced us to the distinguishing qualities embedded within forms of qualitative social work research. These include its capacity to stimulate our imagination and a sense of creativity, as well as extend meaning and our understanding of policy, social need, disadvantage or other practice-related themes. Research may also help us find new ways and means to support service users and is likely to encourage us to question taken-for-granted assumptions, policies, ideologies or practices.

Smaller-scale qualitative research will tend to provoke meaning and critical thought and is arguably more appropriate than larger quantitative projects due to its stronger links to social work practice, especially those applied within community-based settings. Qualitative approaches also tend to provide more engagement with theoretical and philosophical theory or models, which again can help us think deeper and more critically. Despite this, there is also often a 'pragmatic edge' to qualitative social work research.

Further reading

Alston, M., and Bowles, W. (1998). *Research for Social Workers: An Introduction to Methods*. Australia, Allen and Unwin. Chapter 1: Social Work Research

Corby, B. (2006), *Applying Research in Social Work Practice*. Maidenhead, Open University Press, Chapter 2: Research and Social Work – An Uneasy Alliance Over Time

D'Cruz, H., and Jones, M. (2004). *Social Work Research: Ethical and Political Contexts*. London, Sage. Chapter 1: Research, Social Work and Professional Practice

Humphries, B. (2007). 'Research mindedness', in Lymbery, M. and Postle, K. (eds), *Social Work: a Companion for Learning*. London, Sage

Leven, P. (2001). *Excellent Dissertations, Student Friendly Guide*, Open University Press

McLaughlin, H. (2007). *Understanding Social Work Research*. London, Sage. Chapter 1: Why Research for Social Work?

Ragin, C.C. (1994). *Constructing Social Research*. California, Pine Forge Press. Part II: Strategies of Social Research

Social Care Institute for Excellence (2004). *Knowledge Review – Improving the Use of Research in Social Care Practice*. Bristol, Policy Press. Chapter 2: Review Methods and Findings

2 The Research Process

Introduction

This chapter discusses the stages followed when undertaking qualitative social work research. This rostra or journey is also known as the research *process*, in which tasks, skills, techniques and procedures are applied in order to achieve specific results, or research *outcomes*. Although few qualitative research projects follow a logical or linear progression of planned stages (due to unforeseen circumstances such as the discovery of new findings), there are still important processes that we must follow, and stipulating such tasks and roles provides a guide that can help us to clarify what it is we intend to do and how this might be achieved. It may also help us to identify in a brief overview what we are likely to be doing in the near future. In practice, most qualitative research stages tend to flow into one another and overlap, whilst also regularly changing over the course of any research journey. Some may also begin at different timeframes to those originally planned. This is often due to changing circumstances and other factors outside of our control, such as when participants decide they are ready to be interviewed. In essence, qualitative methods and stages are difficult to predict and control, yet inevitably we can and need to make some general plans ahead.

Typically the stages followed within qualitative social work research projects involve:

- The selection of an appropriate topic and development of a research question/problem.
- Reviewing literature relating to a topic.
- Creating a research proposal and defining research objectives.
- Constructing or developing a research methodology.
- Applying research method(s).
- Analysing data.
- Writing up findings and drawing conclusions.
- Disseminating any findings.

Each stage is now explored in more detail.

Stage 1: The selection of an appropriate topic and development of a research question/problem

The first thing we must do is to try and decide a suitable topic of study. A research topic might be represented by a component of social work practice of particular interest, or a social problem or general issue which may require further investigation. We might instead wish to evaluate a service or ask practitioners for their viewpoints regarding a specific policy initiative. This can sometimes be a difficult choice to make because it cannot be just *anything* that 'springs to mind' or stimulates our interest. To begin with, as qualitative research emphasises extending meaning we are likely to consider topics that avoid generalisation or merely quantify hard 'facts' and instead look to explain and unpack themes which might inform our practice and extend our understanding. For example, if looking at day-care provision for older people we are not likely to stress global or national trends of provision (although this may be part of any later discussion in a final report or dissertation) but may instead look at the opinions, attitudes or experiences of residents or staff employed at such centres.

Due to mitigating factors, there may also be other constraints regarding what we can study. These might include the extent to which we have access to related literature or are able to gain access to a reliable sample of research participants. Some course requirements may also limit any choice of topic or there may be other factors which make a more ambitious project practically *unachievable*, such as limited available resources or time. Ethical concerns can also limit our choice, such as whether interviewing children or vulnerable adults remain appropriate under specific circumstances. As any research is likely to take place over an extended period of time it is important to consider something that interests us whilst also recognising that we may have to compromise a little on our precise topic.

A topic of study will eventually be represented by a more focused *research question* or *problem*. This is a statement or query that neatly summarises what it is we wish to investigate and discover. A research question is usually represented by a detailed question or statement exemplified by one sentence which pinpoints our project and concern. Aveyard (2010: 30–36) offers some valuable tips about forming a research question. These include undertaking background reading around any relevant topic, ensuring that you are interested and motivated by the topic, developing and honing a focused and answerable query, and making sure that any statement is clear and unambiguous. In addition, you will again need to be realistic about available time and resources, ensure that there is enough available literature to support the project and that the question answers at least one or, at a push, two questions relating specifically to social work theory or practice. Although research questions/problems may, and indeed often do, adapt or are revised over time, it is still worthwhile attempting to construct a provisional question/problem in order to know what it is we are hoping to achieve.

Two of the most common problems associated with the selection of a suitable topic remain that the research question is too broad and general or, in contrast, narrow or vague. A broad question (generally more common) is likely to generate too much work and draw upon significant resources and time whereas a narrow focus may not be able to generate enough supporting information (such as from other people's research and publications) to help define the focus of the study or to compare your own findings with.

Two examples of feasible research questions/problems are listed below:

> Do older people with mild learning disabilities benefit from day-care provision each week?

> What factors affect the success rates of the foster care of physically disabled children?

Each question is specific and also relates directly to forms of social work theory and/or practice. For example, the first question has carefully narrowed the focus of the study to one particular service user group (older people with a mild learning disability) whilst also linking this group to a common support service (day-care provision). The research question also presents an assumption (the *benefit* of this service to specific service users) that can be tested, such as through interviews with service users or social workers or by considering the available research evidence from associate studies. In a similar vein, the second question remains feasible because it has linked a service user group (parents who provide or young people who receive foster care) with a support service (foster care) whilst again aiming to evaluate the impact of the service. Both questions not only identify our problem but also help us to consider how we might direct our study.

Royse (1991: 38) suggests that ideas for a research question may emerge 'from observations of clients, personal experiences, discussions with colleagues, or reading the literature pertinent to a certain problem'. There also persist distinctions between choosing to investigate what is familiar and what is unfamiliar to us. Familiar themes can include a topic that relates to our personal experience or current social work role. The advantages of any such themes include that through experience we have a 'head start' prior to gathering more knowledge about the topic, and we also may find it easier to gain access to research participants with whom we work (including on a work placement as part of a social work course). Disadvantages include risks such as 'being too close' to participants or maybe having strong preconceptions about the area of study due to personal experience. In contrast, unfamiliar topics are likely to offer a new direction which should help maintain our interest and encourage a more objective distance to be kept between ourselves and research participants or the subject matter.

The unfamiliar, however, also generates inevitable risks. Potentially these include possible ignorance of aspects of the subject area, prejudices regarding groups of 'Others' that we are not over-familiar with or the problem of gaining access to a large enough sample. As Padgett (1998: 27) suggests, researching the unfamiliar also typically requires 'patience and persistence' as well as a need to avoid 'stereotypical assumptions' about participants or related issues. Consequentially, there may emerge a related 'vigilance of self' by which 'one's own assumptions [are recognised] as potential sources of bias'.

Five pertinent questions can help to narrow the focus of a potential research topic. These include asking:

- *Why is the research necessary?* For example, is it likely to inform our practice and assist service users or carers regarding their needs?
- *Is the research relevant to what it is we are doing?* Does it relate to our role or will it benefit us in some other way? For example, research may not necessarily provide an explicit improvement in any social work service provided but may help in other ways such as increasing our knowledge of particular needs or groups that we have only limited experience of working with.
- *Is the research likely to offer new insights regarding our understanding of theory, the law or policy?* Each of these components of knowledge are likely to relate directly to social work practice either now or in the future and a strong case may be made that improvement in any of these core areas is beneficial and justifiable.
- *Do you have some experience relating to the topic?* As discussed above, this is likely to generate both pros and cons; yet again you should be aware that limited knowledge or experience relating to a topic may require more effort, time and commitment.
- *Do you have adequate time and resources to complete the study?* Both tend to be essential requirements but, if they cannot be met, one solution might be to narrow the focus of your study.

Whittaker (2009: 21) draws attention to the difficulties sometimes experienced by researchers attempting to develop a research question from their initial topic:

For some research projects, the transition from having a research topic to formulating a specific research question is smooth and unproblematic. For others, it can take considerable time to narrow down the research project and this is usually something that happens in parallel with developing the literature review. When you see how others have approached your research topic and the range of methodologies they have used, this is likely to focus your thinking.

This again provides an example of how different stages of research relate to one another as well as the importance of looking at related projects for comparison and new ideas. In practice research topics and questions tend to be revised and adapt over time as a project builds up momentum. Although not compulsory, this process usually develops as gradual or incremental change which brings more and more focus to the project as time moves on.

Below, with examples, are five common subject areas within which qualitative social work research projects often develop:

- *The impact of specific types of social work intervention*: such as analysis of the impact of traditional or alternative social work practice upon service users or carers; possibly including those previously applied or used by the researcher.
- *Theory related*: including an analysis of the differing examples of conventional or radical theories and how they might influence our beliefs, values and practices.
- *Social policy and/or law*: the links between policy, law and their application are complex and creating such a bridge through discussion, evaluation and analysis often provides fertile ground for an engaging thesis.
- *Social trends*: new or established trends such as the 'ageing population' or how social work practice might link to asylum and migration trends or consider their impact upon the delivery of social work services.
- *Service user or carer related*: discussion of specific needs or related themes provides one of the most popular and relevant aspects of qualitative social work research.

Williams et al. (1995) reduce the criteria for any project to four sections and ask the researcher to consider if the planned project is *relevant, researchable, feasible* and *ethical*? The final criteria relating to research ethics is especially significant within qualitative social work and is addressed further below as well as in chapter eight. Kumar (1996: 15) stresses pragmatic criteria when he asks if any planned project is valid (i.e., serves a clear purpose), workable (can be achieved according to the limited time and resources available) and manageable (i.e., do we have the necessary skills to maintain the project). For example, consideration of 'your own and your research supervisor's expertise and knowledge in the field of study' should be a priority. Such keen and penetrative questions again help us to focus our intentions and are likely to again aid us in attempts to define what it is we are going to do and how. Overall, such criteria tend to promote humble expectations and pragmatic sensibilities; often born from a realisation that grander or broader schemes generate considerable work that can increase the risks of success. Despite such potential reservations, if you are confident and fascinated by a particular topic then you should pursue your chosen project.

Stage 2: Reviewing literature relating to your topic

The literature review represents a crucial component of all qualitative research. As Alston and Bowles (1998: 64) stress, a literature review allows us to:

- discover what knowledge is already available about the issue we wish to investigate;
- determine how our study 'will differ from existing work and hence add to our knowledge in the area';
- 'conceptually frame [our] work'.

The literature review denotes an essential *foundational* stage because it provides the researcher with insight into not only current thinking regarding a topic but also related themes such as how policy, law or theory might inform the answering of a research question or problem. A literature review will also reveal other people's findings regarding their own research undertaken within similar areas of analysis: this may be recently or over a longer timeframe, but most importantly it allows us the opportunity to *compare* and *contrast* alternative methods and findings with our own intended research. Finally, a literature review should be able to assist us in defining a methodology or how to frame and manage a research project practically, theoretically and philosophically.

Hart (2001) proposes that there are two sections to a literature review. They are literature that relates to, first, your research question/problem and, second, your research methodology. Your first priority will be to focus and narrow your topic, at which point you begin to consider your methodology. As Alston and Bowles (1998: 64) note, an initial concern can be that there is simply too much literature that relates to your topic:

> Some researchers find themselves overwhelmed by the amount of literature available on a given topic. If you find yourself in this situation, you should *selectively* choose works which:
>
> 1. Represent the argument of a larger body of works;
> 2. Present opposing views;
> 3. Reflect current debate, legislation and policy.

In such circumstances there is also a general strategy to narrow any focus according to more specific themes; such as concentrating upon opposing stances or issues relating to specific acts of legislation or distinct policy. If there is not enough literature regarding your topic this problem is more difficult to accommodate and you may need to broaden or reconsider your research question.

The main sources of a thorough literature review include journal articles, textbooks, and official and legal publications and documents. As we shall see in chapters four and five there are however other sources, and also specific databases, to consider.

Stage 3: Creating a research proposal and defining a research methodology

Once we have completed our initial review of the related literature we are then able to create a research proposal. The proposal clarifies what it is we intend to do and how and comprises information on core components of our intended study. This includes the research *aim* and *objectives* and the intended *methodology* of the study. The research aim – like the research question – briefly clarifies *what* we will achieve and the objectives provide details of what will be achieved and *how* this will be done. The methodology relates to both the intended research methods used to collect data (or an ongoing literature search in the case of a literature-based study) and the theoretical and philosophical foundation upon which the project will rest.

One of the distinguishing attributes of qualitative research remains its tendency to be more aware of the role that social or cultural *context* can play in all aspects of social research, from forming a research question, to the collection of data and then to writing and reporting any findings. For this reason we try to learn and understand early on as much as we can about the issues that link to the topic of study. This is so we can decide an appropriate method of data collection and possibly also select and utilise some kind of theoretical perspective to help us further contextualise or understand the subject material we are exploring. The link between theory and methodology is explored further in chapters six and seven.

Typically the components of a research proposal will include the following:

Title This should be brief, succinct and also clear. It is also likely to be provisional yet should be able to capture your intended study in one sentence.

Background   This is a brief overview or abstract of your study that summarises the topic whilst also indicating to the reader why it is that you are undertaking this research and why it is needed? You may also wish to refer to two or three key studies that relate to give the reader an introduction to the topic and the current state of affairs.

Aim and objectives   This is a crucial section of any proposal. The research aim is usually represented by a clear and succinct statement (usually one sentence) that indicates precisely what it is you intend to research. Not unusually any research aim is similar to the overall *research question* that you will seek to answer throughout your research project. The objectives link to the research aim and will provide more details, notably how we intend to accomplish our attempts to answer the research question. Objectives are usually represented by three to five brief statements of intent.

Below is an example of a typical qualitative social work research project complete with its research question, title, and aim and objectives:

Research question: How do social workers specialising in mental health needs apply counselling skills as part of their practice within a hospital setting?

Title: *The use of counselling skills amongst hospital-based social workers specialising in responding to the needs of patients with mental health needs.*

Aim: To critically evaluate the use of counselling skills amongst social workers who practise in a hospital base with patients with mental health needs.

Objectives: The research seeks to:

1. Discover through semi-structured interviews the types of counselling skills used by social workers based in a hospital specialising in support for patients with mental health needs.
2. Through interviews identify what factors promote the use of counselling skills by social workers specialising in support for patients with mental health needs.
3. Draw from interviews to elicit possible restrictions which hinder the use of counselling skills by social workers specialising in support for patients with mental health needs.
4. Utilise interpretive theory to understand the use of counselling skills by social workers specialising in support for service users with mental health needs.

Figure 2.1   Example of the aims and objectives for a research proposal

As can be seen in figure 2.1, it is apparent from the research question, title and aim of the study what it is the researcher is attempting to achieve. For example, there are clear links made between the use of counselling skills, social work practice and the provision of needs for service users with mental health needs. The research objectives then set four targets that stipulate how the research aim will be accomplished. For example, by interviewing social workers the researcher is able to discover how each utilises counselling skills within their practice, and to what effect, for service users. There is also a link made between interpretive theory (discussed in chapter six) and the findings. As stated earlier, the use of theory is typically paramount in qualitative research as it helps us to understand, explain and contextualise any findings.

Methodology and method(s)

This part of the proposal identifies the ways in which data is collected and analysed, including the philosophical and theoretical framework that will support the project. Both aspects are discussed further in key chapters throughout this book (chapters six and seven). Research methods are discussed in the next section further below.

Ethics

This refers to rules of good moral conduct, and for the researcher typically relates to sensitive themes such as:

- the wellbeing and safety of research participants as well as the promotion of their welfare;
- the avoidance of discrimination, including through the use of language or research methods applied;
- the promotion of confidentiality and security, especially relating to sensitive information collected and stored.

The reader of any proposal will wish to know what plans you have made to ensure that your research will be ethical. The priority is very much upon ensuring the safety and security of research participants and any subsequent findings. Often a consent form for participants to sign will be developed, which may provide evidence that participants have agreed to be involved with the project.

Timetable

As part of any proposal it is helpful to set approximate dates for the completion of core tasks such as data collection, writing up, and so on. As with much else within a proposal, it is possible that any such targets will alter over time due to delays or other unplanned occurrences. Nevertheless, such targets offer some structure to the general project. Try to consider possible factors that can impinge upon the time it may take to complete tasks. These may include potential difficulties in gaining access to participants or available resources within a library. In general, it is advisable to give as much time as possible for tasks such as undertaking interviews or writing up.

Stage 4: Applying research method(s)

Research methods are the practical procedures and techniques which researchers follow and apply in order to collect and analyse information or data. The most common and traditional research method is the one-to-one interview in which a researcher will ask a group of participants set and/or improvised questions over an extended period of time. However, many more methods are now commonly used in qualitative social work research and other examples include the focus group interview, participant observation or internet research, among others. It is also not uncommon for more than one method to be combined, such as if a researcher asks participants to first complete a questionnaire and then to participate in a focus group interview. Deciding the most appropriate method by which to broach a topic is not always an easy task, yet careful consideration of this dilemma is likely to save time and improve the outcomes for a project. Chapters nine to sixteen detail the key methods and methodologies used in qualitative social work research.

Stage 5: Analysing findings and data

Analysis is represented by activities in which we look for patterns, groupings, similarities and differences within our collected data: general themes or trends that help us to answer or explore our research question or problem. Although much analysis intensifies later during the research process – and most notably once we begin to collect data – it may also begin earlier, such as during the literature review. Indeed, for many qualitative projects, analysis can continue throughout a project; and even beyond if we carry our findings into practice.

The diverse topics and related social trends or themes that we explore within qualitative social work research are often equivocal, contested or fluid. That is, findings can rarely be reduced to simple black or white conclusions but instead are as likely to be uncertain as clear cut. As noted earlier, rather than seek to quantify or measure facts much qualitative analysis instead looks for meaning and understanding.

Although there are different types of analysis, two of the most common approaches utilised include:

- *Thematic analysis*: in which we look for emerging themes, relationships and dynamics that appear from our findings and data.
- *Comparative analysis*: where we compare and contrast patterns and themes that emerge from interviews, cases or observations, or look at two separate social care services or similar policies applied in two different countries.

Analysis is discussed in much more detail in chapter seventeen.

Stage 6: Writing up the findings

As with analysis, writing up is often regarded as something that occurs towards the end of a project. However, it is often beneficial – if not essential – to begin writing as early as possible. This is because this allows us to develop our thoughts and style of writing. Our writing may also represent our 'data', such as if undertaking ethnographic observation (chapter twelve). As Ramazanoglu and Holland (2002: 161) note, writing may also help us to develop other aspects of research such as analysis or ethics, as well as represent the validity of any thesis:

> [Writing] is, in part, a continuation of the general process of analysis, but it is also a matter of persuading your audience that you have a compelling case. Persuasion means constructing a text or presentation in a particular genre, with a particular take on reasoned argument, and with a particular rhetoric and ethics. Feminists have experimented with different styles of communication and persuasion, but they are still under pressure to make their social research believable or otherwise convincing.

As the final document may be perceived by the reader as representing all that has been achieved during the previous months, it is important to ensure that the standard is as good as possible. Beginning to write early allows us the opportunity to develop not only our style and arguments, but also to ensure that we are confident what it is we are presenting to a wider audience. Writing up is discussed further in chapter eighteen.

Stage 7: Dissemination

Dissemination represents the different ways our findings are passed on to other people or applied in practice. This might include through presentations, in writing or publications and later policy or within social work through direct practice and communication. As it is not likely to be a compulsory part of any taught course, dissemination is often neglected as a priority. Despite this, some politically orientated groups such as feminists believe that dissemination can represent the most important stage of the research process. Within social work research, dissemination can also offer a bridge between theory and practice.

Conclusion

This chapter has summarised the research process. It has illustrated that most research projects can be divided up into seven key stages. Despite this, it has also noted that within qualitative social research such stages are often linked to one another, and they are rarely likely to unfold in a predictable or linear fashion. In addition, regular movement between research stages over time is also likely. Any lack of predictability should not, however, hinder any project, and might instead be viewed as embodying the rich and diverse nature of the topics explored within qualitative social work research.

Further reading

Crotty, M. (1998). *The Foundations of Social Research: Meaning and Perspectives in the Research Process*. London, Sage. Chapter 1: The Research Process
Gilbert, N. (2008). *Researching Social Life*. London, Sage
Greene, J., and Browne, J. (2005). 'Framing a Research Question', in *Principles of Social Research*. Berkshire, Open University Press
Holt, N. and Walker, I. (2009). *Research With People: Theory, Plans And Practicals*. Basingstoke, Palgrave

Padgett, D.K. (1998). *Qualitative Methods in Social Work Research – Challenges and Rewards*. London Sage. Chapter 3: Choosing a Topic and Designing a Study

Punch, K. (2006). *Developing Effective Research Proposals*. 2nd edition. London, Sage

Ramazanoglu, C., and Holland, J. (2002). *Feminist Methodology: Challenges and Choices*. Sage, London. Chapter 8: Choices and Decisions: Doing a Feminist Research Project

Social Care Institute for Excellence (2004). *Knowledge Review – Improving the Use of Research in Social Care Practice*. Bristol, Policy Press. Chapter 3: Three Models of Research Use in Social Care

Shaw, I. and Gould, N. (2001). *Qualitative Research in Social Work – Introducing Qualitative Methods*. London, Sage. Chapter 11: The Consequences of Social Work Research

Whittaker, A. (2009). *Research Skills for Social Work*. Exeter, Learning Matters. Chapter 1: Planning Your Research

3 Core Social Work Research Concepts

Introduction

This chapter looks at some of the key concepts that underpin all forms of qualitative social work research. We begin by placing qualitative research in context and in particular its priority given to meaning and understanding. We then look at the distinction between applied and pure research whilst noting that qualitative research can undertake each form. We also note other important distinctions, such as between realist and constructive theory, inductive and deductive reasoning and data and evidence. Finally, we look at the different types of sample we may work with, noting the smaller sizes used in much, if not most, qualitative research, before exploring research reliability, validity and rigour.

Qualitative research in context

As was noted in the first chapter, qualitative research seeks to explore in great detail trends or 'social facts', such as the attitudes, behaviour or experiences of specific social groups. More broadly yet often in fine detail it might also seek to identify and unpack a social trend or problem or examine a specific ethical problem or dilemma which has come to light. Qualitative research uses a range of creative methods to collect information, and then seeks to understand or explain this 'data', whilst eventually offering cultural and/or political meaning and examining context alongside explanation. Through direct empirical approaches, such as the intense interview, observation or focus group meeting with a group of people the qualitative researcher seeks to answer unexplored or under-researched experience, concepts or trends (Daly, 2003; Crotty, 1998). Findings are then likely to be used to support recommendations regarding new practices or policy, revise or create a new theory and/or compare our findings with existing theories and revise

31

established ideas. In some instances, however, we may seek to instead undertake theoretical or conceptual research, which is more concerned with examining literature and creating new ideas or theory; such as if critically examining a piece of policy or practice from another perspective.

Daly (2003: 193) notes how meaning and context remain vital elements embodied within most qualitative research, including how 'all aspects of the same phenomenon [are explored] to see their inter-relationships and establish how they come together to form a whole'. Other strengths of qualitative research can include:

- Investigating 'lived' experience, interpretations and meaning of people in their living or working environments. This includes viewing the world from the perspectives of people being studied and also probing beneath surface experiences. This tradition may, however, risk a lack of focus over time, especially if we wander too far from our original research objectives following close affinity with research participants.
- Offering rich descriptive detail of peoples' experience capability, relations or attitudes so as to place a study in context – that is link people to their organizational or environmental experiences so as to better understand their behaviour or values. Researchers should, however, avoid too much description, which may swamp and undermine understanding.
- A stress upon *process* or how social events, traditions or small-scale trends gradually unfold over time. This might include examining how an organisation changes from the perspective of a small group of social work practitioners or looking at a service user's changing life experience according to their disability. The stress is often upon the individual in relation to groups, family, key events or within an organisation over time.
- Emphasising flexibility including a capacity to change research approaches according to the findings as they develop.

Qualitative research however can sometimes lack structure which may mean that a project is difficult to replicate or we cannot generalize from perhaps limited findings. Some such projects also lack transparency and are unclear as to how the findings or conclusions were drawn. Qualitative methods and methodologies are also influenced by quantitative approaches: in particular, regarding the need of qualitative researchers to plan ahead, collect and analyse data and write up findings as part of a dissertation, report or paper. Subsequently, although usually involving fewer interviews or less data collection due to the use of smaller samples, a qualitative research methodology may still be as complex or intricate as any quantitative survey. This is due to the detailed and rigorous nature of the inquiry and the tendency to examine many interrelating layers or causes of a research problem. As stated in the first chapter, some research may also benefit from a merger of quantitative and qualitative approaches (see also 'triangulation' in this chapter).

Applied and pure qualitative research

There are two key types of qualitative research, applied and pure. Applied research concentrates upon direct empirical investigations such as undertaking interviews, and also how subsequent findings influence the relationships held between theory and social work practice. In contrast, pure research does not involve empirical methods but is more theoretical, conceptual or historic. It looks at what we mean by knowledge, how we organise and arrange theory or apply ethics and generally examines more abstract concepts or trends. Pure research is also more likely to draw extensively from previous research findings or ideas.

Applied research within social work often concentrates upon themes that link to policy, legislation and practice. This might include how a piece of legislation is interpreted and applied at a local level by practitioners or within a social and health care institution. Other topics abound, such as the impact of discrimination upon stakeholders within social care or health sectors. Since 'pure' or basic research deals with knowledge production and theory its intention is more to expand our understanding and awareness. Common themes explored in pure social work research relate to ethics, the use and meaning of social work theory, the meaning of social constructs such as ageing or the life process, the impact of discrimination, poverty, identity formation or social exclusion upon service users or practitioners, and so forth.

Realist and constructivist perspectives

Although there are different theories attached to and which influence qualitative research (for example, phenomenology, feminist) there are two broad groups of theory that influence the ways by which we approach the undertaking of research and how we interpret our findings. Such distinct *cultures* of research are known as realist and constructivist perspectives.

Realism draws *directly* from the influence of science and proposes that knowledge should reflect a world which is regulated by general laws. The researcher perseveres to be objective and therefore tries to avoid value-laden preconceptions regarding their topic of study or when interviewing or observing people. The emphasis is also very much upon describing, predicting and seeking to control the processes and outcomes of research. Research findings may also be further reduced to measurable facts or 'data' (discussed further below), and ideally research projects should aspire to be replicable or able to be repeated in other settings and at different times. Hence the realist attempts to standardise and control research projects and power is very much viewed as sitting with the researcher as opposed to any participants or 'subjects' of research. Finally, realists tend to believe that the purpose of research remains a quest for objective, unambiguous and single forms of scientific 'truth' from which we can make generalisations and hopefully predict future social trends or the behaviour of people. Realism has been widely criticised by feminists as being narrow in focus, politically conservative and as undermining and exploiting research participants.

Although they share some similarities regarding how research is planned in practice, constructivist approaches tend to differ from most tenets of realism. Constructivism looks at how human practices and culture help to create and define social reality. For example, constructivists look more at the importance of meaning and relationships held between people in the social world, and how they might develop and change over time. They also argue that there are many possible interpretations possible from any single research project and emphasise change and the fluidity of knowledge production. Constructivists stress the importance of relationships and the impact of contingent factors such as knowledge, learning, tradition and culture upon people's perceptions and understandings of what constitutes 'reality'. Meaning is viewed as uncertain and ambivalent in the social world and the researcher is likely to at best be able to offer one of many possible interpretations of a participant's understanding of events. Alongside multiple interpretations, change is also viewed as ongoing. Research should, however, if possible, be owned and shared between the researcher and participants. A key part of constructivist research remains the discovery of the ways by which individuals and groups participate to construct their understanding of reality. How do social actions and thoughts become interpreted and known, how are events and institutions understood and how do traditions form? Constructivists recognise that people have choices and influence their present yet also realise that such choices are rarely free and open but are instead also likely to be restricted by group norms, traditions, institutional rules, etc. Therefore, human relationships are just as important as interpretation. Some constructivists have been criticised for ignoring the fact that there are single forms of 'truth', such as the existence of poverty or discrimination, or for lacking rigour and consistency in their methods and for exaggerating claims that participants will be able to directly influence a research project (see Carey, 2010).

Once again, as with the distinction drawn between quantitative and qualitative research, it is important not to exaggerate the differences between realist and constructive approaches to research *in practice*. For example, many realist researchers recognise the importance of disadvantage experienced by service users whilst many constructivists do not always allow participants to be involved directly in research. We look in more detail at realism (and positivist theory) and constructivism (interpretive, critical and post-modern theory) in chapter six where we take a closer look at research theory.

Inductive and deductive reasoning

Another distinction drawn within social research is between inductive and deductive reasoning. The former is associated with qualitative research whilst the latter influences quantitative and realist approaches. Inductive research sets out to discover and create theory rather than test established theories which look to explain the social world (Hek and Moule, 2006: 42–3). Observations or interviews are completed by the researcher and from this information or 'data' patterns or trends are identified which are then used to create a summary of statements of the overall findings. From the statements we begin to revise or develop a theory or a set of proposals that help to explain and better understand what it is we have discovered. This approach is summarised below in figure 3.1.

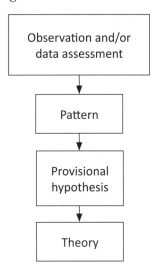

Figure 3.1　Inductive reasoning

Deductive reasoning interprets research from the opposite direction to inductive approaches. The emphasis is very much upon *testing* rather than *developing* theory. From a theory we build a hypothesis or research question, such as 'female carers are more likely to support older male relatives than men'. This hypothesis/question is then tested through observations or interviews with female carers to find out if the original hypothesis holds true or not. We may then reject, accept or revise our theoretical assumptions based on our new research findings. This process is summarised in figure 3.2 below.

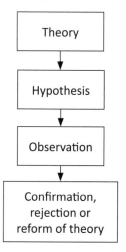

Figure 3.2   Deductive reasoning

Once again, this general rule set between two opposing camps pitted against each other within social research (qualitative/quantitative, realist/ constructivist, and so on) is rarely as clear cut in practice. Generally, most qualitative research is a 'messy' and unpredictable business and it is also possible, therefore, that inductive approaches may draw from core aspects of the deductive tradition, such as if referring to established theory when undertaking observations. Also long established deductive cultures of research increasingly look to integrate some components more commonly utilized as part of inductive traditions. For example the now widespread integration of participative research that involve patients or service users into projects that are either inductive or deductive in principle. Although opposing traditions form, there is also the possibility – in our diverse and ever-changing world that the researcher seeks to describe, detail and understand – that boundaries become blurred. *Cultural* distinctions within social research tend to reflect general observations and traditions rather than conform to static or fixed rules of practice.

Data, variables and evidence

Data represents the foundation of all research and can be characterised by figures, numbers, words, images, quotes and so forth. Essentially, data is anything that can be counted, measured or collected by a researcher. In most cases a researcher will attempt to identify or define the data which they wish to collect early in their project. Gathered data then leads to the formation of patterns or themes of information, which are subsequently used through analysis to construct new knowledge and understanding. Essentially, data represents the basic building blocks of research and is used to promote the expansion of knowledge.

Although much quantitative research can identify a reliable type of data to collect (such as numbers or words) in some qualitative projects it may be less easy to define a source of data. For example, if we are examining the personal experiences of poverty from an older person's perspective, it may not be straightforward identifying what will represent our data. Might we look to collect and transcribe quotes from an interview or instead look at a person's weekly income or basic possessions? Some dynamics such as human emotions may be even more difficult to quantify: for example how do we measure love or anger? Typically, the use of words or phrases in conversation or events witnessed through participant observation can offer our 'evidence' or source of data in most projects. For example, tape recording and transcribing an interview or notes in a diary kept by a researcher can represent data that contributes towards analysis.

There are two main types of data: primary and secondary. Primary data is generated from direct observation, experience or interviews by a researcher. It will rely upon our senses and subjective interpretation of what is happening around us. In addition, it might also be represented by the meaning that a person is trying to convey during a conversation. Secondary data is where primary data has been collected, processed or analysed by other researchers. Examples include academic papers, chapters in books, newspaper reports, or findings from large surveys such as the National Census. Although already processed, this form of data is still open to re-interpretation. Most 'pure' research undertaken as part of literature-based research or a dissertation relies upon secondary data sources, whereas empirical research will more often rely on a combination of primary and secondary sources. Finally 'raw data' is information that has not yet been analysed, such as notes in a diary.

A variable is a characteristic or form of data that differs or varies between individuals and can be measured within research. For example, age, gender, height, feelings, and so forth. Data also provides 'evidence' on which to build a study and thesis. This evidence is represented by collected data that has been evaluated and analysed by the researcher and is then presented as part of a thesis to substantiate or confirm claims. Evidence is typically compared with contrasting evidence such as presented by another researcher in a similar study.

Research concepts

Data and evidence link closely to the emergence of research concepts, which are abstract themes, trends or categories that can have a wider social or cultural meaning or which represent traits discovered regarding a group or person during research. Concepts can also include more general phenomena such as class, gender, homelessness or ethnicity, or more specific themes such as anger, despair, or family ties and relationships. In grounded theory (chapter eleven) and more generally through the stages of analysis concepts *emerge* from data and are then used to support the explanation and understanding of what it is we are attempting to investigate. More often we use concepts to revise an established theory or taken for granted assumption(s) but in some instances concepts can be used to build a new theory.

Typically a research project or dissertation will be built around two or more key concepts that help to locate and direct the project. If we seek to explore social work assessment processes with disabled men, it is likely that that we will initially need to investigate the more general concepts of *disability* and *gender*, and then locate and reduce more specific elements of these concepts by concentrating upon the relationships that form, or emotions which emerge, between service users and professionals during the process of assessment. Concepts are likely to be enriched if we consider data from different angles or perspectives, as is often the tradition within qualitative research as part of triangulation (discussed further below).

Sampling

A sample is a part, portion or section of a wider *population* (total group being studied such as older people with later stage dementia, children and family-care social workers, and so on). Sampling remains the possible techniques and strategy used to select and access a portion of a population. There are two possible types of sampling, probability and purposive. Probability sampling is a scientific approach which seeks to allow all people within a research population an equal chance of being selected as part of the sample. It is a common approach within quantitative research where the priority is to be representative and able to predict and generalise. Purposive sampling is much more common in qualitative research, where the emphasis is not placed upon facts being representative of a population, but more upon gathering rich data to help us understand and explain the answers to a research problem.

There are several types of purposive sampling used in qualitative research. They include:

Purposive sampling   this is one of the most common and effective approaches used in qualitative research. Here the researcher deliberately chooses people who they believe will provide them with the basic and, most likely, best data that they require. In selecting the sample, the researcher might consider factors such as the relevant experience or knowledge held by members. There must of course be clear links between the research problem or objectives and members of the sample.

Convenience sampling   although less reliable, this is a popular approach in which the researcher gradually builds a sample by contacting members of a population that are easier to gain access to. For example, you may wish to interview one or two of your colleagues if they can help to fulfil your research objectives. This approach is not likely to yield findings that are representative or entirely reliable but the findings may still be valid.

Snowball sampling   his is where a researcher begins with one or two participants and then builds their sample by moving on to interview other people recommended, or introduced by the initial participants. This approach is most common with people who are difficult to gain access to, including some service user groups such as homeless people or hard drug users or members of senior management. This is a popular approach used in qualitative social work research.

Theoretical sampling   one of the more complex qualitative approaches which is closely tied to grounded theory (chapter eleven). Striving to be representative is again not the priority, instead greater understanding of the meaning of 'cases' remains the priority, as does theory development. The researcher begins interviewing and then builds up a sample around their findings and analysis so that their understanding of the research problem extends as interviews continue. Essentially the sample is directed and grows alongside the meaning and understanding gained from interviews. There is no set or planned sample size, instead interviewing stops once any findings begin to repeat and no more can be learnt, a stage also known as the 'saturation' point. This approach can be problematic for smaller projects or if members of a sample are difficult to gain access to.

(Adapted from Denzin, 1970; Hek and Moule, 2006)

Denzin (1970: 89–94) further identifies five 'interactive sample models' specific to qualitative research which include those based upon:

- *Social relationships or dyadic structures*: long-lasting bonds including marriages, friends, work colleagues, etc.
- *Social encounters*: people held together by chance or interest but with no real lasting bond, such as members of a jury, couples dancing or people playing cards, people meeting at a charity event, etc.
- *Social groups*: typically long term yet a convergence of relationships and encounters in which two or more people are bonded by 'symbolic encounters' including a common interest or focal activity, such as a group of trustees who meet as part of a carer's advocacy committee. Such groups 'take on a life of their own' yet 'some are shortlived, lasting only a few months, as in certain work groups, while others last a lifetime, as in marriages and families'.
- *Social organisations or bureaucracies*: perhaps most suitable if interviewing social work practitioners, this refers to 'situations of interaction among large numbers of like-situated persons who are engaged in legitimated, coordinated action'. This may include people working in a hospital, GP surgery, voluntary sector organisation or social work team, etc.
- *Communities and whole societies*: by far the largest sample group, comprising local areas or settings, yet there should be some evidence of interaction or bond between participants. The intended research may locate users or carers affected by a particular service within a locality (e.g. residential care or supported living accommodation).

Sample sizes will tend to differ depending upon the nature of the research question or problem as well as possible access-related issues. However, within most small-scale qualitative studies anything from four to eighteen participants is the norm, although larger numbers may be possible. In most qualitative research projects size is not the priority, rather the quality of data collected and then analysed remain the core objective. Finally, 'sampling bias' refers to the under- or over-representation of characteristics of a population found within a sample. Most qualitative samples have some form of sampling bias, which should be acknowledged when presenting your findings in a dissertation, report or presentation (typically in a 'methodology' section).

Reliability, validity and rigour

Reliability relates to the extent to which our findings are consistent and dependable. Reliability also looks at repetition and whether a project can be repeated to produce similar results. For example, if exploring the attitudes of social workers towards older service users with mental health needs, will any conclusions drawn from our study be the same if the research were repeated in a different location at a later date? Reliability is increased with factors such as using appropriate questions in interviews, asking questions in an appropriate setting (such as an office rather than noisy pub) that can also be easily found in most areas or targeting a sample of people who live in most areas and who are relatively easy to find elsewhere (for example, child care social workers or foster carers). Because of the varied issues often explored in qualitative research, as well as the different social groups and locations where such research is undertaken, reliability is not always easy to achieve. Since the priority in qualitative research is upon meaning and understanding, reliability is not always considered with the same priority it may be given in much quantitative research.

Validity is less concerned with methodology, or how our research is organized or *proceeds*, but more with the *findings* and in particular the extent to which they are authentic and sound. For example, regarding validity we might ask ourselves what are the strengths of our findings? If we again explore the attitudes of social workers to older users with mental health needs, were our findings a *true reflection* of the group of social workers being interviewed? Validity is more achievable within much qualitative research due to the many questions asked, themes explored or longer periods of time spent with participants. Although a generalisation, what qualitative research loses in reliability it tends to gain in validity, and vice versa for many quantitative approaches. Validity in qualitative research can be further increased by contacting research participants at a later date following interviews and discussing any results and conclusions with them so as to increase any likelihood of knowing if any of our previous findings were truly accurate (Bloor, 1978).

Reliability or validity will not necessarily be the priority in much qualitative research, or at least from the point of view of the researcher. Among others, Svennson (1995) notes that due to its varied approaches and topical interests it is unrealistic to expect reliability and validity to be given precedence by the qualitative researcher. Other objectives such as achieving greater meaning or drawing attention to an otherwise unknown social problem may instead be seen as more important. Reliability and validity relate to rigour, which looks at the quality of data collected, analysed and presented as well as how the research was undertaken to achieve such aims.

Rigour is typically presented in the methodology section of a final report or dissertation (see chapter eighteen). Here the researcher informs the reader and general audience of how they undertook the research, what methods or theories influenced the project and so on. A question to ask yourself following fieldwork is how reliable and valid are any results and findings? Rigour is not part of a mechanical or abstract process but should instead involve the researcher thinking critically and reflexively about their research and findings and how accurate or meaningful these are. For example, could anything in retrospect have been done differently to improve the results?

Triangulation

Triangulation is when two or more methods or sources of data are used together to fulfil research objectives. Ideally, research methods, such as the one on one interview and focus group interview, should be used together as they complement each other (Bryman, 2004). However, a detailed questionnaire might be used alongside focus group interviews to collect standard data. That is the questionnaire can collect information such as the age or gender, etc., of participants and the focus group interview collects richer and more varied data, such as the opinions and attitudes of the same participants.

Humphries (2008: 124) adds that triangulation may help to give us 'a more holistic picture of the phenomenon to be studied than the use of only one method' and that the aim 'is for misrepresentation or distortion to be avoided, and for findings to achieve a measure of validity'.

Conclusion

This chapter has considered qualitative social work research and its emphasis upon meaning and understanding. Such research can be either pure (theoretical) or applied (empirical) and is likely to also be inductive (move towards theory development). It will also tend to draw significantly from a rich source of data, and rely upon evidence and the related building of concepts and revision, or building, of theory. Qualitative researchers also tend to rely upon smaller purposive samples when they undertake empirical research, and may not prioritise reliability or validity to the same degree as many quantitative researchers. Despite this, priority should always be given to achieving rigour for all projects wherever possible.

Further reading

Bryman, A. (2004). *Social Research Methods*. Milton Keynes, Oxford University Press. Chapter 13 – The Nature of Qualitative Research

Hall, D., and Hall, I. (1996). *Practical Social Research – Project Work in the Community*. Basingstoke, Macmillan. Chapter 1 – Philosophy and Practice of Applied Social Research

Hek, G., and Moule, P. (2006). *Making Sense of Research: An introduction for Health and Social Care Practitioners*. London, Sage. Chapter 5: Approaches to and Design of Research in Health and Social Care

Padgett, D.K. (1998). *Qualitative Methods in Social Work Research – Challenges and Rewards*. London, Sage. Chapter 8 – Rigor and Relevance in Qualitative Research

Royse, D. (1991). *Research Methods in Social Work*. Chicago, Nelson-Hall Publishers. Chapter 2 – Basic Research Terms and Concepts

Sarantakos, S. (2005). *Social Research*. Basingstoke, Palgrave Macmillan

4   The Literature Review

Introduction

This chapter and the next concentrate upon a crucial component of all qualitative social work research, that of the literature review. Literature typically provides not only the foundation of so much social research but also its life-blood. We draw upon other people's work not in a parasitic sense but to help us support, better understand and contextualise our study and findings. We look in this chapter at the purpose and key stages of a review and also how to carry out critical evaluation of any literature. We also then look at some key sources of information and evidence as well as other priorities such as keeping records. The next chapter then explores the methodology of a review, including for a literature-based project or dissertation.

The purpose of a literature review

The literature review not only fulfils core tasks such as allowing us to more clearly define our objectives and unearth what other related research has discovered in the past, it also helps us to better understand our subject of inquiry and research problem. In addition, the literature review should also be able to provide us with an overview of any theoretical perspectives that surround our topic of interest. Indeed the quality of so much social research is based upon the extent to which the researcher has undertaken a focused and thorough literature review. A good review can also save us time and effort later on by helping to steer us in the right direction and offer focus and clear intentions. Inevitably therefore, the review is not something to leave to later stages as it impacts upon all the other stages of research, including, not least, analysis and writing up.

A literature review will seek to:

- examine existing literature relating to your research question/problem and objectives;
- critically evaluate and contextualise, or place into perspective, such literature;
- discover policies and best social work practices relating to our topic;
- improve our understanding of our research topic, including by critically evaluating historic trends, policies, practices, etc.;
- help us identify key themes and issues relating to the topic.

As discussed in chapter two, one of the more difficult stages in any research project is the identification of a relevant and feasible topic to research. From here we look to define our research aim (briefly clarifies what we will achieve) and objectives (how we will achieve our aim through techniques and specific areas of investigation). A thorough literature review will offer vital support in helping us to achieve these tasks by allowing us to read around what other authors and researchers have discovered in relation to our topic. The benefits of this are that we should be able to clarify what it is we intend to do and how.

Stages of a review

For small-scale projects and dissertations there are usually two key stages to a review. These include a brief yet intense *initial* stage that consists of an overview of core literature relating to a topic, and then a more prolonged *ongoing* search that becomes more detailed, focused and thorough. In figure 4.1 we can see how a broader initial review develops into the core ongoing review that becomes more specific regarding attempts to read around themes that link to our research problem and objectives. A typical timeframe for a research project or dissertation over six months will include an initial review for two weeks to a month followed by five months or more spent undertaking ongoing research. In essence an intense early review is following by continued reading to support our research.

Although not compulsory, held within the stages there are typically four components to any literature review, that include exploring:

- **Theory and philosophy**: this may include investigating the intellectual context(s) of any research related to a topic. For example, what theories have been used to explore the themes that you are attempting to address? Might they also be of use to your own research?

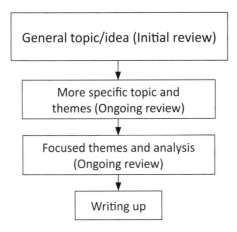

Figure 4.1   Stages of a literature review

- **History of developments in your subject**: this concerns the 'background to current thinking'. How did we come to practise in the way we do *today* as part of child safeguarding or adult protection? Has this changed over the past two decades and if so in what ways? Such historical trends are often prioritised because of their cumulative impact upon policy, legislation and practice. There will generally also be a need to consider both older publications and more recent works.
- **Latest research and developments in your subject**: this addresses present issues and also 'latest thinking and practice'. Try to bring the reader up to date with major developments in social work practice or research that link to a topic under investigation. For example, calls for greater priority given to evidenced-based research or praxis within education and training or multidisciplinary practice in the field.
- **Social research methods and methodology**: this concerns approaches used by other researchers . Looking at how other people design their research or approach a similar topic can be a useful way to stimulate ideas about your own methods .

(Hart, 1998; Walliman, 2006)

Warburton (2004: 9–22) provides some helpful guidelines for reading around any topic. Points include trying to avoid being a passive reader such as by maintaining careful thought about arguments presented by any author(s). This can encourage more insight and clarity to be gained from reading. Also try to get an overview and identify the core arguments within any article. Keep notes and make references where possible and avoid too many details, remembering that the central points that link to a topic tend to remain the priority.

It is also important to explore material relating to research methodology as part of a literature review. This should help to:

- understand how different approaches are applied in *practice* by other people;
- appreciate research approaches that differ from your own;
- understand methodology and extend your research knowledge base and skills;
- learn how to present and detail a methodology from examples set by professional researchers.

Another strategy or skill is to discern between different types of literature in relation to their *relevance to your topic*. One way of achieving this aim is to set parameters or draw a distinction between background, relevant and very relevant literature (Walliman and Buckler, 2008). You may of course wish to set two or four criteria relating to your topic but overall drawing a distinction between literature according to their relevance or otherwise can help to offer organisation, focus and clarity to your reading and literature review.

In figure 4.2 a case example is presented in which a researcher has broken down her literature review into four stages. Upon deciding to study the 'long-term impact of day-care support upon older men with Aspergers syndrome' the researcher has begun by looking at the broad themes relating to social care provision and the support needs of older men, including not least related historical and more recent policies and practices. This general and broad initial review has gradually made way for an exploration of much more specific themes: including a critical evaluation of care management and personalisation policies in the UK and more particularly the various social care support services provided to older men with a disability, including Asperger's syndrome. Following this stage, the researcher has focused her critical reading around evaluating empirical studies undertaken into the impact of day-care support for older people with Asperger's. Finally, in drawing upon her reading and analysis the researcher began to write up her findings. A key part of this final stage, among others, will include drawing upon historical and theoretical developments (drawn from the initial review) that relate to the topic in the early chapters of her report, and also comparing other researchers' findings (drawn from the ongoing review) to her own as part of analysis throughout the study. Some researchers do begin with a focused review (such as in much health care or science-based research) but we may subsequently miss important historical or policy-related themes which tend to be given more precedence in social care.

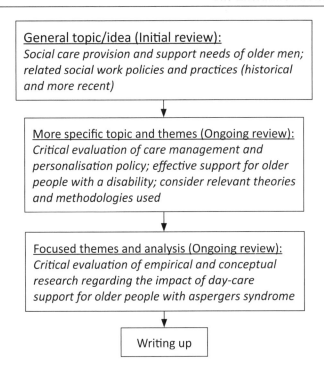

General topic/idea (Initial review):
Social care provision and support needs of older men; related social work policies and practices (historical and more recent)

More specific topic and themes (Ongoing review):
Critical evaluation of care management and personalisation policy; effective support for older people with a disability; consider relevant theories and methodologies used

Focused themes and analysis (Ongoing review):
Critical evaluation of empirical and conceptual research regarding the impact of day-care support for older people with aspergers syndrome

Writing up

Figure 4.2   Case example of the stages of a literature review (long-term impact of day-care support upon older men)

Critical evaluation

A key part of any literature review is critical evaluation as opposed to passive reading. As a reader, this will mean providing a personal and professional assessment of the quality of relevant publications. This might include looking carefully at an author's methodology for possible weaknesses, or maybe considering carefully their presentation of arguments and conclusions for possible inconsistencies or deficiencies. As Dawson (2006: 43) suggests:

> Do not believe everything you are told. Think about the information you are being given. How was it collected? Were the methods sound? What motives did the publishers have for making sure their information had reached the public domain? By developing these skills early in your work, you will start to think about your own research and any personal bias in your methods and reporting which may be present.

Aveyard (2010: 93–8) highlights the significance of critical appraisal when undertaking any literature review:

> In principle, all the published material you use in your literature review should be critiqued for relevance and for its strengths and limitations. You should never cite an author without some analysis of the contribution this author makes to your debate, unless you are summarising well-known arguments at the beginning of your literature review, or summarising arguments in your discussion.

Critical evaluation or appraisal may be achieved by a combination of methods which include:

- Considering carefully the *arguments* presented by author(s) and whether they are sound and consistent.
- Assessing the quality of *evidence* presented to support a thesis and general arguments – for example new data or the coherence and logic of new arguments.
- Asking how does an article *link* to your own research question and topic.
- Assessing whether evidence originates from, and is supported by, *credible sources*, such as other people's research, data or arguments.
- Evaluating how an article or chapter compares with other publications, arguments and research findings. Is it more convincing and better argued or deficient and lacking in evidence? What is the relevance of the work in comparison to others?
- Exploring whether the use of *supporting theory* is sound and how this compares to competing theoretical standpoints. For example, the conflict between different feminist perspectives regarding class-based or power relations.
- Asking what are the strengths and weaknesses of any *findings* and *discussion?*
- Considering if the author(s) is presenting material that is *new* or *different* regarding any debate. Is this unique or distinct stance adequately supported by evidence?
- Appraising the *research methodology* utilised, including in comparison to others.

In practice, it is unlikely to be possible to achieve each of these aims in the limited amount of time available. The priority is instead to aim to be influenced by these principles and in general to consider published or online arguments, trends or 'facts', carefully and with a healthy degree of scepticism. It is certainly not intended that you become 'cynical' or 'incredulous' about other researchers' intentions and methods, but instead that you take a careful stance and remember that information or arguments should never be accepted at face value. Instead, they should be open to careful and ideally balanced (with evidence) criticism. Aveyard (2010: 121) offers some core tips for undertaking any critique of literature within a report or dissertation:

- Remember that critique means to 'give the positive and negative points about a paper'.
- Bear in mind that no research paper or chapter is ever perfect!
- Try to summarise the aims of a paper, what the authors did, what the results showed and your overall opinions of the quality of the paper.
- There is usually limited space to evaluate other people's research. In general, a paragraph per paper offers some guideline although this may be more depending on the topic and discussion.

Key sources

A literature review relies upon key sources of information, debate and other forms of knowledge. A distinction is commonly drawn between primary and secondary sources of information. The former refers to information collected from direct personal experience or research methods such as interviews or focus group meetings. Less common sources such as statistical data bases and film or video material may in some instances be suitable if they are closely linked to a topic. Table 4.1 offers a list of examples of primary and secondary sources.

Table 4.1   Primary and secondary sources

Primary	Secondary
Historical records and texts	Monographs
Experience	Textbooks
Relevant people	Government publications
Organisation records	Popular media
Personal documents (letters, diaries, reports, etc.)	Research reports
Observation	Journal articles
Film/video	Chapters in books
Statistical data	Previous dissertations
Original works of literature and art	Specialist Magazines
	Internet articles
	Databases (such as the Census)

In practice, however, the majority of sources for a literature review for qualitative social work research will be secondary sources. The most commonly utilised include journal articles, monographic textbooks, chapters in edited books, research reports and government publications. They are likely to be accessed at, and drawn from, a library, an inter-library loan or the internet.

Key sources of secondary information include:

Journals articles contain a rich source of empirical and/or conceptual or theoretical findings and usually represent the most reliable sources of information for most social work research. This is because journal articles are peer reviewed and are more up to date and focused than other sources. There are a variety of journal formats including those dealing with local, national and international issues, interdisciplinary and subject specialties, as well as applied and practitioner-led approaches. Core social work journals such as the *British Journal of Social Work, Qualitative Social Work, International Social Work* and *Practice* should always be checked first for articles that are linked to a topic area. In addition, core journals in associated disciplines such as social policy, sociology and health care should also be checked.

Table 4.2   Examples of reliable social work and other journals

Discipline	Journal
Social work	*Child and Family Social Work*
	Child Abuse Review
	British Journal of Social Work
	Journal of Social Work
	International Social Work
	European Journal of Social Work
	Australian Social Work
Social Policy	*International Journal of Sociology and Social Policy*
	Contemporary Crises: Crime, Law and Social Policy
	Journal of Social Policy
	Critical Social Policy
	Social Policy and Society
Psychology	*Psychologist*
	Self and Society: a Forum for Contemporary Psychology
	British Journal of Educational Psychology
	British Journal of Developmental Psychology
Sociology	
Research Methods	*Action Research*
	Qualitative Social Work
	Research on Social Work Practice
	Sociological Research Online

(Carey, 2009)

Journals tend to vary in quality and not all are peer reviewed. It will help to consult with your supervisor if unsure about reliable journals. You will also need to use the critical analysis skills discussed above when considering their merit or otherwise.

Monographs   a monograph is a published academic thesis which carefully examines a single subject or related topics (for example, social care support for women with depression and anxiety or the impact of counselling on younger men, etc.). This format will differ from textbooks because of the rigour and detail of the study, many of which tend to be adapted from a PhD study. Often the content includes extensive analysis.

Text books   regarding popularity and accessibility, course textbooks dominate published academic material in book form. They offer a general and relatively easy-to-follow guide to a discipline and may be beneficial in offering an initial overview. It is nevertheless advisable not to over rely on such books as content tends to be general and this may limit analysis and rigour.

Legislation   Green and White papers in Britain and forms of Guidance are accessible from academic libraries or relevant websites. If concentrating upon the impact of a specific act of legislation upon a form of social work practice it is essential to read as widely as possible from different sources, including critical responses to the impact of policy upon service users or other vulnerable groups.

Edited collections and subsequent chapters   This is a set of articles held in a textbook which link to a specific topic. There are many edited collections linked to social work, and chapters within edited collections may be helpful in examining your study. Edited collections will tend to vary in quality across individual chapters.

Government publications   a number of government publications relate to social work research. Many can be found in an academic library or can be ordered or downloaded from websites such as the Department of Health or Department of Education in the UK.

Specialist magazines   professional magazines including *Community Care, The New Social Worker* and the *National Bulletin* offer up-to-date and (sometimes) critical guidance on current research, policy and practice in social work. They may also have their own websites with latest news regarding social work and social care policy and practice.

Reliable internet sources   potentially, the internet may offer an invaluable resource but try not to over-rely upon internet sources and use your discretion, as the lack of regulation attached to the internet as a whole means that information may not always be accurate or perhaps may be extremely biased. In chapter sixteen there is a list of some extremely reliable websites that includes search engines specifically designed for academic research.

Keeping records

It helps to keep some kind of record of any literary sources accessed and subsequent information and knowledge gained. During the research process and writing-up stage this may offer a quick recollection of previously explored information and knowledge. The main details to keep a record of typically include the names of authors, title of papers or books, dates of publication, the publisher and place of publication and a detailed summary (aims and objectives, core arguments, strengths and weaknesses, conclusions) of the contents of the article, paper, chapter, etc. In addition to general notes, index cards can also help provide a more comprehensive system. This will allow key points and authors to be quickly compared and contrasted, as well as different arguments and general ideas.

Conclusion

This chapter has highlighted the key role of the literature review within qualitative social work research. All qualitative research will be supported and influenced by a literature review. A key reason for this is because the literature review can provide the *foundation* of any research project or thesis. An incomplete or 'last minute' literature review will not unusually lead to inappropriate research methods being applied. In addition, an incomplete review will undermine analysis since much of this is based on comparison with, and understanding of, other studies. It is always advisable to begin your review as early as possible and typically it will continue in some form till the end of your research project or dissertation.

The next chapter offers further information on methodologies used for undertaking a literature review and also details literature-based dissertations and reports.

Further reading

Aveyard, H. (2010). *Doing a Literature Review in Health and Social Care.* 2nd edn. Maidenhead, Open University Press

Fink, A. (2005). *Conducting Research Literature Reviews – From the Internet to Paper.* London, Sage

Hart, C. (1998). *Doing a Literature Review – Releasing the Social Science Research Imagination.* London, Sage

Ridley, D. (2008). *The Literature Review – A Step by Step Guide for Students.* London, Sage

Whittaker, A. (2009). Research Skills for Social Work. Exeter, Learning Matters. Chapter 2 – Undertaking a Literature Review

5 Literature-based Research and Methodologies

Introduction

We saw in chapter four that a crucial foundational stage for any type of qualitative research remains the literature review. The review of literature allows us to more clearly define our research objectives and also gives us insight into what previous researchers have discovered and emphasised regarding our research problem. This chapter aims to explore two related themes: those of literature-based research (without empirical methods) and literature review methodologies, or the way in which we plan, organise and theorise our literature research. The three distinct methodologies of narrative, systematic review and critical interpretive synthesis will be presented and compared for use within literature-based research. We then look at critique before finally exploring some of the ways by which literature-based studies might be structured and presented.

Literature-based research

Literature-based research will usually be built around a research question or theme that attempts to gain new insight into a relevant topic. The topic may link to current practice, ongoing debates within social work theory, ethical dilemmas regarding a recent policy or component of practice in the field, historical trends or specific Acts of legislation and how they influence our capacity to meet service-user needs or our interpretation and constructions of applied practice within specific settings. Because empirical research is not undertaken, the researcher should have more time available to locate and carefully examine relevant literature and associate research themes in an attempt to explore and answer their research question/problem. In so doing, analysis of the literature may be more thorough and extensive and, in some instances, may also be more theoretical and philosophical.

The first obstacle is to choose a topic and then attempt to develop a research question. As was explained in chapter two, topics may relate to a wide variety of issues or topical interests, including an aspect of practice or policy, among other potential subject areas. Although coming from a nursing perspective, Aveyard (2010: 27) prioritises practice-related topics, because the research is then likely to be 'relevant to your professional life and a truly useful project'. Despite this, the author also stresses that it is 'critical that the research topic you select is a topic in which you have a genuine interest'. In contrast, however, Fairclough (2001) argues that applied social science subjects such as social work should instead target social *problems* or *issues*, a cultural response which is more likely, it seems, to challenge established functional or normative practices. Whilst drawing from feminism, Dominelli (2005) advocates attempts to stimulate change and empowerment with service users or carers as part of any research process. There are then many different types of literature research to undertake and this choice may have political ramifications.

Next we attempt to identify or develop a research question or problem. This is again explored in chapter two with examples, yet the priority remains stating in one sentence what it is we hope to investigate and answer. Aveyard (2010: 29) summarises the aim of a research question as a 'search for unaddressed questions, identify[ing] unexplored areas, identifying apparent contradictions, find[ing] perspectives that have not been considered before or an area in which you have some new ideas'. The priority is to be clear and unambiguous about your question/problem, focused yet not too narrow and trying to avoid assumptions that might suggest you already have a strong opinion about the research findings and results. Significantly, any research question should also be grounded and answerable within the available time and link to a body of literature that will support the project. For example, there is little point in pursuing a topic or research question if there is little available empirical research or literature to support this quest. Topics in social work that are likely to contain less or little literature may be those that link to a recent or proposed piece of legislation, a new policy initiative or a relatively recent social problem, support service or form of practice. In contrast, historical or established practices and policies, international trends or universal themes such as poverty, child safeguarding or the ageing process, among many other examples, are all likely to generate a wealth of literature. The examples below offer both an unsuitable and relevant research topic.

> *What factors influence the opinions of social work practitioners felt by service users?*
> Although this question touches upon a relevant topic (the relationship between service users and practitioners) and also has focus, it is unclear and somewhat vague in its objectives. Many factors might

influence the opinions of service users regarding their social worker: available time, personality, their sense of empathy, any support provided or even their dress code or time keeping. Such a high number of potential influences may prove difficult to locate and analyse amongst the literature. Both the practitioner and user are also generically or broadly defined, which again makes this task more of a challenge.

Which, if any, personality traits do service users with a physical disability regard as valuable for social work practitioners?
Although a similar project, this question is much clearer and more focused. It is specific about the service user group (and therefore also the type of social worker likely to be allocated) and isolates what it is we wish to know about the opinions of social work clients. Here, 'personality traits' remains a much clearer aim to account for rather than the more ambivalent 'factors' which 'influence the opinions of social work practitioners' cited in the earlier example. The question for the researcher will be to discover if there is much available research that either implicitly or explicitly relates to this topic. If there is limited available literature, we can still broaden the focus of this study: such as by looking at international rather than national research and comparing examples from two or more countries.

The next important stage involves deciding your research methodology. First you might wish to frame your research within an explicit theoretical approach: as discussed earlier in chapter three and further in chapter seven, there are two core theoretical schools that include realist and constructivist paradigms. Constructivist approaches can, however, be further subdivided into interpretive and critical theories. Such broad paradigms have a wide range of related theories, for example within critical theory there are feminist, anti-oppressive, Marxist and post-Marxist theories. Such insights project a specific view of the world (for example Feminists stress the negative impact of patriarchy and gender exclusion) which can be used to support debates and discussion as part of your research. This might help to draw attention to themes that may otherwise be ignored or a generate debate that challenges or supports some of the related the views of key feminist theories. When you frame your research around a specific theory as part of your methodology, the reader is typically made aware of your influences and also understands that your direction and wider project have been supported by clear objectives. Chapter seven offers clearer guidance on the difference theories that can be used to influence a thesis as part of a methodology.

However, more specifically, you may wish to simply compare your own findings with other people's research or allow your research findings to speak for themselves as part of a traditional inductive process. The example above, which looks at the personality traits cherished by service users with a disability, might draw influence from the extensive canon of critical literature dedicated to 'disability studies' or instead might pay attention to interpretive approaches which highlight and stress the importance of interpretation and meaning between people.

The next aspect of methodology relates to the practicalities of how your research is undertaken or what technologies and framework are used to search for available literature. Three examples of such reviews are provided below.

Narrative Review

Traditionally, qualitative research within social work, and more generally the social and human sciences, has relied upon a pragmatic and often less structured approach to the literature review. This is referred to as a narrative review, in which the search for available literature relating to a topic does not always follow predetermined or exact procedures. Indeed, in practice many students or academic researchers may simply visit their library and check relevant publications such as textbooks or journals for suitable leads. Alternatively, a series of internet searches might take place, sometimes loosely based around a relatively broad topic. Subsequent criticism suggests that such pragmatic approaches lack coherence and may also be biased or even ineffective. While there may be potential risks, this assumption is based upon prejudicial assumptions that narrative reviews *inevitably* lack focus or rigour. In practice, however, as many are likely to be methodical and thorough, and for significant types of social work research (historical or theoretical, among other examples) a narrative review may still be the best approach to utilise. In general, the following guidelines will help to promote a more rigorous narrative review:

- Ensure that you begin with as clearly defined research topic and/or question as possible. This is likely to be revised as the review proceeds.
- Try to develop a search strategy which relates to your topic of enquiry and research aims and objectives. For example, isolate key concepts or words that fall within the remit of your investigation and attempt to clearly define these concepts as the review progresses.
- Try to privilege more reliable sources, such as peer-reviewed journals, official reports and monographs. Most journals have their own search engine online which can provide a useful resource to look for articles

and also publishers such as *Sage* again have a search engine which allows you to look for specific articles. Other online resources such as the *Web of Science* or *Google Scholar* can also be used to look for articles that relate to your study.

- Avoid over-reliance upon less reliable sources of information, such as more general course textbooks or generic internet sites that lack any peer review or regulation.
- Develop a strategy for critical analysis whereby a consistent and coherent attempt is made to carefully consider and possibly question the methodology, empirical findings, conceptual or philosophical arguments, and so on, of each paper, article or report. This process should link to the research topic/question that you are attempting to explore (see also chapter seventeen and four for guidance on analysis and critique).
- Utilise a means of synthesising, summarising and developing your core findings. This may simply be achieved by taking notes or highlighting key sections of papers, etc.

Although narrative reviews are often sometimes caricatured by promoters of more systematic approaches, there is no reason why a narrative approach cannot be used as effectively as more 'scientific' methodologies. Two examples of such systematic methodologies are now discussed.

Systematic review

A distinct methodological approach for literature reviews to emerge in recent years remains the systematic review (SR). An SR seeks to provide a rigorous, transparent and scientific means by which to locate and summarise all the available 'evidence' for clinical, health and, more recently due to Government pressure, social care questions and practices. Perhaps inevitably, this approach is more commonly suited and applied to health-based and clinical research or practice. Aveyard (2010: 14) advocates and details central components of this approach:

> One of the main features of an SR is that reviewers follow a strict protocol to ensure that the review process undertaken is systematic by using explicit and rigorous methods to identify, critically appraise and synthesise relevant studies in order to answer a predefined question. The reviewers then develop a comprehensive searching strategy, leaving no stone unturned in the search for relevant literature, and do not regard the process as complete until the search is exhausted.

Unlike the narrative review, there is an *explicit* rationale that research bias and error be minimised, but because of the health and clinical ideological culture which motivates so much of this approach, priority is also given to quantitative and realist methods (see chapters three and six) or findings. Indeed, much alternative 'narrative based' reviews or qualitative methodologies and some research are largely viewed as anecdotal or unreliable sources of evidence. Reviewers utilising an SR go on to develop an inclusion and exclusion criteria for relevant academic papers, reports or other studies, and then seek to rigorously critique each publication, such as in relation to their methodology, findings and recommendations (Macdonald, 2003). From such processes of critical analysis there should emerge findings and recommendations from the best possible sources of evidence which can be combined as part of a systematic approach for better professional or clinical practices.

In practice, search engines such as the *Web of Science* or *Social Care Online*, among others, tend to be used to do much of the initial review work and then the researcher reads through and evaluates papers or reports identified as valid. Researchers may, however, also decide to search through the abstracts of published journals 'by hand' or contact experts in the field (including service users or practitioners). In practice, however, narrowing down and locating relevant articles can be time consuming, and unless exact and precise search words are used this approach may prove frustrating. There may, however, be aspects of qualitative social work research which are more suited to the SR approach. For example, in relation to health-orientated social care needs – such as around dementia-care or HIV-related domiciliary support or residential care – or another topic that requires specific health care perspectives or support.

There are, nevertheless, deficits to the SR approach that include its sometimes dogmatic attachment to scientific principles. This includes its association with the arguably reductive 'medical model' or 'evidence-based' ideological approach to applied social care. For example, such stances are criticised for emphasising what a patient or service user is *unable* to do due to their disability or condition or for helping to justify the rationing of support services in health and social care (Webb, 2001). There are also concerns which prevail regarding bias that may emerge from a general disregard for much qualitative social research. Many researchers within social care and social work also prefer a more *political* – rather than merely *methodological* – critical approach that is holistic, perhaps uncertain, yet driven as much by recognition of the contingencies of social work and life itself. For example, it is proposed that social justice should be as much a priority as any quest to discover (largely unattainable) objective 'truth'. Much of the SR stance also privileges methodology rather than other research processes or outcomes: a case of the methodological tail wagging the research dog? Finally there are times when a summary of best practices or evidence may not be what is required by the researcher or organisation: most obviously regarding theoretical or specific ethical, political or historic projects or some forms of action and evaluation research.

A less-prescribed alternative to the SR remains the critical interpretive synthesis.

Critical interpretive synthesis

A critical interpretive synthesis (CIS) approach aims to utilise more reflexive and critical approaches which include: formulating a review question, searching the literature, sampling, determining quality, extracting data and conducting an interpretive synthesis. Through interpretive synthesis the generation of concepts of analysis is pursued alongside a more precise understanding of initial research objectives (Dixon-Woods et al., 2006).

The benefits of CIS include its capacity to overcome some of the limitations of a systematic review: for example, any tendency to prioritise things that can be measured rather than identify concepts that are considered important by the researcher or participants, or privilege 'answerable' rather than 'useful' research questions. Just as significantly, a CIS can also encourage us to theorise findings or question taken-for-granted research assumptions (Dixon-Woods et al., 2006). Importantly, a CIS does not prioritise quantitative over qualitative methods or findings and also instead looks to critically interrogate all sources of evidence whilst attempting to build and develop theory. Key processes followed include:

1. Start with a focused research topic and develop a question but accept that any research question may be revised following findings.
2. Follow search sources (as in an SR) but also draw creatively upon sources that don't fit but still have relevance (from the researcher's point of view).
3. The researcher decides if a critical appraisal (of strengths and weaknesses) is suitable or not for each paper or report, etc.
4. Identify and also be critical of research concepts (relating to the question/aims/objectives) as they emerge from all sources.
5. Synthesis of findings emerges from concepts and critiques. This can be viewed as a form of thematic analysis (chapter seventeen) whereby themes that emerge from reading are built up and evaluated for their relevance to your research.
6. Sampling of articles and theory generation develop at the same time.

The essential components of a CIS are clearly influenced by traditional narrative techniques yet each is presented as part of a seemingly more coherent, organised and rigorous approach. In some respects this might be interpreted as a combination of both the narrative approach and the SR, or at least as utilising the strengths of each according to a project. The clear advantage remains that this approach may offer greater structure or even legitimacy to your research in contrast to more diverse and possibly inconsistent narrative reviews. Importantly, principles such as anti-oppression or more holistic analysis within social work can also be integrated into a CIS (especially whilst reading articles found) and many of the disadvantages recognised within an SR may be reduced or avoided. There is, however, very little published on this approach and it is still developing.

The importance of critique

A vital, if not principal, skill to utilise when undertaking a review of relevant literature remains critique. Critique is not only expected for a dissertation or report it also represents a central component of analysis (chapter seventeen). Indeed it would not be possible to adequately explore a research question without recourse to a critical engagement with relevant literature. Aveyard (2010: 90–91) identifies critique as emerging from two related questions which ask if any identified literature is *relevant to the review or not* (i.e., does it help to answer the research question/problem) and also is it of *high enough quality to include* in a study? The first question is generally easier to answer but the second question will take up more time since you will need to read and evaluate each publication in order to assess its worth.

Answering the second question is also known as critical *appraisal*. Aveyard (2010: 96–9) suggests beginning by classifying each publication (for example is it a paper based on empirical research, literature review, chapter, book, report, etc.). Then as we read each we can begin to ask ourselves a series of questions and keep notes and an individual record on each. Crucial questions to ask include:

- What is being said?
- Who is the author?
- Why have the authors written this?
- How did they carry out the research?
- When was it said or written?
- Where does the information come from?

- Are the information and the arguments relevant to your research topic?
- What are the strengths of the publication?
- What are the weaknesses?

You may also look at the methodology that the authors used and whether or not the research methods utilised were appropriate or lacking in some way? Was the sample too small or could more have been done or was the original research aim too broad or unclear, and so on. How has theory been utilised or developed according to any findings or previous research? Inevitably, so many questions may prove too much, especially if you have discovered a high proportion of relevant publications that link to your study. In this instance you may wish to concentrate upon the most significant questions that link to your research objectives.

Jones (2009: 3) takes a broader perspective which is linked much closer to the critical traditions within social work. In particular, the author stresses additional skills that include:

> *Critique*: seeing the less apparent nuances (arguments and findings) as well as the obvious in what is read. Striving to be balanced rather than merely stressing the negatives.

> *Analyse*: be 'discerning about how you gather information and recognise the significance of its structure and significant parts'. This will include recognising *relevant* points raised that counter your own opinions.

> *Evaluate*: judge the quality, worth or value of an article or book and how these points relate to your study.

> *Synthesise*: this involves fusing together different ideas to make a new, and often more complex, whole. It may also involve the resolution of opposing views with an insightful resolution or compromise.

> *Reframe*: this is the taking of a new position for an argument and leads to new understanding.

As can be seen there are numerous techniques and skills to apply when undertaking a review. In general, we seek to avoid passively internalising information (assuming this is possible) and then summarising and describing it for a reader. Instead, we look to critically engage, evaluate, synthesise, and so on, in our endeavour to answer (or revise and better understand) our research question/problem. Our next role relates to the structure of a report, and then the presentation of our findings.

Case Study: Using a systematic review to critically evaluate the links between social work, poverty and social exclusion

Johnny wanted to critically explore the links between social work practice, poverty and social exclusion. He decided to draw upon and utilise a 'systematic review' to critically evaluate existing published literature. Once he had set clearly defined research objectives he then sought to:

- be systematic in how he searched for available literature, that is be clear and transparent regarding how he undertook his review (for example, which databases were drawn upon, any other resources utilized, developing a series of inclusion/exclusion criteria for his literature search, and so forth);
- offer a rationale in his final report underlining on what basis his search proceeded (for example, why he chose to use specific words and synonyms as part of his search of specific sites and why he selected discrete search engines or web sources);
- draw from relevant internet based search engines and other sites;
- search 'grey' literature such as reports included those held within government websites.

Johnny undertook a three stage review using both explicit (for example, poverty, social exclusion, poverty + social work, and so forth) and more implicit (for example, deprivation, neglect, and so forth) words for his search. First, he utilised key search engines such as *ASSIA* (Applied Social Sciences Index and Abstracts), the *Social Science Research Network*, *Web of Knowledge* and *Social Care Online*. This led to a wide range of relevant articles and other publications being found which he read and critically evaluated, including in relation to themes of relevance. Second, Johnny then undertook a more specific search with the help of search engines attached to relevant academic journal websites such as the *British Journal of Social Work*, *Qualitative Social Work* and the *Journal of Social Policy*. Finally, Johnny accessed 'grey' literature, or literature that cannot be found easily through conventional search engines or sources. This can include voluntary sector and charitable websites, not for profit reports, government sites and publications, think tank assessments and reports attached to University sites, and so forth. For example, Johnny looked at websites such as the *Joseph Rowntree Foundation* and the *Department of Education* and *Department of Health*, among others.

This three pronged search is relatively typical for a literature based dissertation and collected extensive literature which was then reduced by concentrating upon material that linked explicitly to Johnny's original research question

Structure of literature-based dissertations and reports

Typically, research that draws from empirical findings is often presented in a format that adheres to the following structure: introduction; methodology; literature review; findings; analysis; discussion and/or conclusion. Because literature-based research does not draw upon new empirical findings, and also concentrates specifically upon conceptual or theoretical themes throughout, different structures are possible which better reflect the findings. Indeed there is typically an array of potential structures for literature-based dissertations and reports. Table 5.1 below offers some examples.

Table 5.1   Different ways of structuring empirical and literature-based dissertations or reports

Empirical-based research dissertation/report	Type 1. Literature-based dissertation/report	Type 2. Literature-based dissertation/report
1. Introduction	1. Introduction	1. Introduction and methodology
2. Literature review	2. Methodology and Background	2. Background
3. Methodology	3. Topical Theme 1	3. Findings and analysis 1
4. Findings	4. Theme 2	4. Findings and analysis 2
5. Analysis and Discussion	5. Theme 3	5. Discussion
6. Conclusions	6. Discussion/Conclusions	6. Conclusions

In the first example, the traditional structure for an empirically-based dissertation or report is presented. This differs from the first literature-based dissertation, which has instead presented three core topical themes that relate to the general findings from within the thesis. The discussion and conclusion section then presents debates around themes discussed within the three-tier theme chapters. In the second literature-led dissertation or report, the researcher has instead presented his methodology as part of the introduction chapter. He has then offered a general 'literature review' styled chapter that presents previous research, and also concentrates upon findings uncovered which more explicitly link to his topic. Finally, both a discussion and conclusion chapter ends the report/dissertation.

Literature-based research typically provides us with more choice of how to present and structure our work. How best to do this may also depend upon factors such as your topic or findings.

Conclusion

This chapter has discussed literature-based research, methodologies and writing structures. It has argued that literature based research can permit more time to concentrate upon research themes and analysis, yet also that the establishment of a research topic and question/problem early on again remain important for this type of thematic or conceptual research. Different methodologies have now emerged to support literature-based research, yet the traditional narrative approach can be just as effective as any other method, especially if it is planned carefully. Despite this, a systematic review or critical interpretive synthesis may be more appropriate in some instances, especially for more practice-orientated or health care related research. Finally, it has been noted that literature-based research will tend to critique, evaluate and synthesise information from publications, as well as encourage a wider variety of ways to structure and present any findings.

Further reading

Alvesson, M. and Skoldberg, K. (2000). *Reflexive Methodology*. London, Sage

Aveyard, H. (2010). *Doing a Literature Review in Health and Social Care.* 2nd edn. Maidenhead, Open University Press

Dixon-Woods, M., Bonas, S., Booth, A., Jones, D.R., Miller, T., Shaw, R.L., Smith, J., Sutton, A., Young, B. (2006). 'How can systematic reviews incorporate qualitative research? A critical perspective'. *Qualitative Research* 6: 27–44

Hart, C. (1998). *Doing a Literature Review – Releasing the Social Science Research Imagination*. London, Sage

Hart, C. (2001) *Doing a Literature Search: A Comprehensive Guide for the Social Sciences* London, Sage.

Jones, S. (2009). *Critical Learning for Social Work*. Exeter, Learning Matters

Macdonald, J. (2003). *Using Systematic Reviews to Improve Social Care*, SCIE Report Number 4. London, Social Care Institute for Excellence

Wallace, M., and Wray, A. (2011). *Critical Reading and Writing for Post-Graduates.* 2nd edn. London, Sage

6 Theoretical and Philosophical Perspectives

Introduction

This chapter looks at the use of theory within qualitative social work research and its relation to philosophical perspectives. We also explore what we mean by theory and also how it may support the role of the researcher. We consider three key types of theory within qualitative research, including positivism, interpretive and critical theory, before finally looking at some of the philosophical components of qualitative research, including with a case example from a recent project. We begin by looking at the meaning and use of theory within qualitative social work research.

Using theory in qualitative social work research

Theory has been defined as a set of interrelated concepts, principles, statements or ideas that 'guide actions and conceptualisations [so to] provide clues or suggestions for intervention [that] help to explain things that we don't understand very well' (Royse, 1991: 16). A theory should also be able to offer us a way of *interpreting* events and provide a framework or means by which to *make sense* of the world in which we live and practise. Theory relating to social work can serve four possible purposes which include a capacity to help us:

- *organise* our activities and resources
- *explain* and *understand* the social world
- *assess*, *evaluate* and *predict* human behaviour and needs
- encourage social and political *change.*

Theory may not only help us understand what it is we are doing but also assist us to plan ahead, organise, arrange, intervene, evaluate, reflect upon and improve our practice and values: inevitably, such attributes may be valuable to qualitative researchers within social work.

Despite this, a question that continues to be asked within social research circles is whether or not theory should be central or explicit throughout any research project. Whatever the benefits, some researchers instead prefer to either avoid an explicit engagement with theory or relegate its overall use through a project. The rationale for this stance remain that the findings or data should be able to speak for themselves and should not be corrupted by numerous external or imposed theories. The reality is that theory rarely achieves this aim but is instead utilised by the researcher to help explain and interpret their findings, often during or following the analysis stage of research. Possible different relationships or options available to the social work researcher regarding theory and qualitative research include:

1. utilising one theory from an early stage (such as feminism or social ecology theory) in the cycle of a project;
2. drawing upon a variety of theories (e.g., different critical or practice-based theories);
3. allowing theory to influence a project (such as other people's findings or an exclicit theory such as phenomenology) yet privileging your own findings;
4. not having any explicit link to theory and allowing your data or information to speak for itself.

Potentially, any number of possible options may emerge within your own project. You may decide to take option four and have no clear or conscious link to theory and allow your findings to speak for themselves, itself a relatively common outcome for students certainly. Often, however, at least some link to theory persists, simply because we need to draw from other people's research findings to help make sense of our own. Sometimes this may be part of an open and explicit process – such as a researcher who strongly identifies with feminist theory and believes that this will help explain her to organise her project and help explain the wider world – often it is just part of the natural rituals held within a project. Although not compulsory, more sophisticated methodologies often have some form of systematic link to a theoretical framework. That is, although they do not allow a theory to constrain a project or determine findings, theory or theories stand to support and frame project when it becomes part of a methodology (chapter seven).

Theory tends to be more pronounced within most qualitative research projects for a number of reasons. Quantitative approaches tend to prioritise methods and objectivity above theory, whereas for some qualitative approaches the opposite can be true. There are also more theoretical models for researchers to choose from that link with many qualitative projects, and many researchers can feel a particular commitment to a specific theory or wider belief system. On a more practical level, comparison, context and understanding are also central to qualitative analysis. As an example, commitment to feminism or the principles of anti-discrimination tend to be popular within social work, and their advocates argue that research should not simply be about mechanically collecting and processing information to maintain systems and institutions as they are. Research should instead also be about encouraging positive change. There are, nevertheless, dangers in embracing openly ideological research, not least because it may distort your 'real' findings.

Professional researchers, students or practitioners are not expected to transform an established theory or create a new one. Instead, awareness and engagement with theory is a more likely expectation. If we are comparing our own findings to other similar studies our relationship to theory is embedded in the fact that we confirm, reject or more likely revise the findings of other researchers. Indeed, criticising or revising established theory tends to be the most common outcome of most qualitative research. However, evidence must be presented to support whatever stance is taken.

Levin (2005: 85–6) details some traditions followed and questions asked about a theory within research. These can include describing a theory for the reader, locating it within current academic or policy-related thinking, asking why a theory is needed or whether it is still valid, reviewing publications relating to a theory (including critiques) and considering alternative theory. We might also seek to test the theory and evaluate the theory or seek to improve it. There are then many different ways that our research may link to theory or be used by the researcher. Although not compulsory, at least some association is often inevitable yet one theory is rarely allowed to constrain or determine our findings, rather it will more often provide subtle support and guidance.

Core qualitative research theories

There are three key schools of theory which relate directly to qualitative research in social work. They are positivism, interpretive and critical theory (as well as various associated 'mongrel' and 'post' theories). Perhaps a little confusingly, each are also related to one another yet have distinct philosophical and practical qualities. For example, although positivism influences the application of all research – most prominently regarding the way by which research is planned and arranged – its view of the world is distinct and largely separate from the two other core theories. Indeed, the other two theories largely reject the view of the world projected by positivists. We shall now outline and explore each theoretical school and how they influence qualitative social work research.

i. Positivism (and post-positivism)

Positivism (drawn from 'realist' philosophy) assumes that scientific methods drawn from the natural sciences such as physics or biology may be applied directly to the study of people and wider society. It promotes the values of reason, logic, truth, objectivity and validity. Until the 1960s, positivism remained the centre of social scientific theory and philosophy (Brewer, 2003), and indeed in many respects this outlook has always influenced social work policy, practice and research (Jones, 1983). At its most basic, positivism seeks to construct and apply scientific laws to human behaviour, and also tries to promote measurement (of behaviour, attitudes, etc.), objectivity and a lack of bias in social research. Positivism assumes that 'evidence' and 'data' can be collected and accurately measured by researchers and also that the social life of people remains 'independent of human consciousness' (Jones, 1993: 118).

Positivism also seeks to encourage approaches which individualise human behaviour. It looks to isolate and carefully study a personality (or 'case') with only limited reference to other influences. Examples include theories attached to psychology, such as attachment or behavioural theory. Generally, these theories neglect the impact of wider structural or historical forces on human behaviour and attitudes and the impact of 'factors' or 'variables' such as poverty, gender, class, etc. There is a search for objective or uncontaminated 'truth' as part of this research philosophy and also an assumption that the neutrality of a researcher can be an explicit part of any project. There is an assumption that the researcher may be able to predict future human behaviour, based upon collected 'data' and establish laws to enhance this process. Positivism also privileges the use of statistical information and the gathering of social 'facts'. It attempts to discover causations and correlations and links between two or more 'variables'.

Particularly in science-based disciplines such as medicine, nursing and psychology the dominance of positivism has never really been challenged. Despite internal criticism, social work has nevertheless always retained a close link to positivism. For example, such as in its support for professionalism and 'casework' through which the 'expert' maintains a healthy and objective distance from the 'service user' and rationally assesses or evaluates their problems. There are also popular theories within social work – such as evidence-based practice, systems, task-centred approaches and classical Marxism – that draw directly from positivism. Such examples underline that positivism is more than just a methodology or theory – it is also a philosophy or ideology which encourages us to make many assumptions about the world around.

In contrast, post-positivism retains core elements of the positivist outlook but differs in two key respects. These include that post-positivists:

- accept that objectivity within social research cannot be guaranteed. Despite this, there is still an assumption that an unquestionable 'truth' may be acquired from qualitative research if proper procedures have been followed;
- question whether research can be value-free and instead recognise that the opinions held by researchers may influence their findings.

'Critical realism' is a form of post-positivism that draws from both the social and natural sciences and holds that there are forms of reality which are independent of our own existence. Such 'reality' can be captured by the social researcher yet research is not recognised as always being value-free. Critical realists also argue that theory requires regular revision and maintain that no one theory will be able to capture 'truth' for long periods. Inevitably the need for regular 'updates' generates demand for ongoing research to take place. There are also some advocates of critical realism who recognise the political implications of social research. This includes a belief that when psychological, organisational or structural mechanisms are discovered which promote disadvantage or social exclusion (as detected by the researcher) they should be challenged (via calls for reform or drawing attention to disadvantage, and so forth). Houston (2010: 88) stresses the link between critical realism and anti-oppressive social work research, and also notes its capacity to support more egalitarian methodologies such as action research (chapter seven). Houston argues that critical realist approaches examine:

> how human agency (actor's choices, meaning, understandings, reasons, creative endeavours, intentions and motivations) interacts with the enabling and constraining effects of social structures (durable, enduring patterns, social rules, norms and law like configurations). To understand social life, it is argued, we must comprehend the interplay between these two, central spheres.

There is then within environments and relations a complex and stratified set of social bonds comprising 'an array of interlocking domains' in which the task of the researcher is to:

- understand the empirical interconnections between human agency and social structure;
- recognise the social world as essentially open and complete with 'a heterogeneous assembly of different causal mechanisms';
- combine the personal with the political.

On a philosophical level, critical realism stands somewhere *between* positivist and interpretive theory (discussed below).

Although the explicit use of positivism or post-positivism has tended to be relatively muted in qualitative social work research, it has become more popular in government-funded (and arguably more conservative) social work research. Most dissertations or research projects within social work instead tend to rely upon more in-depth analysis: either accommodating a small sample of participants, an evaluative study of a small- to medium-sized organisation or thorough investigation of aspects of specialist literature. Each may struggle to fit within a traditional realist approach, and indeed there are serious questions as to whether more general social work research can fit with this type of narrow ideological research. Also, the largely unpredictable *qualitative* nature of the social work role; based as it nearly always is within diverse and unpredictable 'community' settings, and the ethical or political principles that are apparent within practice, provide significant hurdles. Despite these reservations, at least some aspects of positivism remain in all forms of qualitative social work research and critical realist approaches offer more recognition of disadvantage and the many contingent factors that influence the social work role.

ii. Interpretive theory

Interpretive approaches (or 'hermeneutics') look to unearth meaning and try to discover how people interprete and understand their direct experiences in the social world. A researcher tries to gauge, reach and comprehend the perspectives, opinions, emotional responses and attitudes held by participants. Interpretivists argue that researchers should

- unearth people's *interpretations* of the worlds around them;
- better understand the *beliefs* and *actions* that people hold and engage in;
- explain the impact or role that participants' themselves have in creating the micro-worlds around them.

Douglas (1984: 8) defines the interpretive view as seeing:

> the social world as constructed *by* social actors through their vastly complex interactions in concrete situations.... Society is not a separate level of reality outside of individuals determining what they do, as structuralists argued. Society is what individuals are and what they do.

Interpretive researchers challenge the realist view of the world which argues that we can *objectively* evaluate and predict the behaviour of social actors or groups being studied. Instead, a *subjective* personal understanding of people and their interpretation of the 'worlds around them' becomes the goal of the researcher. Interpretive theorists also reject the idea that we can acquire or measure quantifiable 'facts' as in the positivistic tradition. In contrast, the sometimes tedious skills of listening and/or observation take priority.

Although there are different interpretive theories, each shares common attributes that include a tendency to:

- Concentrate upon the individual and the personal *strategies* of research subjects. This includes participants' use of language and behaviour so as to understand how the world appears to each.
- Through often unstructured interviews sometimes drawn over a long period of time try to understand the diverse and unique social worlds of research participants and/or related social group(s).
- Stress participants' response to external stimuli (symbols, knowledge, language, etc.).
- Aim to capture participants' subjective meaning of their own world.
- Empathise with, and therefore try to better understand, research participants.
- Encourage research participants to take a lead role within the research process rather than be directed by the researcher.

Interpretive theory is closely linked to constructivism (chapter three) which:

- views meaning as uncertain and ambivalent, open to interpretation;
- stresses people's choices, which are not however free but restricted by tradition and rules;
- looks at the importance of human relationships;
- considers how people negotiate meaning, including in groups, and construct and understand their reality (e.g., being homeless, a lone parent, a disabled man, a social work practitioner, etc.).

Ethnomethodology is an example of an interpretive theory. It seeks to investigate the ways by which people create order in their lives and as a consequence looks at people's use of 'common sense knowledge'. More particularly it attempts to 'analyse the methods, or the procedures, that people use for conducting the different affairs that they accomplish in their daily lives' (Coulon, 1995: 2). Ethnomethodologists scrutinise 'members' methods' or their 'practical actions as part of the accomplishment of 'organised artful practices' within everyday life' (Roberts, 2006: 89). Livingston (1987: 10) adds that ethnomethodology is the study 'of the common, everyday naturally-occurring, mundane methods that are used by people to produce and manage the common, everyday activities of the everyday world – activities like shaking hands, taking turns in a conversation, reaching a verdict, standing in line [etc.]'. This approach can be especially valid for understanding the practical role of the social work practitioner: including their engagement with activities such as undertaking an assessment, making telephone calls, keeping a diary, presenting evidence in a court of law or using and interpreting professional ethics or a theory, among many more.

Overall, the impact of interpretive theory upon qualitative social work research (and practice) has tended to be relatively muted. However, this trend would appear to be changing with greater use of theories such as phenomenology and ethnomethodology within social work research. One reason for this relates to the links between interpretivism and social work's use of casework, assessment and evaluation to understand and organise their role. Such tasks and others can be better understood by a researcher who uses an interpretive approach to guide their study. Another interpretive theory and methodology, that of phenomenology, is discussed in chapter seven.

iii. Critical theory

This approach to qualitative research views the role as offering more than just a series of tasks in which we collect, analyse and report data, so as to better explain or understand society. Instead, social research is viewed more as a political activity which can highlight disadvantage, power imbalances and question established normative practices, values, traditions, and so forth. In essence, research 'should…seek to change society for the better' (Porter, 2003: 60).

As with interpretive theory, generally diverse critical approaches reiterate a distinct cultural and political challenge to the 'reductive' posturing seemingly embedded within positivism. They reject the relevance of applying scientific methods to social research and instead ask deeper questions about the ethical consequences of such potentially damaging research processes for participants who become reduced to 'objects' of study. Critical theory is recognised as a relatively consistent yet disparate methodological approach that includes a tendency to rigorously explore *cultural* forms of disadvantage, including ways by which language and knowledge production is used to maintain dominance and control for privileged groups and exclude others. It also looks to identify and explain the *causes* and *impact* of social or economic inequality and many other forms of social exclusion, discrimination and disadvantage. In doing so, it draws particularly from feminist theory but is also influenced by Marxist and post-structural ideas which stress the role of class and power in maintaining privilege and social exclusion.

Critical theory emphasises 'structural' forms of disadvantage and exclusion: such as service users' restricted and limited access to resources, including those that relate to circumscribed employment and education opportunities, housing, health and social service support, among other types of 'life chances'. It also stresses the importance of alternative ideas and practices, especially those that seek to alleviate discrimination and emancipate disadvantaged social groups. There may persist a tendency to also try to link the personal experiences of service users or practitioners with wider structural forms of disadvantage. For example, by exploring the personal statements and experiences of service users, such as regarding their past relations with professionals or wider institutions such as schools or the health and social care system. Critical theorists often look at *reflexivity* or the values of the researcher, which are identified as always influencing the research process, and reveal their own beliefs, and how initial beliefs and values might have changed throughout a study.

Standpoint theory within feminism offers an example of critical theory for research. Hekman (1997) lists its main attributes, some of which include:

- To link *knowledge* with *power* as opposed to the realist priority given to 'reality'.
- To ground the researcher's experience as an oppressed female in the research process, drawing upon past knowledge to empathise with participants.
- Recognising the identity of feminists and research participants as fluid and changing rather than, again amidst many positivist assumptions, fixed and stable.
- Realising the potential dangers of knowledge and power held by the feminist researcher over the participant.
- Recognising diversity and different power relations held between women, including as subjects of research.
- Always being willing (within reason) to question the researchers own 'truth' claims, including from their own research findings.

Critical theory also links to and encompasses postmodernism, which emphasises the use of more eclectic theory and methodologies. It highlights diversity, social fragmentation, and questions essences of truth that traditionally have compartmentalised complex knowledge and social occurrences into convenient packages (Positivism especially but also core aspects of Marxism and some feminist theory). In particular, postmodernists promote social diversity, ambivalence and the use of research to permit 'excluded' voices to be heard. In relation, Interpretive and Critical approaches can also be combined as part of a sophisticated and applied social research methodology that may even accommodate aspects of critical realism.

A critique that holding strong preconceived views may undermine a project is a relatively common complaint made against 'value-based' or 'openly ideological' critical researchers (see Lather, 1986, for a related discussion). Might the researcher already have made key decisions about their findings in advance of their research beginning, or just as questionable perhaps, attempt to 'fit' their findings within their own preconceived political ideals?

We may, however, draw from different theories to organise our research project through our methodology (chapter seven) or instead utilise critical approaches to analyse or better understand our data and findings, including when we write them up in a final report or dissertation. Whatever the limits of critical theory regarding demands for a seemingly 'objective' political perspective, there is no doubt that such varied and rich approaches have helped to extend knowledge and understanding to previously never-ventured-into terrains, and their sustained influence continues within qualitative research of all forms. The influence of critical theory within social work is most prominently felt within models of practice such as anti-oppressive and anti-discriminatory practice as well as the widespread expansion of participative research (chapter fifteen).

Philosophical perspectives

Epistemology and ontology

In addition to the three core theoretical schools we can also link our research according to the philosophical implications of what it is we hope to investigate and how. Along with theory this may sometimes be neglected as a priority – especially regarding the physical act of undertaking applied research – but it can again help us to better understand how our study and methodology fits with important wider debates and processes.

To begin with, there is an important distinction to be made between epistemology and ontology. Epistemology relates to the study of knowledge and science. It also represents the nature of knowledge and knowledge production, including what the researcher counts as knowledge. Regarding a research project, the epistemology is represented by the theories we use to support a methodology and also then gather and analyse findings. It also refers to the theory we may create or extend as part of our research. Each of the theoretical schools discussed earlier in this chapter represents epistemology, as do more specific theories such as feminism, phenomenology or anti-discrimination, among others.

Ontology in contrast has much broader consequences and meaning than epistemology. It refers to 'the nature of being or social entities', it represents 'the study of what is real' and asks wider questions such as 'why do we exist' or 'is there a god' (Elliott, 2005)? In the context of social work research there may be an ontological question(s) held within our research project or question such as do older people experience discrimination or what does life in a residential home actually mean to its residents?

Ontology, epistemology, methodology and method

Any research project or dissertation can be divided up into four inter-related sections that include its ontological, epistemological, methodological and method related components. As stated, ontology reflects the nature of social reality and what the researcher understands reality to be like, whereas epistemology represents the nature of knowledge and knowledge production. Methodology is the theoretical and philosophical assumptions linked to a topic and the ways in which any such topic will be interrogated and, finally, methods remain the procedures followed in order to gather data relating to a topic.

Each research project is held together by a bridge that stands between epistemology and ontology; with recognition that knowledge and its production support the investigation of ontological themes. In essence, more detailed knowledge helps us to better understand why we are here and what this means to us all. The broader claims or statements that represent ontology – and which are usually held within a research question – require exploration and evidence to confirm, revise or reject their claims.

Methodology and method(s) represent research processes that use knowledge to support the production of more detailed knowledge. This new knowledge is then used to answer the ontological question set at the beginning of a research project (Carey, 2009).

This set of relationships is summarised in the example below (figure 6.1).

In the example illustrated in figure 6.1, the researcher has made an ontological statement which argues that informal support or caring undertaken primarily by women reflects a personal response (on behalf of the carer) to wider cultural and group expectations and norms. That is, the tendency for women to fulfil a caring role for an ill or disabled relative embodies a response to peer and family pressure – and wider established norms – as opposed to seemingly 'natural' *biological* influences. To test and confirm this through research and subsequent knowledge production the researcher has used an interpretive methodology because it rigorously explores personal experiences and meanings from a participant (carer's) perspective.

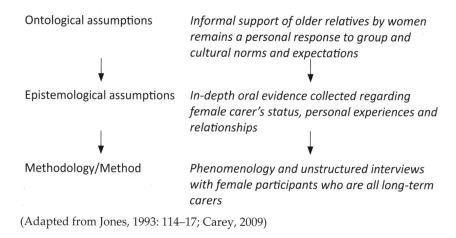

Ontological assumptions

Informal support of older relatives by women remains a personal response to group and cultural norms and expectations

Epistemological assumptions

In-depth oral evidence collected regarding female carer's status, personal experiences and relationships

Methodology/Method

Phenomenology and unstructured interviews with female participants who are all long-term carers

(Adapted from Jones, 1993: 114–17; Carey, 2009)

Figure 6.1   Ontology, epistemology, methodology and method in action: A research project supported by interpretive theory

As a method, unstructured interviews fit with an interpretive methodology as each permits space and time for participants to engage with the core intention of the research, and also allow the researcher to explore the meaning and experiences of the carers, as well as the context of the experiences for each participant. Overall, it is hoped that evidence collected from such interviews, as well as previous published research or evidence, will help the researcher to fully understand and then explain the experiences, attitudes and values of each participant regarding their carer roles.

Although not essential, constructing such a table may help us to better understand what it is you are hoping to achieve and how this might be done. It may, for example, also help us to see how the various tasks, roles and theory relate to the overall project so to give it greater clarity and purpose.

Conclusion

This chapter has looked at the three schools of theory used in social research: positivism, interpretive and critical theory. It has been shown that each theoretical school has different qualities and world views yet also takes a different stance regarding how to fulfil research objectives and explain and understand research findings. For some projects there may be no explicit or conscious link to theory use: a researcher may decide to allow data to 'speak for itself'. Often, however, a researcher or student will commit to one theoretical approach alone as part of their methodology, or use a more eclectic mix of related theories. This chapter has also detailed the distinction between ontology, epistemology, methodology and method, and highlighted how each relates and is applied when undertaking qualitative social work research.

Further reading

Alvesson, M. (2002). *Postmodernism and Social Research.* Buckingham, Open University Press

Corby, B. (2006). *Applying Research in Social Work Practice.* Maidenhead, Open University Press. Chapter 4 – Paradigm Wars

Crotty, M. (1998). *The Foundations of Social Research – Meaning and Perspective in the Research Process.* London, Sage

Humphries, B. (2008). *Social Work Research for Social Justice.* Basingstoke, Palgrave Macmillan. Chapter 7 – Critical Social Research

Lather, P. (1986). 'Issues of Validity in Openly Ideological Research: Between a Rock and a Soft Place'. *Interchange* 17(4): 63–84

Ramazanoglu, C., and Holland, J. (2002). *Feminist Methodology: Challenges and Choices.* Sage, London

Roberts, B. (2006). *Micro Social Theory.* Basingstoke, Palgrave Macmillan

7   Methodology

Introduction

This chapter introduces an all-embracing, indeed paramount concept within qualitative social work research, that of methodology. A good methodology will be able to guide and add coherence to any research project and also limits the dangers of wandering away too far from the original intentions and objectives of our study. Methodology offers not only direction but can also furnish the research process with theoretical understanding and purpose. This chapter defines and discusses methodology and then gives two examples: first, a theoretical perspective (phenomenology) and, second, a practice-centred approach (action research). We then look at methodological pluralism and some of the criticism held against methodology before concluding with the summary.

Methodology

Methodology is often assumed to refer to the different methods (interviews, focus group meetings, etc.) we apply to collect our information or 'data' as part of our research. This is not the case. Instead, methodology refers to the set of ideas, theory or philosophy that surrounds, encompasses and, literally, 'holds together' a research project. As Cohen et al. (2007: 47) indicate, a methodology will help 'us to understand, in the broadest possible terms, not the *products* of scientific enquiry but the *process* itself'. The analogy of a bag conveniently holding all our different possessions together is sometimes used.

Crotty (1998: 66) privileges the importance of the theoretical perspectives central to methodology and the assumptions that the reader of a final report or paper can draw from this. Different methodologies draw from different theories that influence how the researcher applies their methods and interprets their findings. Payne and Payne (2004: 151) highlight the ways by which a specific methodology will indicate clearly and succinctly to the reader the values of the researcher and how their project has been moulded.

Methodology offers us a theoretical and philosophical foundation (such as realism, feminist, critical, etc.) which in turn will then influence the methods that we deploy to collect our information and data. For example, we saw earlier in chapter six that interpretive perspectives stress the importance of people's experiences, meanings, understandings and interpretation of events 'in their own world'. Within such a methodology or applied philosophy will fit a method such as the unstructured interview, which allows people to discuss their opinions, attitudes and values at great length. It also allows the researcher to focus their intentions by helping to make sense and explaining what the participant is discussing. In contrast, a more critical methodology, such as one influenced by standpoint feminism (chapter six), might instead encourage the researcher to get closer to participants and engage over a longer period of time to understand and detail their person experiences of discrimination or whatever else. Therefore, a narrative interview (chapter fourteen) approach, in which the researcher looks carefully at how participant's express their views through language, may be more suited to this methodology (see, for example, Skeggs, 2001).

Since methodology looks also at the philosophical implications of research it will also influence other stages in the research process. For example, as well as influence how we interpret our findings it can also affect how we write them up. So a researcher driven by a feminist methodology is likely to draw upon other research findings undertaken by critical thinkers who highlight the disadvantages faced by women in the home and workplace, as elsewhere. In addition, any such methodology will also influence the ethics of the research process. This might include the practical extent to which and how anonymity is maintained or more philosophically to what extent any participants are involved in decision-making processes regarding how the research develops and is applied. A science-based (or 'realist') study is instead likely to encourage stringent procedures to follow regarding anonymity and the storage of data, but may also limit or exclude participants from being involved as a co-researcher. Specific methodologies can therefore embroil their influence throughout a research project, and in so doing provide a foundation upon which any project is based.

In practice, a methodology will tend to be decided relatively early within the research process. However, it is also not unusual for it to adapt and change as the research progresses: once again, it is the flexibility of qualitative approaches that distinguishes such methodologies. A methodology can also be drawn from a combination of different strategies and types of theory.

Examples of methodologies that can be utilised in social work research are now discussed below. First, we begin with a theoretically-centred approach and then continue with a practice-based methodology. Critiques of methodology are then considered.

Phenomenology

This theory looks at 'conscious experience' from the points of view of research participants who are each perceived as drawing upon a 'stock of knowledge' to guide them through the world. This knowledge is made up of beliefs and perceptions which guide us all through life but which is also open to change based upon new forms of knowledge. Such new knowledge can be gained from different sources, yet group belonging and identity are seen as offering an important source of knowledge (alongside past experience and education). There is subsequently 'a common knowledge of shared "systems of relevances" of what is deemed to be natural or appropriate by ... group members' (Roberts, 2006). The role of the researcher is to tap into and understand such acquired/held knowledge. Phenomenology does not entirely concentrate upon the individual but also the influence of wider cultural and structural factors upon behaviour and values.

Phenomenology belongs to the interpretive school of theories which search for *meaning* among research participants; especially the ways in which people interpret and make sense of the world in which they live. This may relate to a role fulfilled or a part played within an organisation by a social worker or volunteer. In practice, phenomenology as methodology looks to discover what it means *to participants themselves* to be human, and how any sense of all that is around – including the sometimes apparently mundane – helps to achieve understanding and purpose for people themselves. By using this methodology, a researcher also seeks to understand the strategies that people employ in their day-to-day lives. As Wilson (2002, my emphasis) explains:

> [Phenomenologists assume that] people are engaged in an on-going process of making sense of the world, in interaction with their fellows and we, as scientists, are seeking *to make sense of their sense-making* .... What distinguishes the social scientific enterprise, however, is that the social scientist assumes the position of the disinterested observer. He or she is not involved in the life of those observed – their activities are not of any practical interest, but only of cognitive interest ... the social scientist may focus on aspects of behaviour that are taken-for-granted by the ordinary person, but that are topics of cognitive interest to the social scientist.

When physically undertaking research into a topic the methodology can often appear *descriptive* in practice, although forms of analysis do filter into, and become a part of, any research process, especially during later stages. As with most interpretive theories, phenomenology is most commonly utilised during one-to-one interviews, as this method allows us to directly uncover and explore ways by which people express their experiences, opinions and values. The approach can also fuse with observations of group interaction or activities alongside one-on-one interviews. However, phenomenology as methodology also looks to uncover hidden meanings and themes beneath the surface of participants' 'reality' – this may include implicit meanings within parts of an interviewee's conversation that is linked to a researcher's research topic, and which might also be indicated by a participant's use of body language. A researcher will often take notes as well as transcribe during any interviews so as not to miss gestures or expressions that may have significance (Holloway, 1997: 118–21).

Colaizzi (1978) suggests seven stages that are followed during phenomenological research. These include:

1. Questions for interviews are prepared, and interviews are then undertaken with a small sample and each is then (ideally) taped and transcribed. Bear in mind that transcribing is time-consuming and sufficient time should be allocated in advance for this task. Semi-structured interviews generally remain the best format for a social work dissertation or small project due to the relative freedom allowed to ask additional questions if necessary (please see chapter nine for further information regarding interviews). *Transcripts are then read several times over so that the reader is able to understand and fully appreciate the participant's meanings regarding what has been discussed.*

2. *Researchers isolate significant statements within each transcript. Statements that link to relevant themes are translated and summarised into notes that exemplify their analytical significance.* For example, the statement 'I want more time alone and also wish that staff would not enter my room without knocking on the door first' becomes 'service user antipathy regarding lack of privacy; especially from staff members'.

3. This is a crucial stage in which *significant statements (from 2 above) are interpreted by the researcher into the participant's 'meanings'.* This stage is likely to include any understanding by the researcher of participant's *hidden* meanings, and will draw upon the researcher's skill and ability to interpret the person's meanings from each interview using implicit and explicit 'evidence' drawn from transcripts, observations and notes.

4. The *process in stage 3 above is then repeated for each interview and all 'meanings are organised into clusters of themes'.* From here onwards 'common patterns' become apparent and each is considered and compared against the full transcripts and notes for confirmation and any possible new interpretations that could emerge.

5. *A detailed 'exhaustive description' of the participant's feelings and ideas are summarised in written form;* these are based upon those extracted from the themes identified in 4 above.

6. From the exhaustive description above, *the researcher looks to uncover a 'structure' of meaning that has emerged from the participant's themes and transcripts.*
7. *The themes, structure, etc., are summarised and presented individually to the participants who then consider and feedback any responses.* This process allows for any gaps to be filled and may also mean that data or themes not included are added.

The means of identifying, exploring and *developing* themes from a source of (participant) data, rather than preconceived prejudices or assumptions, provide the essence of the phenomenological technique. As Holloway (1997: 120, my emphasis) insists: 'researchers should read with an open mind and suspend prior assumptions by making them explicit and being aware of them. They *follow the ideas of the participants rather than imposing their own.'* This process has been criticised for underestimating or excluding an appreciation of wider structural and cultural factors, especially those that impinge upon participants' values and actions (for example, social norms, prior education, religious beliefs, employment opportunities or organisational regulations, among others).

As a part of the phenomenological method other skills used include an assumption that:

- Participants are treated as individuals (who nevertheless rely upon other people) to help them to understand and create the world around them. This is also known as 'intersubjectivity'.
- People rely upon 'classifications' within their worlds to typify what it is they are doing, and also this occurs as part of a need to create a source of pragmatic knowledge to draw on. An example of this classification process would include the ways by which a social worker might label or rank different service users, relatives or other professionals, as being 'competent', 'demanding', 'caring', 'warm' or 'neglectful' *types.*

In practice, phenomenology can offer an extremely beneficial methodology to a social work researcher. This is because it seeks to explore and investigate in-depth a small sample of participants via a rigorous set of interview techniques. Exploring the 'micro-worlds' of people from their own perspective may be an ideal way to study the identity of a carer, a person who works with challenging children or a volunteer who helps older people with their gardening. Phenomenology can also be relatively easily applied, such as within a practice placement or work setting, and is also useful for exploring the world of the social work practitioner, another professional or occupational group within or attached to social care. It is less likely to be able to allow us to generalise about a social group being researched.

Interpretative phenomenological analysis

Interpretative phenomenological analysis (IPA) is a methodological approach influenced by phenomenology and which is 'committed to the examination of how people make sense of their major life experiences' (Smith et al., 2009: 1). It draws from hermeneutics (the study of interpretation), phenomenology and psychology. Typically through one-to-one semi-structured or small group interviews, IPA seeks to examine in great depth and detail individual experiences, including major events in a person's life (for example, schooling, relationships, work, etc.). IPA seeks to avoid predetermining findings by limiting or avoiding pre-interview theoretical or conceptual engagement. Great emphasis is placed upon encouraging research participants to discuss at length and reflect upon their specific experiences under examination. IPA is particularly effective for examining major life events (having a first child, loss or bereavement, close relationships, beginning school or work, etc.) and therefore strong links to social work abound. Smith et al. (2009: 1) highlight that the key to IPA is building trust between the interviewer and interviewee(s), and for the former to be able to suspend belief and see through the eyes of the participant:

> IPA shares the view that human beings are sense-making creatures, and therefore the accounts which participants provide will reflect their attempts to make sense of their experience. IPA also recognises that access to experience is always dependent on what participants tell us about that experience, and that the researcher then needs to interpret that account from the participant in order to understand their experience.

The key is not so much an event or isolated experience itself but instead *how the participant makes sense of such an event or experience.* A small sample (between 1–14 people) is selected, with participants chosen according to their capacity to help us investigate and answer a research question or social problem. There is typically an implicit bond held between participants in that they have in common personal experience relating to the topic of investigation (for example, parents who have adopted children with mental health needs, support workers based in residential care homes, newly qualified mental health social workers etc.). Interviews can be person-centred or group led and may take place as single events or run over an extended period. In contrast to many other methodologies, however, IPA interviews are likely to last for a longer period of time, typically for at least an hour. Another method sometimes used alongside the individual or group interview remains the 'participant diary' by which a daily account of the subject's experience (relating to the research theme) is kept by the participant and then evaluated by the researcher.

Typically, interviews are recorded and transcribed, although for a student dissertation notes may suffice. The researcher then reads and re-reads printed transcripts (or notes) to capture, reduce and evaluate salient themes that link to the research question: a similar process is followed if a diary has been kept by each participant. Inevitably, the process of gathering and evaluating data is time consuming and can be strenuous for any researcher. Codes for transcripts can be used as a part of analysis (see chapter seventeen) but the essence of the approach is for the researcher to identify and understand the experiences of the research participant. Ideally this is without being influenced by previous assumptions or knowledge gained about the people or topic being interviewed or explored.

There are likely to emerge 'hierarchies of experience' from interviews or diary accounts. For example, if exploring the early stages of adoption from a parent's perspective many participants may prioritise their emotional difficulties experienced and neglect the advice or support offered by professionals. Such responses regarding personal and group experience will represent an important aspect of the findings. A table which represents and frames the findings (including any hierarchies of experience) can be constructed by the researcher: this can help to summarise the different experiences of participants and may also distinguish and scale the more significant themes discovered from the least. The writing-up of any findings will generally involve a merger of descriptive accounts of participant's experience (including the use of quotes from interviews or diaries) set alongside the researcher's interpretation of any discussion of the findings. IPA does not generally seek to accept or reject established theory but, as with much qualitative research, is likely instead to revise or extend an established theory.

Action research

Action research (also known as participatory action research) involves the researcher working closely with participants to the point that participants are *actively involved* in the research project. Contrary to many traditional research methodologies, participants become researchers themselves. Usually this collaborative approach involves diagnosing a social or organisational problem (that will link to, or become, the research question), to which a solution is developed jointly with participants based on a diagnosis initiated by both the researcher and participants (McNiff, 2000).

It often involves collective tasks and roles – such as reflection, evaluation, planning, task completion and action – which co-exist within on-going 'cycles' of action with a collective aim.

Action research became popular during the counter-cultural and activist political movements of the 1960s and 1970s, although its roots lay in the critical response to positivism or 'scientific' research initiated by the Frankfurt school of critical theory (Miles, 1993: 66). The spirit of action research is exemplified by attempts to utilise social research in tandem with efforts to 'fuse knowledge building with empowerment and social advocacy'. In a practical sense, the activist traditions of action research mean that researchers endeavour to ensure that participants 'maintain substantial control over the study from start to finish' (Padgett, 1998: 11). Despite this, the widespread dissemination of action research has inevitably led to a diverse range of permutations and incarnations emerging, some of which have diluted or become distracted somewhat from their original form. This has included a tendency to promote efficiency, teamwork and effectiveness as organisational and management-led priorities, rather than the emancipation and empowerment of disadvantaged groups such as service users.

Grundy (1990) subsequently proposes three distinct models of action research – the technical, practical and emancipatory. Each is summarised below:

1. *Technical*: this model is detached from the original critical intentions of action research but it does maintain some links, chiefly relating to a degree of involvement enjoyed by participants and a will on behalf of the researcher to encourage *change*. However, the researcher is expected to lead the project and seeks a 'more efficient or effective practice as [their] objective'. This might include eventual changes in response to the research findings, such as reforming aspects of an organisation: for example the role of staff, management practices, or changing staff relations with customers or service users. Participants are largely passive throughout the research process and consultation is kept to a minimum with the researcher's direction taking priority. Humphries (2008: 73) warns that aspects of the technical model are 'contrary to the ethical standards of much social work research'.

2. *Practical*: again within this model a relatively marginal role is played by participants and much direction is provided by the researcher. The researcher identifies and looks to improve aspects of an organisation which will subsequently benefit participants, who may include service users. Consultation involves the researcher *stimulating* participants. Although responsibility is held within parameters defined by the

researcher, there may be scope for a co-facilitator role on behalf of at least one participant.

3. *Emancipatory*: the closest model to the original aspirations of action research in which the 'system' is seen as constraining the actions of individuals and groups. Participants are deliberately exposed at regular intervals to critical theories which seek to question and undermine the status quo; and this should lead to the (Marxist and critical feminist) notion of *praxis* emerging in which critical theory binds with and influences practice. This cultural process is then supplemented by group reflection and enlightenment, and further engagement with praxis in the field of research. This mutual or 'symbiotic' ritual is then repeated and recurs. Importantly, dialogue is encouraged between service users and organisation members, such as employed staff, who *together* represent the participants. The researcher oversees this process but allows participants to lead and direct the research process.

Additional themes identified within action research include a tendency to:

- encourage change for individuals as well as associated groups, organisations and communities to which participants belong;
- change the 'language and discourse, activities and practices, and social relationships and organisation which constitute the interactions of the [participant] group' (Kemmis and McTaggart, 1990, cited in Humphries, 2008: 75);
- support reflexive critique, especially the capacity for participants and researchers to become more aware of their own 'perceptual biases';
- enhance collaboration between people and encourage democratic processes and group understanding;
- encourage researchers and participants to question their role and wider purpose;
- support an appreciation of wider critiques among all involved in the research process rather than one single definition and understanding of 'truth';
- encourage the interdependence and application of theory and practice through praxis.

Before deciding to pursue and initiate a piece of action research, the following questions should be considered:

- How many participants are you likely to involve?
- How long will the project take to complete?

- Are enough participants likely to agree to be involved with the research project? Who is likely to recruit the participants and how?
- Are any participants likely to require some training regarding research methods prior to the project beginning? If so, who will provide this training?
- Are participants likely to remain involved in the project, especially if it is long term?
- If required, do you have adequate financial and other resources to sustain the project?
- Will you be able to manage the project from start to finish?

It may not be possible to answer all of these questions at once. Nevertheless, it will help to consider as many as possible prior to beginning what is likely to be an ambitious and time-consuming piece of research. As a methodology, most forms of action research fit well with many of the emancipatory and ethical principles of social work. This approach also fits neatly with critical theories – including anti-discriminatory, feminist, Marxist and anti-oppressive practice, among others; so it provides a relatively clear, if not contested, theoretical and philosophical framework to draw from. Despite some interpretations involving strong principles, action research is nevertheless flexible and adaptable and can be interpreted in differing ways depending upon personal projects, course or organisational requirements and specific topics selected to study.

Due to practical restraints it is unlikely that an ambitious interpretation of action research can be fulfilled for most researchers or courses due to the relatively limited amount of time and resources available to social work students or practitioners. It may also be an inappropriate methodology for some placements or social work courses. For other research it is likely that more control of the research process may be necessary to save time. One possible way of coping with this problem is if selective and/or core aspects of action research are utilised within a methodology. For example, core aspects might include a tendency to:

- Involve, wherever possible and within reason, participants in the research process.
- Wherever feasible, endeavour not to dominate and control research proceedings.
- Consider how you might balance the principle of participant involvement with any need to explore the initial research question.
- At an early stage set realistic aims and objectives that can be met.
- Carefully contemplate the implications of any restrictions regarding time, resources, ethical consequences, and so on, by which to complete the research.

Critics have tended to highlight the loss of control and rigour that action research can sometimes encourage (Cancian, 1993) as well as the potential for bias in the findings. Some interpretations of this methodology also seem to assume that participants will act as a united and collective group who will follow a predictable response to the delicate matters raised and agree upon how to proceed with the research. Practically, this is unlikely and disagreements may be difficult to plan for and accommodate. Also, this approach can be extremely complex and is likely to draw upon much knowledge and demand many interpersonal skills, especially those relating to communication and diplomacy. In general, action research is most suited to research projects held over a longer period of time and when the researcher has good access to a particular organisation or group. It may not be suitable for many social work courses as the time-commitment and engaged practices are likely to impact upon other course requirements, such as the completion of portfolios, essays, and so forth. For some researchers, ethical permissions may also be more difficult to attain.

Criticism of methodology and different approaches

Although popular as a means of organising research, methodology has been criticised. Seale et al. (2004: 7–8) promote a more flexible or fluid methodology and ague that otherwise we are drawing too heavily from rationalist or scientific practices that constrain research projects. Aveyard (2010: 37–8) argues that theoretical frameworks typically support research but are not essential. Instead, we can build our research around endeavours and methods that seek to answer a clearly defined research question. Implicit within such criticism is an attempt to allow findings and data to take priority. Hindess (1973) argues that methodologies remain contradictory, and maintain only a tenuous link with what researchers go on to do and apply *in practice*. More of a concern, perhaps, they may also draw attention away from any data collected and also encourage bias.

Rather than advocate a type of research anarchy, many such critics are suggesting that any research methodology should be able to alter according to specific or unplanned circumstance, so that they more readily relate to the discovery of new information. This more flexible approach can help permit more discretion, as well as allow the researcher to remain in control of their project (rather than at the mercy of a predetermined methodology). More importantly, perhaps, this more flexible stance may better reflect findings and support analysis. Other approaches might avoid any link to a specific school of theory, and instead compare or combine emerging ideas with different sources (such as other peoples' research findings), build theory from data or use theory as a *negative* reference point.

Nevertheless, some researchers prefer the support offered by a clear methodology and this approach also suits some projects more than others. For example, there are obvious benefits regarding the setting of clear plans prior to undertaking a piece of action research or if drawing upon Interpretative Phenomenological Analysis prior to and during any interviews with social work practitioners. It is important, however, to use your discretion. It is also possible to combine different approaches and theories when constructing and developing a methodology to suit specific research aims and objectives. This is commonly referred to as 'methodological pluralism'. For example, if we wish to discover the preferred support available to female carers of older disabled male relatives (for example, respite, day or domiciliary care) then we may look to combine a core interpretive approach (such as phenomenology) with some aspects of feminist theory as part of our methodology. The former will allow us to better understand and interpret the meanings articulated by female carers interviewed whilst the latter will help us to analyse the findings by comparing them with past feminist research that has analysed the expectations placed on women to fulfil caring roles. As we shall see later, combinations of different methods, such as interviews and focus groups or case study research, are again common as part of a methodology. Clearly, utilising a methodological pluralist approach will demand a sense of creativity and imagination.

Conclusion

This chapter has highlighted the role played by methodology in helping to support research. A methodology can provide us with a recipe of method(s), scheme of ideas, a framework in which to organise a project and a theoretical and philosophical structure around which to support a project or dissertation. There are many methodologies which can be applied within qualitative social work research. The use of a specific methodology is never a compulsory requirement; you may instead decide to build the core of your research around a research question or the objectives. Also, you can chose to design the methodology as your research progresses or allow the data to speak for itself (see Grounded Theory, chapter eleven). Some research projects will, however, demand some recourse to methodology (for example, ethnographic or life history research and discourse analysis, each discussed in later chapters).

Further reading

Alvesson, M. and Skoldberg, K. (2000). *Reflexive Methodology.* London, Sage

D'Cruz, H., and Jones, M. (2004). *Social Work Research – Ethical and Political Contexts.* London, Sage. Chapter 4 – Methodology

Humphries, B. (2008). *Social Work Research for Social Justice.* Basingstoke, Palgrave Macmillan. Chapter 5 – Action Research

McNiff, J. (2000). *Action Research in Organisations.* London, Routledge

Reason, P., and Bradbury, H. (eds) (2000). *Handbook of Action Research: Participatory Inquiry and Practice.* London, Sage

Smith, J.A., Flowers, P., and Larkin, M. (2009). *Interpretative Phenomenological Analysis.* London, Sage

Radnor, H. (2002). *Researching Your Professional Practice – Doing Interpretive Research.* Buckingham, Open University Press

Ramazanoglu, C., and Holland, J. (2002). *Feminist Methodology: Challenges and Choices.* Sage, London

8 Research Ethics

Introduction

This chapter details the significance of ethics within qualitative social work research.

Most if not all social research generates ethical implications; however, they are likely to be more pronounced if you intend to interview people or gather data through a similar method where contact is a prerequisite. Although it depends upon which research method(s) you intend to utilise to collect your data, qualitative social research will often tend to raise more intense ethical questions, as Padgett (1998: 33) proposes:

> The uniquely close, dynamic and ongoing nature of the relationship between the researcher and respondent in qualitative research raises a number of ethical questions that quantitative researchers do not usually encounter.

The essential ethical rules of good conduct are covered in this chapter alongside requirements set by professional codes of ethics and committees. First, we briefly define and look at the relationship between ethics, qualitative research and social work.

Ethics, qualitative research and social work

Ethics within research refer to 'rules of morally good conduct' (Gomm, 2003: 298) and seek to ensure that research participants do not experience physical or psychological harm, receive informed consent for their participation or are not deceived or violated in other means, and so forth. More generally, ethical codes within research seek to avoid deceit, exploitation, abuse or other forms of malpractice. Ethics, in principle at least, also seek to maintain sensitivity, respect and honesty towards the subjects of research. One of the difficulties, however, of discussing ethics within qualitative research relates to the many different stances that may be taken by individual researchers or sometimes institutions: in many respects this reflects the disparate nature of qualitative research. Nevertheless, Bryman (2004: 508) highlights the four most common ethical stances held within qualitative research, which include:

- *Universalism*: the most rigid if not conservative approach, which maintains that certain ethical precepts and rules should *never* be broken as part of social research, regardless of circumstance.
- *Situation ethics*: a more pragmatic stance that recognises the importance of leverage and discretion regarding each individual case. It is acknowledged that ethics represent a crucial component of qualitative research but we must also take a more holistic view and accept that the moral implications of any study depend upon the situation and circumstance. Unlike universalism, situation ethics recognise that it is difficult to generalise in a complex social, political and culturally diverse world.
- *Ethical transgression is pervasive*: Gans (1962: 44) proposes that there are times when 'the researcher must be dishonest to get honest data'. From this logic flows an assumption that few competent, sincere or organic projects can ever truly be ethical and a *degree* of dishonesty is essential simply to fulfil our research objectives. This is not a stance that seeks to promote the exploitation of research subjects or encourage dishonesty but instead merely recognises that a degree of discretion may be required in order to fulfil most research aims. This largely pragmatic view at the time would now be considered almost radical when ethical codes and rulings have intensified significantly.
- *Anything goes (more or less)*: at first glance this appears the most extreme component within any research ethics discourse. However, closer inspection again reveals a plea for flexibility and fairness (rather than anarchy) as well as recognition of the many barriers that social researchers typically encounter in their quest for knowledge. This is perhaps even more so the case for those within social work hoping to apply 'emancipatory' or 'anti-oppressive' principles; since the dynamics of power or discrimination are likely to be even more difficult to identify, access and analyse. We may also follow an ethical research 'process' yet our 'outcomes' in findings and dissemination may be unethical in not challenging disadvantage and exclusion. Douglas (1976) highlights the comparative deception of the researcher as being mild in comparison to the activities of the mass media: any 'dishonesty' may also be of little significance in contrast to say big business greed or mistaken military interventions, etc. Again, as with the 'transgression' stance above, this relative view would now be considered extreme within most Universities and some other institutions.

From the four stances above we can further reduce and distinguish between two key positions: the privileging of knowledge, scientific enquiry and relative truth (e.g., ethical transgression; anything goes; situation ethics) and the prioritising of regulation and the safety and well-being of the research participant, subject and, importantly, professional interests and institutions (Universalism). We can also distinguish between *absolutist* (one true and valid view or interpretation, e.g. Universalism) and *relativist* (all points of view equally valid yet generally moral rules have only limited validity; there is no absolute truth) ethics. For a more balanced approach we might seek to combine the two less-pronounced or extreme stances (ethical transgression, situation ethics) and consider carefully the important attributes of our own research (research question, aims and objectives, methodology, etc.) and how these might best be achieved whilst prioritising principles such as honesty and respect for participants. Nevertheless, core institutions such as Universities, Health Trusts and professional associations including those linked directly to social work (for example, the Social Care Institute for Excellence) increasingly adhere to a universal stance, at times to protect the organisation/profession as much as any research participants.

In relation Banks (2002) notes social work's tendency to aspire to the universal ideals of the philosopher Immanuel Kant. In particular, this includes the importance given to maintaining dignity and respect for others, complying with universal moral rules and determining the qualities of *individual* actions. Such sometimes rigid stances are of course not without criticism. Dominelli (2002), for example, draws significantly from feminism to argue that much more is required. Indeed, social workers should instead seek to engage in struggles for equality and social justice – especially on behalf of less powerful groups, including women, disabled people, minority ethnic group members, and so forth. In essence wherever possible we should try not to individualise or institutionalise our understandings of ethics and, where possible, must also acknowledge the disadvantages experienced by participants *outside* of any research project.

Core ethical rules for research

Robson (1993) provides a useful list of practices to *avoid* if undertaking ethical qualitative research. These include:

- Coercing potential 'subjects' into participating (through manipulation or threats, etc.).
- Deceiving participants such as by telling lies or concealing any research intentions.

- Invading privacy.
- Lacking respect for participants.
- Undermining the confidence or self-esteem of participants during research.
- Violating the human rights of participants such as by forcing your own values or opinions on participants.
- Inducing participants to commit specific acts that undermine their confidence or which are inappropriate.
- Generating or exposing participants to mental or physical stress.

In most cases at least, it is safe to declare that each of these practices remains morally suspect and are to be avoided. Nevertheless, we must acknowledge that there are critical thinkers, such as Douglas (1976), who maintain that seemingly unethical acts such as telling lies are justifiable *if* subsequent research outcomes go on to make numerous, or indeed many, disadvantaged people's lives less oppressive. Again, there are relative questions which remain according to particular circumstance and we must recognise that morality and ethical questions are rarely answered with black and white answers but are often instead more uncertain and nuanced.

Although there still are variations across institutions, authorities and professional groups, the most commonly applied rules for ethical conduct within research relate to and include:

Non-malevolence and dignity   potentially at least research, participants could be harmed by a researcher's enquiries, especially if discussing sensitive topics such as domestic violence, neglect or abuse. Reasonable steps should be taken to ensure that adequate support is available if this remains a potential risk. Inevitably perhaps, such risks should be avoided or minimised wherever possible. For example, you may wish to revise questions to make them more sensitive in particular circumstances or have information available of local counselling services.

Access   permission to undertake your research is crucial and should be gained in advance from relevant authorities, institutions, associations and persons. For example, most Universities now have their own internal ethics committees to which an application to undertake any research may be made (discussed further below). Other likely 'gatekeepers' include Health Care Trusts, local authorities and professional associations such as the Association of Directors of Children's Services (ADCS) in the UK. ADCS have their application process and provide helpful information on their website. Alongside a University or Trust this is a good place to start in order to gain permissions. The key is to begin the process of ethical application as early as possible as this is nearly always time consuming, to pass through successfully may take up to six months, if not longer in exceptional circumstances. In some instances however, such as if you are not employed by a University, you may only require permission from a Charity or manager of a social care organisation and then can seek permission from each member of your sample. Typically it is best to approach an organisation through a letter, email or telephone initially for general advice. In most instances any 'gatekeepers' will wish to know what your research aims/ objectives are, how you will collect any data and for what purposes your findings might then be used.

Respect   participants should always be treated with respect and thanked for their participation in your research. Perhaps more so than most other forms of social research, vulnerability is more prevalent within social work because of the sensitive nature of the role and the many disadvantaged or vulnerable groups whom the work affects. Age, class, disability, sexuality, race and gender, among others, are all potential sources of vulnerability and this should be recognised by the researcher, who carries potential power and influence over participants.

Avoid discrimination   all types of discrimination or prejudice should again be avoided at all times. This includes preconceived assumptions or stereotypes relating to the cultural habits, behaviour or attitudes of particular groups of people (for example, older people, minority ethnic groups or people with mental health needs).

Voluntary participation   potential and recruited participants should be made aware of your overall intentions and should also be free to decide whether or not to participate in your research. They should not be coaxed or tricked into participating, and should not be interviewed or observed covertly.

Informed consent   a brief overview of your intended research (methods, objectives, likely dissemination, etc.) should be supplied to participants so to allow them to make an informed decision about whether or not to participate. In relation to this, participants should be considered 'competent' (e.g., *compos mentis*, etc.), provided with full information and be made fully aware of what will happen to any findings following interviews, etc. In special circumstance, such as in the case of children or an adult with a learning disability, informed consent might be gained through a parent, teacher or carer, assuming all other ethical criteria are fulfilled.

Data collection   consideration will need to be given to how collected data (information) can be safely stored, anonymised and who will be able to gain access to it. Are there any contingency plans to accommodate the loss of data? This is always a paramount concern and certainly any formal committees or institutions will want to see some evidence of pre-planning and foresight around this potentially delicate matter.

Confidentiality and anonymity   how will participants be protected from any risks of their opinions, actions or attitudes becoming open to public scrutiny? Are you planning to anonymise your discussions or time spent with participants, and if so how? Do you, for example, plan to use pseudonyms when presenting your findings in a final report?

Research ethics also need to be considered *throughout* a project rather than just near the beginning or at particular stages. We also need to remember that any such rules of good conduct do not just apply to research participants but also numerous other people included in the acts and applied techniques of qualitative social work research (e.g., people who provide access to participants, colleagues, carers, and so on).

Research committees and codes of ethics

In most countries there are now formal research committees or panels established to undertake ethical reviews and process relevant applications. For example, in the UK Universities and other education establishments and Health Care Trusts now have research committees. For social work there is also the Social Care Institute for Excellence and its Social Care Research Ethics Committee (part of the National Research Ethics Service) that considers proposals regarding adult social care research, intergenerational studies for both child-care and adults, use of social care databases and some proposals for studies in the NHS. Another option remains the Association of Directors of Social Services (Adults/Children) who again consider applications for ethical approval. All such institutes and associations have websites and other contacts offering further advice. These institutions typically offer guidelines that are linked to professional codes of ethics which researchers are expected to adhere to. Formal application processes typically exist (many online) and researchers may also need to appear before a panel of experts to justify their applications, especially if there is any uncertainty about a proposal. It is only necessary to follow such guidelines if you require participants to be involved in your research project. Literature-based, historical or other conceptual research will not usually require formal contact with committees.

Such committees do not, however, only protect participants, as Bryman (2004: 509) insists:

The ethical guidelines and the ethics committee are there to protect research participants, but they are also involved in protecting institutions, so that researchers will be deterred from behaving in ethically unacceptable ways that might rebound on institutions. Such behaviour could cause problems for institutions if ethically inappropriate behaviour gave rise to legal action against them or to adverse publicity. However, ethics committees and their guidelines are there to help and protect researchers too, so that they are less likely to conduct research that could damage their reputations.

Such committees and application processes can also provide a useful exercise for researchers to clarify their intentions and associate research objectives and methodology. Request for revision of an initial application is a common occurrence after a first meeting (typically more information or clarity required), so don't feel rejected and upset if your application fails at the first attempt. However, such committees or panels are often now led by staff trained within a healthcare discipline, and this can create problems for students and staff within social care. As Darlington and Scott (2002: 23) argue, there can be tensions regarding contrasting approaches and interests towards research, especially unfamiliarity with qualitative methodologies on behalf of panel members. Such panels will also nearly always follow the more conservative 'universal' model discussed earlier.

A more specific code of ethics for social work research now exists. Butler (2002: 243–7) has detailed a fifteen point code of social work research ethics which, among other criteria, seeks to promote research that:

- is anti-discriminatory;
- seeks to empower service users and promote their welfare;
- serves the greater good, and seeks to avoid any harm for service users;
- respects human rights, and aims 'towards social justice', especially for service users;
- informs participants 'of all features of the research' and respects 'individual participants' absolute right to decline to participate in or withdraw from [a] research programme';
- ensures confidentiality at all stages for research participants and service users;
- recognises the part played by participants;
- allows research participants the right to withdraw from a project at any point;
- reports research findings even if they 'reflect unfavourably on agencies of the central or local state, vested interests ... as well as prevailing wisdom and orthodox opinion'.

In relation to this McLaughlin (2007: 52) also proposes that this code can be used alongside Banks' (2002) four-point ethical rules for practice that prioritise:

- respect for people
- the promotion of service user empowerment
- support for social justice
- maximising the interests of service users.

Nevertheless, such ambitious codes and rules are not without criticism. For example, there is the tension that remains between (minority) professional interests (for example, power and status) and what may appear as rhetorical claims to protect and support service users. Also, most qualitative research requires creativity, flair, and initiative, qualities that are again not promoted within the confines of any universal formal code. Indeed Rossiter et al. (2000: 315) propose that codes of ethics seek to 'render the professional an individual subject of correction' and Humphries (2008: 20–21) also criticises codes of ethics for being 'self-interested statements' which bypass concerns for social justice in favour of controlling 'the individual behaviour of researchers'. They may also treat participants as 'passive and dependent' and do not 'take account of the social structures that are the concern of social justice'.

Despite such damning statements, authors such as Butler (2002) implicitly acknowledge the structural limits of universal formal codes of ethics and recognise that they require continual reform and revision. Despite deficits, many do still offer a useful summary of good practices and they can help us to clarify our intended research. McLaughlin (2007: 54) stresses that codes also offer clear guidance 'on how to act and as a means to protect research subjects from malpractice or abuse'.

Conclusion

This chapter has offered a summary of some of the key ethical codes and rules to follow when undertaking qualitative social work research. Key principles include avoiding discrimination, recognising the vulnerability of participants, encouraging voluntary participation, providing informed consent and ensuring plans to promote anonymity and confidentiality. It has also been noted that formal codes of ethics may be detached from the realities and indeed 'messy' components of qualitative research and can seek to protect professions and institutions rather than research participants as claimed. Nevertheless, they may also promote good practice and also help to clarify what it is we intend to do and how.

Further reading

Butler, I. (2002). 'A Code of Ethics for Social Work and Social Care Research'. *British Journal of Social Work* 32: 239–48

D'Cruz, H., and Jones, M. (2004). *Social Work Research: Ethical and Political Contexts.* London, Sage. Chapter 1: Research, Social Work and Professional Practice

Homan, R. (1991). *The Ethics of Social Research.* Harlow, Longmans

Humphries, B. (2008). *Social Work Research for Social Justice.* Basingstoke, Palgrave Macmillan. Chapter 2: Ethical Research and Social Justice

McLaughlin, H. (2009). *Service User Research in Health and Social Care.* London, Sage. Chapter 3: Ethical Issues in Involving Service Users in Research

Padgett, D.K. (1998). *Qualitative Methods in Social Work Research – Challenges and Rewards.* London, Sage. Chapter 4: Ethical Issues in Qualitative Research

Tannsjo, T. (2008). *Understanding Ethics: An Introduction to Moral Theory.* Edinburgh, Edinburgh University Press

Part 2

Qualitative Methodology and Methods

The second part of the book looks at some of the principal methodologies and methods used as part of any qualitative research project. As detailed earlier, methodology can be viewed as a 'recipe' that guides and holds together our project. It may be theoretically informed or instead might be driven by clear plans based around a research question or problem and objectives. Methods are techniques which are held within the walls of a methodology, and are represented by skills, tasks and procedures that help us to gather information and data so to address our research question or problem. In this part of the book we present different research methodologies and methods. Importantly, however, different methodologies or methods can link or overlap. For example, interviews may also offer a form of case study research and ethnographic research can also contain interviews or case studies, etc. We now take a look closer at the variety of different methodologies and methods open to the qualitative social work researcher.

9 Interviews and Questionnaires

Introduction

This chapter explores two of the key methods used in qualitative social work research. They include the interview, which is the most popular method used across the social sciences, and the questionnaire. For most dissertations or projects the use of one of these methods will typically be enough to collect adequate data to support the objectives of a study. However, there are times when both methods can be combined – such as by providing a brief questionnaire for participants to complete prior to, or following, an interview.

Each method is now explored in detail below.

Interviews

Although originated in quantitative research, the interview is now a widely used method applied within qualitative social work research, and indeed more generally within social research. This is primarily because interviews remain a cheap, convenient, uncomplicated yet highly effective means by which to collect an extensive and usually rich amount of data within a reasonable period of time. Crucially, interviews, like communication and relationships, are also embedded in social work practice as Carr (2010: 124) underlines:

> Interviewing plays a significant role in social work research *and practice*. In practice settings, social workers engage clients in intake procedures, needs assessments, and clinical interviews, all of which involve interrogatory routines .... For instance, a homeless shelter may require that workers ask a specific set of questions during intake interviews to determine if interviewees are technically 'homeless', and to establish their eligibility for services.

As social workers, we regularly engage in interviews on a formal and informal level, often alternating in a typical working week between completing complex assessment documentation to engaging in spontaneous and often delicate informal 'chats' that may involve advice giving, empathy and components of counselling and other forms of therapy.

Within research, the interview is also an extremely adaptable and flexible method, capable of collecting more varied data than many other approaches, as Bell (1987: 70) reminds us:

> A major advantage of the interview is its adaptability. A skillful interviewer can follow up ideas, responses and investigate motives and feelings, which the questionnaire can never do. The way in which a response is made (the tone of voice, facial expression, hesitation, etc.) can provide information that a written response would conceal. Questionnaire responses have to be taken at face value, but a response in an interview can be developed and clarified.

Many possible topics can be researched through the interview method. However, there are particular topics that are more suited to this approach. In particular, this includes questions that aim to examine sensitive issues that social workers accommodate, including poverty, neglect, or illness, and others. It can also help us to detail and unpack personal experience, emotions or feelings, again tangible experiences or events that practitioners address and accommodate regularly in their daily practices. The interview may also be an effective way to gather such nevertheless potentially convoluted and complex data, and may provide an ideal platform from which to investigate privileged information, especially if we gain access to 'key players' such as managers, doctors or teachers. This may also allow us an opportunity to gain new insights on issues under-explored in the past.

Through the medium of the interview, participants are able to use language to express their opinions, emotions, thoughts and lived experiences. The interview also recognises the participant as the 'expert' who is 'best able to report how they experienced a particular event or phenomenon' (Darlington and Scott, 2002: 48). Carr (2010: 140), however, also stresses the need for the interviewer to locate and contextualise the interview process itself:

> Considering social work's historical commitment to the person-in-environment on the one hand, and qualitative researchers' attention to the socially embedded nature of social science data on the other, the challenge for qualitative social work research is to connect *content to context* – both in the sociohistorical contexts in which people speak and in the interactive context of the interview itself.

The qualitative interview can take many forms – from the formally structured to the less regulated and unstructured or something in-between. It may instead embrace the more flexible in-depth approaches used in, say, narrative research (chapter fourteen) or life history approaches (chapter thirteen), or the collective interview used within focus group research (chapter ten). Despite differences, the emphasis within qualitative research mostly pivots around a *depth* of investigation and analysis rather than general sweep of many sub-topics or urge to quantify explicit facts (Silverman, 1993).

My previous experience of doing interviews suggests that most participants are keen to engage with, and indeed many enjoy, the one-to-one interview. Most prominently this is due to recognition that someone has taken an interest in their opinions or past experience. In relation to this, Rapley (2004: 15) adds that, if applied with care and skill, the interview may pervade 'our contemporary cultural experiences and knowledges of authentic personal, private lives'.

Some practical concerns

Before fully committing to the interview as your key method to collect data you will need to consider how the topic which you intend to investigate *relates* to this approach. In particular, we must consider the probable viability (or otherwise) of interviews regarding practical concerns such as:

- Will you be able to gain access to enough participants willing to be interviewed? This does not need to be guaranteed for everyone in your sample but you should try to confirm access in principle with at least a couple of participants.
- How long might it take before formal permission is granted to approach or interview people? Permission can take time so begin this process as early as possible.
- Will there be travel or any other costs involved?

The next step will be to speak to potential participants themselves and you then need to decide at what location interviews will take place. Many practitioners like to be interviewed in their work environment and many people will not wish to travel to be interviewed. Some groups however may wish to be interviewed in another setting and you may give people a choice, a decision which is likely to increase your sample size. A setting without any distractions, such as a private room, is likely to be ideal, especially if you are recording the interviews. For all groups including people other than practitioners you will need to think carefully about issues such as people's mobility and access needs, personal requirements such as relating to medication or diet (for longer interviews) and the possible impact that the nature of the discussion may have. Are the topics to be discussed appropriate, including in the likely settings? Obviously discussion of sensitive topics such as bereavement, neglect or abuse should not take place in a public space.

Another alternative is to undertake your interviews over the telephone. In general this is not ideal because of a lack of visual prompts and clues available, as well as the difficulty you may face if trying to take notes whilst interviewing. The advantages will, however, include time or cost saved by avoiding travel. You may also find it easier to gain access to a larger sample.

You will then need to decide which format to utilise in order to collect your data. In qualitative interviews two formats remain: unstructured and semi-structured interviews. Both formats are typically planned with one person at a time, and each is summarised below.

- *Unstructured interviews*: here there may not be any set questions planned, rather a list of pre-planned topics, ideas or prompts regarding what may be discussed. Overall considerable flexibility and discretion is allowed regarding what can be discussed, and the emphasis is very much upon the participant guiding the conversation. This approach is usually prevalent in biographical or life history research (chapter thirteen), in which a person takes time to reflect upon past experiences. Notable drawbacks of unstructured interviews include that they can take a considerable amount of time to complete, and also tend to collect large amounts of data (that will need to be read, coded and analysed).
- *Semi-structured interviews*: this approach integrates a combination of pre-planned and spontaneous questions, with the latter allowing the interviewer some discretion to ask new questions in response to a participant's answers or body language. This format tends to work well within social work research and indeed is extremely popular in all types of qualitative research. It is ideal for exploring a sensitive or extremely focused topic and will tend to take less time than an unstructured approach. Semi-structured interviews can proceed with unstructured/ structured questions asked in any order depending upon circumstance.

Both approaches link in many ways, including the tendency for researchers to be keen to mine varied and often rich data. As Brewer (2004: 320) also adds, 'rambling' is encouraged in most qualitative interviews regardless of structure due to recognition that allowing interviewees to go 'off on a tangent' helps us to gain a better 'insight into what the interviewee sees as relevant and important'.

Once we have decided our format we then need to consider what questions to ask.

Designing questions and interview skills

Once access to a small sample of participants has been gained, and a format has been decided upon, we then need to prioritise two tasks. These include the types and number of questions to ask. Ideally, questions should link to the research question or topic as well as to the objectives of a project or dissertation. They will also be made up of two possible types that include:

- *Open-ended questions*: the most common approach in qualitative research, where interviewees are free to answer and explore queries in their own words and style
- *Closed-format questions*: much more common in quantitative research and questionnaires, in which a limited choice of possible answers are provided. Although often counter to the intentions of qualitative social work research, such questions can still be used effectively for collecting crucial information (for example, age, past work experience, or broad opinions).

Case study: Exploring unemployment among young men who are HIV positive

Lisa wanted to explore some of the practical problems (finding employment, housing, personal relationships, and so on) typically faced by young men who had been diagnosed with HIV for five years or more. Lisa also wanted to know how best to help and support this group in her work as a volunteer with a Voluntary Organisation specialising in giving support to people who use illicit drugs for recreational and other purposes. Lisa first carried out a brief yet intense study of relevant literature (mostly in books, magazines and on Government and Voluntary sector related internet sites) and also asked for advice from friends or work colleagues based in either health or social care sectors about her intended research. Eventually, Lisa gained access to nine men all aged between 22 and 31 years of age and after careful thought, advice and extensive reading, decided to narrow her focus on problems faced by young men with HIV in findings employment.

Lisa designed a brief questionnaire (12 questions) that helped her collect basic data such as the age of each participant, length of diagnosis with HIV, etc., and which each man completed just before their main interview. Lisa then interviewed each of the men for up to an hour using a semi-structured interview format. Lisa pre-planned and designed eight core questions that linked directly to her research problem, and a further four questions which addressed less relevant topics such as how the men spent their leisure time, and so on. However, Lisa also asked between five to eight further questions that were not planned in advance, largely depending upon the response of each participant to the core set questions. Lisa discovered that seven of the men were currently unemployed and each believed that their health status had had a negative impact upon their chances of finding employment. The findings also revealed that this was related to a combination of factors, including prejudice, limited employment opportunities and low self-esteem on behalf of some of the men. Among other findings, Lisa concluded that health and social care professionals have a potential role to play in raising the self-esteem of men with HIV and also perhaps of confronting prejudice among employees. However, Lisa also concluded that although both approaches, alongside relevant training, were likely to offer important support, more could be done by governments and relevant authorities to raise awareness of discrimination and, most important of all, create more employment opportunities for young people. This research helped both Lisa and colleagues with their role and was eventually published in an online social care journal.

Try to limit the number of questions you plan to ask. For example, be selective and as focused as possible so to avoid bombarding a person with too many questions. As well as potentially alienating or confusing the interviewee, you are also likely to collect far too much information to process. Try to create some order in the core themes or topics that you intend to cover (related in some way to fulfilling the research objectives). It may also help to initially rehearse an interview by asking some of the questions you have recently designed to a friend or colleague, so as to judge whether the questions are clear and effective in fulfilling your aims. Finally, keeping a note either before or after of facts, such as where the interview took place, how long it lasted and who attended, etc., will help jog your memory when you come to analyse and write up the findings.

Some tips to designing questions include:

- Keep questions brief, unambiguous, simple and clear.
- Use clear and simple language with familiar words drawn from everyday speech.

- Avoid jargon, acronyms or abbreviations.
- Avoid asking more than one question at a time. For example, 'Do you always feel tired after a meeting or wish to go for a long walk or straight home?'
- Avoid leading questions which may influence a participant's response, such as 'Do you agree that too many social care services have been privatised and that they are expensive and unreliable?'
- Avoid difficult or unclear questions. For example, 'On how many occasions did you attend a day centre to meet a service user last year'?
- Try not to ask insensitive or offensive questions. For example, 'Are you regularly detached and aloof when in contact with the relatives of service users?'
- Avoid at all times questions that are based on negative assumptions or prejudice. For example, 'Do you find it difficult controlling your emotions, and also therefore doing your job properly with your type of mental health condition?'
- Avoid questions with the word 'not' in the sentence as this may be confusing or provoke uncertainty. For example, 'Is it not in the interest of informal carers to ask their opinions about a client's needs?'
- Do not ask questions that assume specific prior knowledge, as this can embarrass participants or make them feel uncomfortable. For example, 'Do you agree with the recent reforms of the greater role that service user participants will play in higher education?'

Alongside the design of appropriate questions we also need to consider some of the many other skills we may draw upon to help us with any interview. Initially, interviews may seem relatively straightforward, but careful planning and attention to detail is essential. Denscombe (2007) also offers the following tips:

Be gentle   let people finish answering their questions and also allow them time to think. Don't rush and be careful not to interrupt people if possible. Remain sensitive to the feelings of the interviewee   you may not agree with the opinions being expressed but it is distracting if you emphasise any disapproval, for example with explicit gestures. Try also to control your body language.

Be ethically sensitive   ensure that the participant is aware of what the research is about and that findings are treated with confidentiality.

If necessary be critical (in moderation)   you are able to challenge some of the responses given by interviewees, such as if there are inconsistencies or a lack of clarity. You will, however, need to use your discretion as upsetting a participant will probably undermine the intentions of the interview.

Be attentive throughout   try to listen carefully to what is being said and minimise potential distractions. Try also to remain in the background and avoid unnecessary 'chatter' outside of any formal interview questions.

Use probes if appropriate   if an answer seems unclear then the use of subtle probe techniques may help. For example, asking for clarification of an answer or requesting more details.

Use prompts if necessary   silences can be productive but prompts may be necessary to move an interview along. For example, subtle tactics such as repeating a question may help, especially if a participant's answer is unclear.

Check for exaggeration, boasting or attempts to please or fob off the interviewer   interviewees may become excited or agitated when discussing something relating to their life. If you believe this is affecting any answers, make notes and think of possible ways to overcome such outcomes (such as changing the subject or moving to the next question).

Maintain suitable eye contact Try not to maintain direct eye contact throughout, and avoid staring at a participant for long periods!
If necessary make notes on non-verbal communication   remember that body language can sometimes reveal the true feelings or beliefs held by a participant.

Try to read between the lines if necessary   for some interviewees you may have to ask yourself what is *really* being stated 'beneath the surface' by the participant, and also perhaps ask what is *not* being said.

Confirm responses if necessary   if an interviewee's response is unclear or vague you may need to verify the meaning intended by the participant.

The points raised above are guidelines to consider. There is, however, unlikely to be such a thing as the 'perfect' interview and you should use personal discretion and instinct and follow whichever guidelines to the extent which suits your project.

Taping or note taking during interviews

It is essential to keep some record of any interview. This remains a priority so as to recall information but more generally to also fulfil the objectives of any project and in relation to the need to analyse the findings. Four options remain open, which include:

Taping and transcribing the interview   tape recordings may be intimidating for some participants, but this still remains one of the most common approaches and permits all of the conversation to be captured whilst allowing the interviewer to concentrate upon the interview without too much distraction. Extensive time will usually be taken up transcribing a full interview but partial transcription of key points remains a viable option.

Making notes during the interview   this is a cheap alternative to tape recording which is also fairly straightforward and often effective. However, you may miss important details and possible points raised and some participants may feel that you are not listening to them or may be distracted whilst you write.

Taping and note taking   combining the two approaches remains a possibility and this is often the approach that professional researchers and academics follow. Typically, the full interview will be recorded and transcribed and notes will also be taken during or after an interview. However, bear in mind that considerable work is likely to be generated which may take up many hours of precious time.

Making notes after an interview has finished   this approach has the advantage of not distracting the interviewee, which may encourage a more open account to flourish. Nevertheless, you are relying extensively upon a very good memory and inevitably there is a significant risk of losing important points raised.

In general the extent of data collection will depend upon the nature of the project, its size and available time. Smaller projects such as dissertations will tend to rely upon the cheapest and least time-consuming options – such as note taking during or after an interview. Much bigger projects are likely to demand some form of transcription, although this depends upon other factors again, such as how large is the sample and how viable is it to transcribe more than, say, eight interviews? In all forms of research there is always a tension between a need to gather as much rich data as possible whilst also being realistic about financial and time constraints. Try to be realistic and avoid over-ambition. You will also need to consider other influences, such as the research objectives, available time and participant needs.

Analysis

All qualitative analysis takes place throughout the research process and will have begun prior to an interview (such as when reviewing the literature and defining the objectives of a project). Analysis will, however, intensify once interviews begin – and there will continue to be a link between data collection and analysis – and especially when they are complete and you begin to fully reflect on any findings.

Analysis is discussed in more detail in chapter seventeen where there is discussion of specific types of analysis. You are likely to use one of these methods (thematic, comparative, documentary analysis) but for interviews within analysis you are attempting to:

- Tease out and explore important trends, themes, occurrences, issues, and so on, which emerge from any interview. This represents the 'evidence' upon which the research objectives can be fulfilled.
- Identify the extent to which trends and issues, etc., are similar to or distinct from those detailed by other researchers. How do your own interview findings link or contrast with the arguments presented by other researchers? Such similarities and/or differences are likely to make up much of the material explored within your analysis.
- What interview findings link to and answer your research question and subsequent objectives?

There are different possible ways to approach analysis. For example, you might rely upon notes taken during the interviews when excavating any findings, or instead link the issues inherent within the notes or transcripts to a set of codes (discussed in chapter three). The main point of analysis is to discover trends and compare and contrast these findings with those of previous researchers. This helps to explain or contextualise findings, which are then used to develop a discussion, conclusions and recommendations for policy and practice.

Checklist and possible problems

Below is a brief checklist to consider prior to beginning any interviews:

- Consider how you might gain access to a sample? Permission to undertake interview research with a sample is essential. Try to secure each as early in advance as possible.

- Based on your research objectives, decide *what it is you need to know.*
- Decide if you need all of this information. If not, then remove or revise some requirements and concentrate on what is left. Could the research objectives be reduced in scale?
- Decide the format which you will use (semi-structured interview, telephone, and so on), the method of data collection (tape recording, note taking) and plan the best setting to undertake the research.
- Construct and check your questions, being careful to be clear, brief, avoid ambiguity and link questions to your objectives.
- Consider a prepared formal introduction to recite prior to the interview. For example, in which you *briefly* introduce yourself and detail the purpose of the study and what you will proceed to do on the day and after.
- Add instructions or reminders next to each question if this seems helpful or necessary.
- Thank participants for their time after any interview. You may also wish to briefly explain what you intend to do with the data.

Qualitative interviews are not without problems. This may include problems of gaining access to enough suitable participants. Assuming access is gained, participants may not arrive or can be late. Sometimes a participant may not respond to questions, can become easily upset or may leave midway through to go elsewhere. Some participants may exaggerate or even lie throughout an interview, which we are unlikely to be able to detect.

Some academics within social work have stressed the power imbalance which favours the interviewer. Hardwick and Worsley (2011) also highlight that there are occasions when little emphasis may be given to the needs of vulnerable service users within the academic interview process. Holstein and Gubrium (1997: 114) argue that respondents should always be viewed as equals in the construction of knowledge.

Questionnaires

Questionnaires draw from quantitative and survey research, and within such realist methodologies most questions included tend to be presented in a closed format (with a limited set number of possible answers). However, the use of questionnaires within qualitative social work research is not uncommon and they can be used alone or alongside other social research methods such as the interview or focus group. Qualitative questionnaires tend to use more open-ended questions (with discretion and choice regarding what answers to give) so that participants can explore their opinions or experience in more detail. Questionnaires are usually completed by themselves but they can also be completed by a researcher in the company of a participant.

The benefits of questionnaires include that they are exceptionally cheap, can save considerable time and may reach a large audience and help to collect considerable data. However, some important questions might be insensitive for issues that social workers deal with, or topics which service users or carers experience, such as neglect, abuse, or discrimination, may not be asked in such a document. There are many topics, however, suited to a questionnaire within social work, such as personal evaluation of specific services, including how to improve such provisions. We might also look at experiences of contacts with professionals, personal need requirements or attitudes concerning a wide range of other topics.

Initial priority and the construction of questions

Many of the general rules for questionnaire-based research are much the same as for other methods. That is, you need to decide what you wish to gain from the research and how the questionnaire method can best help to address your research objectives. To fulfil your aims, formulating the number and type of questions to ask participants remains especially important. For example, you should keep questions as focused and as clear as possible, try not to ask too many questions (less is often more for this method) and always undertake a small pilot or trial – such as with colleagues, family or friends – to test responses to, and possibly revise, the design and questions. In general, the rules for designing questions for questionnaires are much the same as those presented earlier in this chapter for interviews. In particular:

- You should include some brief information that presents a researcher's identity and general intentions.
- Participants' should be thanked for their time and effort in advance.
- Offer some simple and brief instructions on how to complete and return the document.
- Ensure the document is as brief as possible, clear, unambiguous and easy to understand.
- Try not to be too general and broad in either your overall aim or the questions asked.
- Always allow sufficient space for answers.
- Avoid asking more than one question at a time.

Dawson (2007: 91–3) offers some additional tips that include:

- *Avoid a status bias or potential embarrassment*: try not to ask questions which may encourage respondents to give a false answer. Notable examples include those that relate to qualifications or income or sensitive issues such as relating to an illness, bereavement or deeply personal aspects of social care needs (e.g. toileting).
- *Avoid 'leading' questions*: these are questions which make assumptions about a respondent, such as regarding what they own, believe or have done in the past., or which 'steer' responses and encourage a particular answer.
- *Avoid sensitive questions*: a possible alternative is to ask indirect questions relating to potentially difficult themes. For example, by making reference to the wider population that has an illness rather than the respondent.

Although it will often help to ensure that your questionnaire is as brief as is possible, if exploring a complex topic, more questions than the interview method may be required because it is likely to take further questions to extract enough information that you require (as opposed to the interview when more spontaneous questions can be asked). Bear in mind, however, that the larger the questionnaire the less people are likely to be willing to complete it. Again, you need to use your discretion to decide how best to balance the need to collect rich and accurate data with the essential requirement to collect or receive back enough completed questionnaires. Of course, completing a questionnaire alongside a participant is another option and often a good procedure to follow, as within practice-based social work! This will also allow more discretion to the interviewer, permit more options regarding the exploration of a wider range of topics, and the researcher's presence may help to overcome potential difficulties, such as uncertainty regarding the meaning of some questions for the participant.

You will also need to decide what balance you might wish to establish between open and closed questions. Since open questions permit much greater choice for participants when completing, and closed questions only offer a limited selection of possible answers, the former will tend to dominate many qualitative questionnaires. This rule is only likely to reverse when undertaking research with a large sample, such as more than sixteen people.

When constructing closed questions try to ensure that as many possible answers to set questions are available to the respondent. Also try to include a 'don't know' category for those who are uncomfortable or unsure about any question. Closed questions are helpful in collecting important information such as age, gender, time spent doing a job or activity, and so forth (see question 1 in figure 9.1). They tend to be less suitable for more complex qualitative concerns such as those that link to emotions, attitudes, personal relationships or experiences, and many more. It is here that open questions are likely to more common. Try to allow adequate space to complete any open questions that you present. In general, open questions will take longer to construct by a researcher than other types of question. This is because they may be difficult to perfect, especially if we consider the priority that should be given to ensuring clarity, focus, reliability, and so forth.

Another possible option to consider remains closed questions which are 'scaled' (question 1 in figure 9.1 uses a ratio scale which is ideal for locating numerical information such as age, salary, etc.). Nominal scales are the most basic type of scale. They aim to quantify simple yes/no/don't know type queries (question 2 in figure 9.1 uses a nominal scale). Scales are especially helpful for testing peoples' varying attitudes or values. Ordinal scales, for example, typically offer three to six choices to the respondent, and may begin with a strong agreement with a statement and then move gradually to options which disagree or strongly disagree with a statement (questions 3 and 4 in figure 9.1 use ordinal scales). Although intended for larger surveys, the use of scales can still be of benefit for some qualitative research that accommodates smaller samples. This is because they are often able to pinpoint attitudes and values, and also allow the use of simple statistics such as averages to offer an easy-to-read and understood figure which reflects the opinions of a sample. Finally, open questions will tend to be focused yet have no restrictions or control over the answers given by participants (questions 5 and 6 in figure 9.1).

The sequence of questions within a questionnaire can also be important. Although there is no standard format, typically we begin with a simple introductory question that is not too challenging and then usually move to unpack and explore a topic over the course of the document.

Bell (1987: 67–70) and Dawson (2007: 99–100) provide a tips checklist for completing a questionnaire that includes:

- Decide and list what you believe you need to know.
- Ask why you need this information, removing anything from the list which is not essential or which does not link directly with your core objectives.
- Ask if the questionnaire is the best way to collect the information. Might it be used alongside brief interviews, participant observation or some other method?
- Is the questionnaire 'clear, concise and uncluttered'?
- Is the questionnaire well structured and laid out?
- Are there basic and unambiguous instructions regarding how to complete the form on the questionnaire?
- Will intended respondents be co-operative?

1. Total time of practice as an adult social worker (full time equivalent):

☐ 0–12 months
☐ 1–5 years
☐ 5–10 years
☐ 10–20 years
☐ 20 years or more

2. As part of my adult social work role I enjoy working with informal carers (family members, friends, relatives, and so on)?

☐ Yes
☐ No
☐ Don't know

Please place a tick in the circle that represents how you feel about the following statements.

3. I have a good working relationship with a majority of informal carers who support my service users?

	1	2	3	4	5	
Strongly Disagree	○	○	○	○	○	Strongly Agree

4. My past experience suggests that care and support provided by informal carers is more suitable than other forms of care and support (such as provided by a personal assistant or support worker)?

	1	2	3	4	5	
Strongly Disagree	○	○	○	○	○	Strongly Agree

5. What additional support (if any) might be provided by your work colleagues to assist you in your work with informal carers (please list and briefly explain)?

_____
_____
_____
_____
_____
_____

6. What additional factors (if any) not listed above might improve your working relationship with informal carers (please list and briefly explain)?

Figure 9.1   A questionnaire comprising a combination of closed, nominal, ordinal scaled and open questions

- What might be the best way to distribute and/or complete the questionnaire? Postal questionnaires are relatively cheap and easy to administer but respondent rates are low. Might we hand out the questionnaires to people in a closed environment such as a classroom or day centre?
- Might it help to complete the form alongside a participant or could someone else provide assistance (such as a personal assistant or carer)?
- Have you informed respondents of what the research objectives are and what will happen to the results (briefly)?
- Has the questionnaire been piloted?
- Start with easy questions and if possible ask for more personal details at the end.
- Try to use a mixture of question formats if possible (for example, scaled, closed, open, etc.).
- Avoid jargon, offence or confusion and words with multiple meanings.
- Avoid vague words such as 'often' and 'sometimes'.
- Use specific timeframes (for example, two months, three weeks or two days) when asking about behaviour.
- Use specific place frames (for example, 'in what country were you born?' rather than 'where were you born?').

Questionnaires may be highly appropriate for smaller-scale projects such as a dissertation or piece of evaluative research carried out at a local social work department, hospital, day centre, or for service users who receive personal care. As qualitative questionnaires tend to contain more open-ended questions, they will often take longer for a person to complete. Some form of support may therefore be necessary. Larger questionnaires may represent the main or only method used to collect data or they may be used on a smaller scale to support other more person-centred or literature-based methods and methodologies.

Conclusion

It has been shown that the interview remains a viable means by which to undertake qualitative social work research. Concentration on behalf of the researcher is often important, especially regarding concerns such as access, the structure and style of questions and how to analyse any findings. Similarly, with the questionnaire we are offered a relatively straightforward, and cheap, means by which to collect data, but must again be careful to adhere to general and specific rules that will make this process much easier to apply. Both methods are extremely flexible and can be used alongside other approaches and methodologies depending upon the topic and research objectives.

Further reading

Darlington, Y., and Scott, D. (2002). *Qualitative Research in Practice: Stories from the Field.* Open University Press, Maidenhead. Chapter 3 – In-depth interviewing

Denscombe, M. (2007). *The Good Research Guide For Small Scale Research Projects.* Maidenhead, Open University Press. Chapter 10: Interviews

Foddy, W. (1994). *Constructing Questions for Interviews and Questionnaires.* Cambridge, Cambridge University Press

Gillham, B. (2000). *Developing a Questionnaire.* London, Continuum International Publishing Group

Gillham, B. (2005). *Research Interviewing – the Range of Techniques.* Berkshire, Open University Press

Holstein, J.A., and Gubrium, J.F. (1997). *The Active Interview.* London, Sage

Whittaker, A. (2009). *Research Skills for Social Work.* Exeter, Learning Matters. Chapter 3: Interviews; Chapter 5: Questionnaires

10 Focus Groups

Introduction

This chapter details a key research method increasingly used as part of qualitative social work research, that of the focus group. Focus groups offer an extension to the formal interview, the key difference being that a 'moderator' interviews a group of participants rather than one person at a time. In this chapter we will look at the planning of a focus group, the role of the moderator, offer a discussion guide, means of support and some of the ways we can analyse our findings. We conclude by looking at the relevance of this method for social work related research.

Focus Group Research

The focus group method is 'an interview with several people on a specific topic or issue' (Bryman, 2004: 345). This approach originated in marketing and political research, although the method has also been used in sociology (Padgett, 2008: 100). Typically, this flexible and potentially rigorous method involves a group interview in which in-depth discussion takes place around a predetermined topic, theme or series of related issues. Usually the researcher is interested in 'how people respond to each other's views and build up a view out of the interaction that takes place within the group'. In effect, the researcher is interested in participants' attitudes, values and, to an extent, behaviour as a *member of a group* rather than just the responses or beliefs of individual participants (Bryman, 2004: 346).

Group participants may have something in common but usually members do not know each other in advance as this is recognised as helping to encourage more informative debate and discussion. People with different status or rank within an organisation – or from different socio-economic backgrounds – are not usually merged for focus group research unless this is recognised as a priority regarding the aims and objectives of a project. A distinction has been drawn between 'complementary' and 'argumentative' focus groups (Kitzinger, 1994), with the former tending to be more suited to groups working towards common goals (such as in a workplace setting, including of course a social work team or volunteers) or if discussing a sensitive topic (e.g. bereavement and loss, abuse, neglect, informal care) and the latter when exploring a topic that encompasses complex views (e.g., political opinions).

In planning a focus group you will need to consider:

- *How to recruit participants?* Might an advert be presented at a GP surgery or school or will a 'snowball' sample be built around one or two initial participants?
- *How group members will support your research?* For example, how might they be able to help you answer your research question?
- *Possible support needs for members*: for example, might an interpreter be required for deaf community participants or specific catering needs for some members (for example, vegetarian or vegan food, etc.).
- *Likely number of meetings.* When will they take place (morning, afternoon, evening) and how long will each meeting last (usually one to two hours although you may prefer shorter meetings)? Might the number of meetings change as the research develops? You will need to discuss possible changes to the group at the first meeting.
- *How to gather your data*? Might the sessions be recorded or notes taken instead?

Often several related meetings take place over an extended period of time, a process that can mean that relevant topics may be rigorously unpacked and explored. The researcher more often acts as a 'moderator' or 'facilitator' and prompts, or carefully leads, any discussion by asking a combination of planned and spontaneous questions. As Punch (2005: 171) summarises:

> The role of the researcher changes in a group interview, functioning more as a moderator or facilitator, and less as an interviewer. The process will not be one of alternative question and answer, as in the traditional interview. Rather the researcher will be facilitating, moderating, monitoring, and recording group interaction.

In most cases moderators aim to 'promote interaction between participants' whilst looking to 'ensure that the discussion is open and relaxed while addressing the research question, which can be a delicate balancing act'. They should also attempt to promote interest in the topic, as well as discourage apathy, if necessary. Participants may differ in their involvement with any meetings and topic depending upon their experience, and a moderator might try to encourage greater involvement from those 'on the edges'. It is a relatively common occurrence for some dominant group members to sometimes move discussions away from the original intentions defined by a moderator. Moderators must try to monitor this potential hindrance to a meeting and carefully move any discussions 'sidetracked' back to the intended topic of discussion. Focus group meetings are rarely intended to offer therapy or group counseling, so again moderators will need to ensure that the core objectives of the meeting remain the focal point of any discussions. Also, insensitive topics or issues may be introduced by one or two members and the moderator needs to monitor this potentially distressful process, bearing in mind any possible difficult consequences for other members. Tact and subtlety again remain crucial skills to support such roles, although at times the moderator may need to be more assertive. Assistance for the moderator is also recognised as beneficial when dealing with groups of people: for example, whether to take notes or offer other forms of emotional support.

Typically in any discussion plan for a focus group meeting, a series of set questions will be asked. To begin with an *introduction phase* will allow the moderator to introduce themselves, the research topic and some ethical groundrules. You may also wish to summarise what you hope to achieve in the first session and what topics might be addressed. Often meetings then proceed to a *'warm up' phase* whereby one or two 'non-threatening' questions allow participants to get to know one another and also feel more relaxed in a potentially alien or threatening surrounding. Next we have *introductory questions*, whereby broader topics that link to our research objectives are discussed so as to again allow participants to get to know one another whilst also preparing them for the more focused questions that will follow. Next is the crucial stage known as the *key questions phase* where direct questions that link to any research question are asked of the group. At this point, the moderator needs to think carefully about possibly asking additional questions if the set questions have not adequately addressed the intended topics to be explored. Finally, we then move to the *closing questions phase* where topics not addressed might be explored (including those initiated by participants) and the moderator summarises proceedings, details the next planned meeting and thanks participants (Morgan, 1997).

Three attributes relating to focus group research are recognised. They include that:

- *The moderator should facilitate the group.* Complete control of participants' behaviour or talk should be avoided, as should being passive and submissive. Instead, support and prompting, alongside the occasional steering of any debate if the original focus is lost, remain paramount. The moderator may also encourage quieter speakers to contribute, and subtly discourage dominant or overbearing personalities, especially if they inhibit other group members from contributing to a debate.

- *Sessions have a clear focus*: for example, this may be based upon beliefs or experience that participants have in common. Here a group discussion will usually be triggered by a 'stimulus' – often a question that will encourage a lively debate. A prompt may also be used, such as a photograph or topical newspaper report, to kindle debate and discussion. Again, the priority for the moderator is that any discussion remains focused at regular intervals and does not meander.
- *Interaction and lively talk are encouraged*: this assists the core task of gathering information, and the moderator should seek to recognise *beliefs* or *attitudes* from participants whilst unearthing and exploring any *reasons* for, or *causes* of, the general opinions expressed.

Regarding sample size, most focus group meetings tend to have between four and fifteen members. However, fewer members may be more practical and appropriate in some circumstances. This will depend on factors such as available time, the topic of research under investigation, likely participants, a tutor's recommendations, course requirements, etc. For example, between three and four members is usually acceptable for many social work dissertations and four to eight the norm for other research projects.

Another option is to run more than one focus group. For example, it may be possible to have two separate meetings where different questions are provided to the same group. Alternatively, two separate groups of people may be asked the same questions so as to increase the sample size. The length of time of any focus group meeting will differ depending upon factors such as the number and type of participants present, the research objectives being explored and the response of group members to questions asked. Although not compulsory (indeed numerous formats now proliferate), typically focus group meeting are semi-structured, allowing the moderator and participants some discretion whilst ensuring that planning is in place. Questions will usually follow the same general structure as listed earlier in this chapter. During any meeting a good indicator of when to move onto the next question is when initial points raised are repeated by participants.

Other points relating to focus group research include that after the moderator introduces themselves they should thank any people for coming, allow people to introduce themselves, and give a brief outline of their research. We may then wish to set some ground rules, such as stipulating that people be allowed to finish speaking and only one person should speak at a time. At the very least, five key questions that link to your research objectives should be asked of the group. Further questions can be used as a tool to break silences or bring the group discussion back to the initial research topic. Finally, participants should always be thanked at the end of a meeting and the moderator may also wish to inform people what will happen to any of the findings. For example, will the data be used in a report or published in a journal, and so on (Krueger and Casey, 2000).

As with individual interviews, there are different ways that focus group meetings can be transcribed. Generally the most common and effective remains a full tape-recorded transcript. This can then be reduced and summarised in bullet point style themes at a later time, most notably to aid analysis. Alternatively, you may wish instead to keep notes of key points raised and discussed or merely those that link directly to your research objectives (Krueger and Casey, 2000). As has already been suggested, moderating and taking notes at the same time is extremely difficult so you may require support with this task or instead may make notes after a meeting. Always ensure that any electric recorders to be used are working in advance and that you have sufficient batteries.

Regarding analysis, it is also important to concentrate upon the themes discussed that relate explicitly to your research question and objectives. Perhaps more so than other methods because you are dealing with a group, focus groups have a tendency to sometimes wander from any initial priorities established by a moderator. Try to detach group opinion from personal attitudes and experience. Sometimes group norms and values can differ from individual stances and you may wish to decide from the beginning how you deal with this predicament. Sometimes people agree to a group stance to avoid conflict or to 'fit in'; consider if this has occurred, such as in your post-interview notes. Findings from focus group meetings are unlikely to be representative; predominately this is because dominant group norms can take over at an early stage (Krueger and Casey, 2000; Linhorst, 2002).

Relevance for social work and potential problems

Focus group methods are extremely relevant for many types of project undertaken in qualitative social work research. Their benefits are many, including not least the saving of time and money, the collection of considerable data in a short time-scale and the rich variety of data that can be collected. In particular, focus group discussions fit firmly with the community and social issue related concerns of much social work practice, and related topics that aim to explore peoples' motives, attitudes and group experiences. Possible groups that can be interviewed about their experiences or attitudes include social work practitioners, managers, support workers, volunteers, health workers or other professionals such as teachers or nurses. This approach may also be suitable to unpack more sensitive topics that some people may feel more comfortable about sharing within a group rather than as part of a one-to-one interview with someone unknown.

Case study: Using focus groups to develop culturally sensitive material for deaf people

Teresa Crowe (2003) wanted to investigate how to best prepare and develop HIV and AIDS prevention material for members of the deaf community in Washington, America. Crowe used a sample of 31 deaf people (17 women, 14 men; aged between 21 to 46 years; 19 Black/African American, 12 white participants) and undertook five focus group meetings over the course of one year. Each participant drawn from the deaf community represented a variety of sub-cultural groups (educators, volunteers, students, etc.).

The researcher used a relatively complex methodology that combined purposive sampling and three stages of focus group meeting that included: first looking at needs assessment (seven participants x two groups), design of relevant materials for deaf people and finally an evaluation of different designs of posters and other materials. The researcher used a variety of settings to undertake the focus group research (including a coffee house that was hired for the day and which served food to participants, and University seminar rooms). Participants were also paid a small amount for their involvement.

The research drawn from data gathered within the groups revealed that there was a lack of knowledge about HIV and AIDS among many deaf people (including risks of transmission), as well as a lack of available resources and materials that were designed for this specific social group. The group nevertheless helped the researcher to develop new resources, such as posters and brochures, which were later disseminated in community settings and institutions. The research also revealed that traditional materials for HIV and AIDS awareness were often inappropriate for deaf people, including some techniques used by professionals, such as social workers.

For example, poverty, bereavement or the experience of caring or alcohol dependency, and so forth. In these examples, however, the moderator will need to be particularly sensitive, use their discretion and possibly seek advice from a tutor or advocate in advance. Focus groups may also be useful for evaluating and improving services in health or social care or for gauging opinions on policy or practice.

Linhorst (2002: 223) highlights the potential relevance of focus group research for social work. This includes:

- The diverse populations and issues covered by social work practice and research and the related flexibility and suitability of the focus group method.
- The 'consciousness raising', collective, educational, anti-discriminatory and empowering potential of focus group meetings for participants.
- The method fits with and supports social work's 'unique person-in-environment perspective'.
- The capacity of 'flexible' focus group research to be combined with other methods, such as the one-on-one interview or questionnaires.

However, Linhorst (2002: 224) also warns that there is a tendency for focus groups to be used in a 'mechanistic way based upon business marketing's use of focus groups and their early use in the social sciences'. Because of social work's diverse role and qualitative research interests, this process can be challenged but there are nevertheless also limits to using focus groups. These include that focus groups may be difficult to organise and arrange and that the number of issues to explore can be limited in comparison to individual interviews (especially due to time constraints). Also, it is possible that ethical requirements regarding confidentiality may be compromised. The role of the moderator can also be difficult, including for novices. Finally, excess data can be collected, making analysis time-consuming and difficult. Despite such potential problems, there are still significant benefits attached to a flexible method which can usually be learnt quickly by the novice whilst typically providing a wealth of data at a later point.

Analysis tends to follow a similar process for qualitative research, discussed in more detail in chapter seventeen. Briefly, these involve *thematic* and *comparative* analysis, whereby we look for persistent trends, patterns and themes that run throughout our data and general findings, and which may be individually salient or also relate to other patterns (in the case of focus groups the information collected from individual or group discussion). For example, as Crowe (2003) discovered in her research with deaf community members discussed earlier, the finding from interviews suggested that there was a lack of awareness of HIV- and AIDS-related risks among many of her research participants. This research theme may also be analysed from the perspective of its relationship to other findings, such as the lack of suitable available information targeted at deaf community members in a local area. Focus group research may also be combined with other research methods, such as the individual interview or questionnaire, or used as part of a wider methodology such as the grounded theory and case study approaches discussed in the next chapter.

Conclusion

This chapter has discussed and detailed the use of the focus group method, including in qualitative social work research. It has been shown that focus groups offer a flexible and nuanced method upon which to build a research project. It has also been argued that focus groups need to be planned carefully in advance and that they typically demand extensive skills from a 'moderator'. Despite this, such skills can be quickly learnt. Although there are disadvantages to this method – including potential practical and ethical problems – the benefits of this approach include extensive and rich data that can be collected at a low cost and over a brief period of time. Focus group research also fits closely with many of the eclectic topics and issues that social work practitioners accommodate.

Further reading

Barbour, R.S., and Kitzinger, J. (eds) (1999). *Developing Focus Group Research: Politics, Theory and Practice.* London, Sage

Crowe, T.V. (2003). 'Using Focus Groups to create Culturally Appropriate HIV Prevention Material for the Deaf Community'. *Qualitative Social Work* 2(3): 289–308

Krueger, R.A., and Casey, M.A. (2000). *Focus Groups: A Practical Guide for Applied Research.* London, Sage

Linhorst, D.M. (2002). 'A Review of the Use and Potential of Focus Groups in Social Work Research'. *Qualitative Social Work* 1(2): 208–28

Morgan, D.L. (1997). *Focus Groups as Qualitative Research.* 2nd edn. London, Sage

Whittaker, A. (2009). *Research Skills for Social Work.* Exeter, Learning Matters. Chapter 4: Focus Groups

11 Grounded Theory and Case Studies

Introduction

This chapter looks at two separate methodologies which are united in their rigorous, precise and in-depth investigations and analysis. Grounded theory offers a painstakingly thorough collection and exploration of rich data yet also provides the researcher with considerable discretion regarding how to build up a sample and develop theory. Case study research looks instead at one case or example to explore in great detail a theme or set of issues that are at the centre of interest for the researcher. Each is now explored.

Grounded theory

Grounded theory (GT) is a distinct methodological approach which is founded upon a premise of gradually *building theory from data*. This approach is popular in health and education research although it does also have considerable relevance for social work related projects. The researcher initially defines a research question or problem and then collects data (during observations, interviews or focus group meetings, etc.) from participants. They then analyse this new information and steadily extrapolate meaning and build new concepts and theory.

A distinct component of GT remains that the literature review does not usually take place at an early stage as in most other qualitative approaches but instead continues throughout a project. This helps to explain new findings gathered from data and also supports the development of theory. Another distinct trend within GT remains a tendency to gradually build a sample as the research and findings develop (theoretical sampling); thus a set category or fixed number of research participants is unlikely to be planned from an early stage. Sample size is normally moderate in size for GT-influenced research, typically between 20 to 30 participants, although such figures offer only a guide (Gibson, 2003; Padgett, 2008). Importantly, however, for GT to work a small sample (e.g., *less than* 8–15 participants) would prove counter-productive for most projects as this methodology is generally reliant upon a (potentially) larger sample. In particular GT builds a sample until *saturation* point is met, when findings begin to repeat (such as when interviewees express the same feelings as have been identified earlier in previous interviews). At heart GT attempts to combine both inductive and deductive research processes: this is to allow recognition of the subjective or personal beliefs and experiences of participants (constructivist) whilst also recognising the significance of organised processes (realist) undertaken by the researcher within qualitative research.

Glaser and Strauss (1967) are widely recognised as the pioneers of GT and both were critical of 'quasi-scientific' or realist attempts to define social and qualitative research. In contrast, each believed that social rules, norms and the experiences or attitudes of people were more interdependent and complex than realism was able to take account of. As Cohen et al. (2007: 491) note, in seeking 'to catch the complexity and interconnectedness of everyday actions grounded theory is faithful to how people act; it takes account of apparent inconsistencies, contradictions, discontinuities and relatedness in actions'. Nevertheless, because of its popularity a variety of interpretations of GT tend to persist, including attempts to integrate aspects of this methodology with other approaches (Gibson, 2003; Floersch et al., 2010). Nevertheless, although influenced by deductive styles of research (theory influences data collection), the inductive method (new data collected leads to patterns emerging which help to develop theory) that is the hallmark of most qualitative research is followed more closely within a GT methodology. As Cohen et al. (2007: 491) also add, GT assumes that 'patterns and theories are implicit in data, waiting to be discovered'.

For a typical research project influenced by GT the following stages will be followed:

- *A research question is asked or problem identified.* For example, the initial emotions expressed by foster carers when meeting a new child.
- *Theoretical sampling of participants develops.* This is where the building of the sample is pragmatically influenced by emerging findings: that is, the sample is not rigidly fixed in number or the status of participants but instead is ongoing and gradually builds up. Here, sampling is not a separate stage of the research process as in most other approaches. The researcher is guided by the developing findings yet may also look for diverse groups, for example, so as to improve their comparison of findings and build better research concepts and themes for theory development.

- *Interviews or other methods continue to be undertaken to collect and analyse data.* Interviews intensify as the sample builds, and both interview and sample growth remain interlinked and develop together.
- *Transcripts are carefully read and emerging trends or themes defined.* For example, the feelings of apprehension or anxiety felt by new foster carers.
- *Collected data is coded and research concepts are developed.* Codes are typically represented by a letter or number that signify explicit behaviours, attitudes, emotional traits or events experienced and articulated by interview participants (see below for further information about coding).
- *There is movement back and forth between the four stages identified above.* For example, sampling and data collection may influence the slight revision of the research question, or emerging data may affect any decision regarding how to extend the sample of research participants.
- *Notes will be kept of further individual 'cases' following interviews or observations. Analytical concepts or trends continue to emerge from new data and help to revise the categories and concepts which will help to develop the final theory.* For example, the foster carers will continue to be interviewed on an individual basis and such new data may then lead to a revision of any initial findings, especially after further detailed exploration of early notes kept and initial themes identified.
- *The researcher begins to develop a conceptual scheme which leads to the emergence of a core theory.* From this point, additional data will be compared with the gradual building of a core theory. For example, all or a majority of the foster carers may highlight the importance of social work support in their attempts to fulfil their new role as foster carer. Other research undertaken or theoretical concepts (such as systems, attachment or feminist theory) may be integrated into aspects of the analysis without being allowed to overbear or determine this process.
- *Eventually a state of 'saturation' will be reached.* In general, this is where no more new findings or a repetition of outcomes emerge regarding points raised by those interviewed. At this stage, the researcher should exit the field and continue analysis and theory development. (adapted from Strauss and Corbin, 1990).

The different phases of GT generate the following research 'products':

Codes and Coding   this is a central component of GT and represents salient themes or phenomena identified as crucial to the research participants interviewed or observed. Codes are typically exemplified by a letter/number that represents explicit attitudes, emotional traits, behaviour or events experienced and articulated by interview participants. Codes allow us to summarise data and subsequently label, separate or compile key findings or trends. As Bryman (2004: 402) notes, codes in GT are not fixed or static entities as in much quantitative research but instead remain more fluid and open to reinterpretation, most notably following further interviews and the collection of more data.

Concepts   these each emerge from several open codes that have been joined together. They represent labels that are given to discrete phenomena or patterns and will eventually form into even broader categories.

Categories   a category remains a 'concept that has been elaborated so that it is regarded as representing real-world phenomena' (Bryman, 2004: 403). A category is usually made up of two or more concepts and there may be a distinction made between core and peripheral categories. Categories are typically broader and more abstract social or cultural phenomena than concepts, such as relating to several longer-term reflections and experiences. Establishing a small number of categories will often represent the core building blocks upon which a theory rests.

Properties   these represent components, attributes or aspects of a single category.

Memos   these remain notes, such as from interviews or in relation to a researcher's reflection on emerging themes, which alongside transcripts will aid the generation of a concept. Memos can be helpful for developing ideas or recollecting information or thoughts that might otherwise be lost.

Hypothesis   this represents initial ideas or hunches about the relationship between different concepts. A hypothesis like a research question can be summarised into a question that the researcher seeks to answer.

Theory   the end product of GT in which generalisations or statements that epitomise findings are codified and presented to a reader or audience. There is a distinction sometimes drawn between *substantive* (small-scale statements or findings about everyday life or events) and *formal* (more abstract and broad findings, categories or trends) theory. The latter will tend to require data collection in different localities or settings (for example, more than one residential home, hospital or day-centre or possibly such institutions in different cities or regions of a country).

Usually a project influenced by GT will draw from indepth semi- or unstructured interviews, ethnography or participant observation or a combination of these approaches. Focus group meetings are less common but can still support a GT project. In theory, however, GT may be combined

---

A case example: Use of empathy by social workers working with patients who are HIV positive

Barry wished to explore the values and experience of social workers based in a local hospital. He concentrated upon practitioners working with HIV-positive males and followed a set of methodological steps that were influenced by grounded theory. These included:

- Defining a research problem.
- Interviewing for at least one hour social workers over a period of one month in relation to their practical day-to-day experience and beliefs. Eventually this grew to a total theoretical sample of 16 (11 female, 5 male).
- Writing up and exploring transcripts and then identifying codes, concepts and eventually building categories that reflected the majority of interviews.
- Undertaking further interviews that sought to build upon, revise or confirm and complete the first stage of the research, in particular to refine the categories.
- Rereading personal interview accounts and especially those details that linked to the category of how empathy was expressed by practitioners.
- Comparing evidence of 'empathetic events and workers' with those of other accounts of sample members that revealed an alternative set of emotions (including anxiety, uncertainty or a lack of empathy).

Barry analysed his findings with reference to other research within nursing and social work and built a substantive theory which detailed the disparate emotional responses – often influenced by factors outside of work and other case responsibilities within work – of social work employees working alongside patients with a chronic illness within an institutional setting.

---

with any other methodology or method. For example, Floersch et al. (2010: 407) undertook qualitative research into the impact of the use of psychotropic medication on adolescents in the USA. They combined the use of grounded theory with both narrative interviews and thematic analysis to 'produce a multidimensional understanding of medication experience'. The authors propose that this methodology helped their research by offering 'different interpretations' of the experience of the taking of medication by adolescents. In general, GT is increasingly used alongside other qualitative methodologies with a view to offering different perspectives from the same data, and thus extending analysis through comparison. Again, Pieters and Dornig (2011) draw from GT but do so from the vantage point of two separate and different PhD projects: one based in a nursing school and the other in social welfare. However, both researchers aided one another by helping to analyse and code each other's emerging data, thus supporting each other's project up to saturation point by comparing and evaluating one another's data at regular intervals.

The extent to which GT is applied may depend upon factors such as the original research question asked and its related topic, the intended sample group, the expected time available to gather data. As stressed earlier, we need at least to have access to a reasonable-sized potential sample. Also, the extent to which a literature review is undertaken, and when it begins, will depend upon your own requirements: one of the strengths of GT remains its flexibility and capacity to offer specific tools or elements of the methodology to different research settings and projects. Much like some interpretations of participation research, you may feel that this intense methodology is too time consuming and elaborate to justify a full excursion into its vaults: instead, some elements may be drawn upon. For example, in practice it is unrealistic to expect every new GT project to develop a 'new' theory, especially following relatively brief contact with a moderate sample. A more realistic outcome is likely to be the revision of an established theory that had some influence upon your own project. Typically, a strict reading of GT will mean that a project proceeds over a long period of time and utilises considerable resources. Again, the qualitative tradition of investigating experience and attitudes make this approach suitable for exploring related topics with practitioners, carers, users and so forth. It can accommodate sensitive issues or more practical concerns but again is less likely to be representative or allow us to generalise.

As the methodology unfolds over a longer period of time and involves numerous interviews it is more likely to be suitable for a PhD or moderate-sized research project rather than an undergraduate or Masters dissertation. Despite this, the cultural process and some core techniques of GT, such as to build or develop theory from data or allow preconceived prejudices to be reduced, may still be applied within a smaller project.

Case study research

Another distinct methodology remains the case study approach. This is where a single case example is explored in relation to a specific research problem or question. As Bryman (2004: 51) notes, cases are often chosen because they 'exemplify' our attempts to investigate our queries:

Cases are often chosen not because they are extreme or unusual in some way but because they will provide a suitable context for certain research questions to be answered. As such, they allow the researcher to examine key social processes.

A case may represent a number of possible concerns or topics of enquiry. For example, it may seek to explore a small 'clan' of people (or 'group case study') who share something in common: like similar experiences regarding the fulfilment of a certain role or task, such as parenting or coping with a particular illness or disability. It might instead be represented by a single person's life experiences and/or beliefs in relation to a particular concern or habit (e.g., use of illicit drugs) or the ways by which a skilled role is fulfilled by a person such as a community nurse or volunteer. The possibilities are many, however, and might also include studying the 'case' of an organisation such as a social service or health care clinic, a piece of government policy or legislation or instead a nationwide social trend within a particular city. Typically with cases of people the researcher will concentrate upon four or more individual cases.

Whatever the subject-matter, this methodology seeks to explore a predetermined case *in great detail*. Predominately this is to thoroughly interrogate and then better understand the characteristics or qualities embodied within each. Cases are also often seen as exemplifying more general principles, qualities or issues, and can be used to generalise and make recommendations. As Payne and Payne (2004: 32) note, it is the time permitted to explore in great detail a topic of study which provides the merits and strength of case study research. In particular, a researcher can 'complete work more quickly, and in much greater depth and detail, than if the researcher were trying to cover several cases'.

Yin (1994) recognises three types of case which include:

i. Critical case in which a case is chosen because it permits greater understanding of the topic to be explored, and also because it links directly to any research objectives. For example, if exploring the role of informal care skills required for the support of people with dementia we may undertake a series of unstructured interviews with a man who has cared for his wife at home with later stage dementia for many years.

ii. Unique case this might involve the study of a distinct organisation, country or a person who exemplifies particular characteristics or traits which makes them ideal for in-depth study. For example, a female senior manager in a social care occupation dominated by men, or a younger male undertaking an informal carer role when social and cultural norms might expect such tasks to be fulfilled by an older woman, and so on. This is not intended to be the exploration of the unusual or the bizarre but instead is drawn upon because it can greatly benefit the process of enquiry and analysis, such as through comparison with more prominent examples in associate research studies.

iii. Revelatory case   this is usually represented by a case that helps to explore subject-matter which has not been analysed before, perhaps due to problems researchers had in gaining access to a particular social group. For example, Carey's (2006) research into the experience of social workers employed by private sector employment agencies. There may also be a topic that relates to a recent social trend that has not in the past been explored by qualitative researchers and which you are able to gain an insight into because of a current post or new role.

Punch (2005: 145) notes four key characteristics of case study research. They include:

1. Identifying clear research *aims* and *objectives*. We need to be clear about what it is we hope to achieve and how we might fulfil these objectives. Such questions should always link to any case and establish how 'evidence' from any case study might be used to explore our research aims and objectives.
2. Stipulating the prevalence of *boundaries* that delineate a case. For example, if exploring one authority's approach to child-care then we must clarify this early on, and distinguish it from other related policies, such as regarding fostering and other forms of childcare.
3. Recognising what the case *constitutes* and *entails*. For example, if studying a country's policy regarding support for people with Alzheimer's, it can be beneficial to narrow the focus to easily assessed criteria for analysis rather than attempt to study a number of broad and difficult-to-quantify themes. In this example, we might look at how domiciliary support is organised and provided to people with Alzheimer's in France by social workers.
4. Establishing the *means of data collection*. Empirical research methods such as interviews and participant observation can be used, but other approaches such as focus groups are possible depending upon the study. However, we can undertake case study research based upon a literature review, such as by looking at and comparing empirical findings from other studies using a narrative or systematic review (see chapter five).

Humphries (2008: 90–91) also stresses the need for good reasons for deciding to select any case. For example, we may ask what it is that we can learn from this particular case *which is not already known*. Cases should not be selected for convenience but instead because they permit a critical investigation of complex themes to take place. Hitchcock and Hughes (1989) also identify important hallmarks of case study research. These can include a *vivid description* of, or *chronological narrative* of events; a description of case-related *themes* together with an *analysis* of each; or a stress upon a *person* or *group of individuals* and subsequent attempts made to understand their *perception of events*. Also, we may wish to highlight *specific events* or *issues* that are peculiar to a case; may become *intimately involved* and *immersed* within a case study; and can then detail the *richness* and *distinct qualities* of a case in a final write up.

Yin (1994: 21–7) notes five stages of research design, which include:

- A study's research question or topic must be defined as early as possible.
- Research propositions, or preconceived assumptions or statements about the study case must be formulated as they may help us to gain focus.
- A 'unit' of analysis must be identified, which often is the case in question. For example, if studying a practitioner's personal experience of the assessment process, then it is the practitioner's *viewpoints* about assessments that become the unit.
- A clear and tangible link between the data (on which any assessment is based) and the research aims and objectives of the study must be made.
- Some criteria for interpreting and evaluating the case study should be recognised. How will a case be assessed and compared with other related research? Might we look at themes or compare our evidence to findings from other studies (see chapter seventeen for further advice on analysis)?

Yin (ibid.: 27–32) adds that theory often plays a central role in casework. We should, therefore, seek to review the established theories or available empirical information that relate to any topic, either before or whilst collecting data and try to link any current theory to any such study so to analyse findings and analysis. For example, as a means of comparison or to better understand our findings. In addition, it is also possible to use more than one method to collect data, such as combining interviews with the focus group method. As we may be engaged in exploring one or two cases, the researcher may be able to examine the case study meticulously from many different angles by using a variety of methods or theories. Indeed, comparison of two or more cases is often ideal for literature-based or empirical research.

Analysis remains a key process that should be explicit within all case study research. It is not enough to merely describe attributes that link to any one case: any investigation will need to unearth and extrapolate, understand and place into context emergent themes that link to the initial objectives of any study. For example, Helavirta (2011: 13) used a case study approach to analyse the moral standpoints of children who had been taken into care and were supported by adoptive parents in Finland. She used a sample of seven children who had been taken into care within one city as her case. Through a total of 20 interviews over the course of a year Helavirta was able to extrapolate the children's moral views on life within their new home and then used this data to question established normative assumptions regarding adult constructions of what should be right and wrong within an ideal home. In particular, the assumption that children should not take on too many responsibilities for adults is queried:

> In the field of child welfare, [children] assuming responsibility for adults is often considered problematic, and children that have to do this are easily defined as excessively burdened. My findings challenge the social workers to identify established and often unquestioned concepts about children as exclusively the targets of care. If the children's moral standpoint on reciprocal care is appreciated and recognised in child welfare work, the fact that children assume responsibility for their home and parents, does not appear as an unambiguous threat to good life.

Unlike so much quantitative research, a qualitative methodology such as the case study approach will often develop an *analytical frame* as the project develops, clarifying and focusing what it is we hope to detail, understand and explore. Hochschild (1983) famously investigated emotion work or the ways by which employees use or manipulate emotions to cope with stressful roles that include regular contact with the general public. She studied and interviewed flight attendants as her 'case', and the frame of analysis became the employee's expressions and use of emotions in their work, most prominently when engaging or communicating with passengers. We may decide not to develop an explicit frame of analysis, however, and instead decide that the case example can be best explored through the development of themes or comparison with other findings. Case study research can be used alone as a single methodology or may be combined with other approaches. Commonly, this will include the interview but may well involve the integration of types of action research, ethnography or other approaches.

Case study research has been criticised on a number of grounds. These include that any cases chosen may be too narrowly focused and therefore lack the potential to make more general claims. A common criticism again is that cases may instead also be better suited as initial pilot studies for larger projects at a later stage. Research boundaries may also sometimes be difficult to define for some cases, which may mean that any topic is difficult to assess and evaluate to good effect. Nevertheless, my own experience suggests that what a case study lacks regarding objectivity or generalisation it can usually make up for with depth of investigation. An intense level of analysis is also possible due to the additional time available to survey our findings. The case study approach is ideally suited to a dissertation or small-scale project because it represents a manageable piece of work that can provide a rich source of data, explanation and understanding.

> **Case example: Coping strategies used by Team Leaders based in social work settings**
>
> Lisa wanted to know how her senior colleagues coped with the levels of pressure and stress that appeared to be part of their demanding and at times difficult role. What were their strategies for coping from day to day? Were such strategies implicit and hidden or was there at least some evidence of a conscious set of plans to cope? Lisa interviewed two of her colleagues, each based in a different sector of her regional authority: a woman based in a social work area office and a female colleague working in a residential care setting. During the ongoing unstructured interviews, it became clear that different strategies emerged from each person and that each was strongly influenced by a combination of the work setting, role, collegiate relations and personality of each employee.

Conclusion

This chapter has explored two distinct methodological approaches. Although often demanding regarding time and resources, grounded theory nevertheless offers the researcher a solid methodological base on which to rest their study as well as a flexible and thorough insight into research participants' viewpoints or experiences. It may also be able to offer the revision of a key paradigm or even perhaps a new theory as a final research outcome. Case study research more often looks at only one participant or group but nevertheless is equally as precise and in-depth in analysis as grounded theory. Both approaches are united in their capacity to be used alongside other research methods, or as part of a wider methodology. Each approach also encourages the elevation of explanation and understanding above description or the capacity to generalise.

Further reading

Dey, I. (1998). *Grounding Grounded Theory: Guidelines for Qualitative Inquiry*. San Diego, Academic Press

Denscombe, M. (2007). *The Good Research Guide For Small-Scale Social Research Projects*, Open University Press, Maidenhead. Chapter 2 – Case Studies

Floersch, J., Longhofer, J.L., Kranke, D., and Townsend, L. (2010). 'Integrating Thematic, Grounded Theory and Narrative Analysis: A Case Study of Adolescent Psychotropic Treatment'. *Qualitative Social Work* 9(3): 407–25

Gilgun, J.F. (1994). 'Hand into Glove: The Grounded Theory Approach and Social Work Practice Research', in Sherman, E., and Reid, W.J. (eds), *Qualitative Research in Social Work*. New York, Columbia University Press

Gomm, R., Hammersley, M., and Foster, P. (eds) (2000). *Case Study Method*. London, Sage

Helavirta, S. (2011). *Home, Children and Moral Standpoints: A Case Study of Child Clients of Child Welfare*. Qualitative Social Work. Published online: 21 June

Humphries, B. (2008). *Social Work Research for Social Justice*. Basingstoke, Palgrave Macmillan. Chapter 6 – Case Study Research

Pieters, H.C., and Dornig, K. (2011). 'Collaboration in Grounded Theory Analysis: Reflections and Practical Suggestions'. *Qualitative Social Work*. Published online 28 November

Stake, R.E. (1995). *The Art of Case Study Research*. Thousand Oaks, CA, Sage

Strauss, A., and Corbin, J. (1990). *Basics of Qualitative Research: Grounded Theory Procedures and Techniques*. Newbury Park, Sage

Yin, R.K. (1994). *Case Study Research – Design and Methods*. London, Sage

12 Ethnography

Introduction

This chapter explores and details one of the more complex, diverse and in-depth methodologies with a long tradition, that of ethnography. The chapter offers a definition of ethnography and also discusses its approach, philosophy and logic, as well as some of the different theoretical approaches that influence its application by the researcher in the field. We also look at some of the key skills and practical problems faced by the ethnographer, such as access and field relations. Finally, we look at some of the criticisms aimed at this unique approach and then look at a case study.

Ethnography

Ethnography has a long history – initiated within anthropology but since adopted in a wide range of disciplines, most notably the social and human science disciplines. Brewer (2000: 6) acknowledges its ambitious yet delicate scope:

> Ethnography is the study of people in naturally occurring settings or 'fields' by methods of data collection which capture their social meanings and ordinary activities, involving the researcher participating directly in the setting, if not also the activities, in order to collect data in a systematic manner but without meaning being imposed on them externally.

As Edmund Leach (1982: 161) suggests, in comparison to many other approaches the researcher 'tries to understand alien societies from the *inside* rather than the *outside*'. That is, the researcher becomes a part of the social group and/or organisation being studied, and typically immerses themselves into a new and distinct *sub-culture*. As a consequence, ethnography becomes not simply a single technique or set of skills, but is also a philosophy that highlights *culture* within a group, especially any in which the ethnographer is directly involved. Perhaps somewhat surprisingly, there is no great traditional link between social work and ethnographic research. At best ethnographic methods have represented a marginal resource in comparison to say theoretical analysis (especially in the UK) or the interview. Despite this, ethnography holds great potential for the social worker and indeed has been used to great effect in the past (for example, Pithouse, 1987).

Marvasti (2004: 36) maintains that ethnography means to 'write about people or cultures'. Three subsequent priorities remain, which include 'involvement with and participation in the *topic* being studied, attention to the *context* of data collection, and sensitivity to how the subjects are *represented* in the research text'. Skeggs (2001: 426) again identifies attributes apparent within ethnographic research. They include an expectation that:

- The researcher will actively participate (for example in conversations, rituals, building friendships, etc.) and observe *within* the settings of research participants.
- Any 'fieldwork' will be conducted over a prolonged period of time.
- An understanding on behalf of the researcher will develop regarding how *context* (environment; status, role, and the cultural norms and identity of participants) informs the actions of participants.
- An account of the *relationship* between the researcher and the researched will develop.
- The researcher will acknowledge 'how experience and practice are part of wider processes', including those that relate to the expectations and norms of peers, as well as responses to, and engagement, with different settings, institutional traditions, priorities and cultural expectations.
- Different research methods can be applied alongside ethnographic fieldwork. This may include the gathering of statistical information (regarding the setting or participants) or, as is often the case, direct one-on-one or group interviews with participants or the reading of reports, diaries or other sources of information.

Humphries (2008: 137–42) highlights some assumptions made within 'traditional' forms of ethnography. These include that priority is given to the present rather than the past, human behaviour is recognised as unpredictable and ever changing and that the researcher acknowledges their own subjective influence upon the interpretation of events and interactions being observed. For example, individual prejudices or prior assumptions made about people being observed or simply one's presence affecting events. The study of the internal changes occurring *within* individuals is as important as the interactions *between* people. Regarding the direct study of people, Humphries notes the problem of 'deciding what to observe and what is irrelevant to the area of interest', and also highlights the importance of recognising change through observations made within different settings and context:

The individual is not a consistent, static personality, but is always in a state of 'becoming', always undergoing change in interaction with the environment ... it is important to observe people in different contexts, since behaviour, opinions and beliefs change and may even be contradictory, according to the context.

Tedlock (2000: 455) privileges any ethnographers role as an 'ongoing attempt to place specific encounters, events, and understandings into a fuller, more meaningful context'. In relation, Marvasti (2004: 36) maintains how research is not to be considered ethnographic if it ignores 'the context and related conditions under which people's actions and statements [are] observed and recorded'.

In a persuasive book, La Fontaine (1985: 15–19) argues that two motives should be central to any ethnographic approach. They are, first, the necessity of capturing an understanding of the influence of, and engagement with, wider social or cultural forces. Again, this is another call for an appreciation of context, and recognition that the researcher does not merely describe what they see each day. For social work, this might include a description of the *impact* of the policies enacted within a particular organisation upon staff and service users; or procedure, management practices, professional and other peer expectations, etc. It might, instead, relate to the subjective and cultural priorities that people develop and cling to as part of their daily roles fulfilled – which may contrast with, or even oppose, the formal rituals embedded within organisations. This may include a less apparent or even 'unseen' set of informal processes, such as power dynamics embedded within language, relationships or status, forms of disparate class- or gender-based conflict, group support provided during times of stress, or different ways in which people articulate their identities or emotional intelligence, and so on. Fetterman (1998: 17) again underlines the complexity of many observational processes within a research field:

Living in a foreign community for a long period of time enables the fieldworker to see the power of dominant ideas, values, and patterns of behaviour in the way people walk, talk, dress, eat and sleep. The longer an individual stays in a community, building rapport, and the deeper the probe into individual lives, the greater the probability of his or her learning about the sacred subtle elements of the culture: how people pray, how they feel about each other, and how they reinforce their own cultural practices to maintain the integrity of their system.

The second objective that La Fontaine isolates is the importance of comparing and contrasting previous studies; ideally in the hope of (once again) better understanding and contextualising events, processes and relations that are witnessed. Often this process is labelled 'holistic' – that is, it aims to be able to take into account the many different dynamics evident within a research setting and to be able to relate each to one another.

Traditional, critical and post-modern ethnography

Despite the shared significance of themes such as participation, context and integration within ethnography, there have nevertheless developed distinct approaches within the methodology over the years. For example, Harvey (1990: 8–14) isolates three dominant strands – traditional, critical and post-modern. First, traditional approaches stress the acquisition of detailed descriptions of 'forms of social interaction and the meanings which lie behind these'; the subsequent aim being to 'reveal social processes' rather than look to consider any causes behind what is happening (ibid.: 9). Indeed, the meaning of the word ethnography locates writing 'about ethnicity' or detailing 'other cultures'. Here the ethnographer searches for the meaning of their observations of different cultures and also how language, myths, physical objects, traditions, and so forth, are exchanged between people within social groups or institutions. The ethnographer's interpretation of interactions between people is then compared and contrasted with findings from previous studies. There is also a tendency to emphasise an unbiased and detached description of social events and processes as witnessed by the researcher, with only limited, if any, attempt to politically contextualise any findings. As stressed previously in chapter six, such 'realist' assumptions can carry significant drawbacks, including not least their largely fruitless attempts to maintain the objectivity of the researcher 'stood at a distance' or, and in relation, ignore the profound influence of societal institutions, conflict and structures or normative processes (including language, the role of the family and schooling, expectations, traditions, etc.) upon a social group's or individual's behaviour and attitudes.

Second, and in contrast yet also maintaining many of the insights and techniques of traditional ethnography, remains critical ethnography. This attempts to link any detailed findings 'to wider social structures and systems of power relationships in order to get beneath the surface of oppressive structural relationships'. No easy task, yet this may include drawing upon critical literature and research in related studies or topics. In an attempt to build upon and extend this tradition, Skeggs (2001: 437) isolates four underlying themes inherent in feminist ethnography. They are:

1. Recognition of and 'sensitivity to the power effects of the researcher'. This especially regards a realisation that researchers can hold considerable power over research 'subjects' and therefore need to

fully appreciate an ethical commitment to emancipatory and ethical research.

2. An understanding that traditional ethnographic research has a tendency to encourage the 'virtues of objectivity, distance and detachment ... [and] the objectification of the other'; that is, reduce the person or 'research participant' to a series of almost emotionless observations and accounts. Through critical reflexivity the feminist ethnographer should endeavour to look much further beneath what is going on and accept the 'other' as a real and unpredictable person.

3. A contribution of 'important interventions into the debates over the authorising and legitimacy of knowledge production'. Feminist ethnography has raised questions about not only research methodology and process but also inequitable ways by which patriarchal knowledge is created and disseminated. It seeks to counter this trend such as by drawing attention to new forms of critical and rigorous knowledge production that more accurately capture the experiences and attitudes of women.

4. Production of 'some of the most in-depth material about women's lives' and therefore the enablement of 'significant challenges to what comes to be counted as knowledge'.

Harvey (1990: 12) again draws from critical ethnography to stress the need to link research observations and talk in the field with 'structural relations'; that is, how research participants' behaviour, beliefs and actions are influenced, and sometimes moulded, by wider social and cultural forces such as class, gender, 'race', language, discourse and dominant ideology. Again, this is not an easy process, but within social work an attempt should be made by the researcher to examine, discuss and understand such processes rather than simply interpret and describe events and traditions at 'face value'.

Third, both traditional and critical approaches have been criticised by the postmodern stance. As Pink (2001: 19) points out, postmodern thinkers argue that 'ethnographic knowledge and text can only ever be a subjective construction, a "fiction" that represents only the ethnographer's version of a reality, rather than an empirical truth'. In other words, the views of the researcher or ethnographic author offer only one of many possible interpretations of events – typically this is a privileged yet inevitably biased account of a subjective reality. Also stressed by postmodernists remain the centrality of power, fragmentation, contradictions, uncertainties, paradox, ambiguity, and other such implicit or unseen social or cultural dynamics which can (seemingly) be difficult to directly observe and take account of. The emphasis then from the researcher's perspective becomes the uncertain, fluid and the ambivalent, as well as priority being given to enriching and understanding a convoluted research *process* rather than merely seeking to quantify research *objectives*. That is, the researcher recognises complex realities and experience in the field and also questions their own values, assumptions, beliefs and interpretations. Such principles are opposed to traditional ethnography in which the 'expert' researcher may arrogantly assume rational and objective understandings and interpretations of 'subject' people under his professional gaze. The related interpretive (chapter six) theoretical viewpoint of utilising ethnography to *understand*, *involve* and *implicate* the 'views and perspectives of [research participants] and the meanings they attach to things' is prioritised (Corby, 2006: 50). This approach helps the ethnographer to reduce or overcome bias by offering a voice, if not equal say, to participants in how research progresses.

There are, however, aspects of the postmodern stance that may be difficult to apply in practice. For example, involving participants in decision-making processes throughout research can prove difficult, and there must be asked questions about whether such 'interactive' processes can ever really progress on an equal level with all participants.

In practice, whether intending to or not, the researcher is likely to draw from all three traditions of ethnography. That is, carefully plan and organise their research (from a realist perspective) whilst recognising cultural and structural disadvantage (from a critical stance) and acknowledging uncertainty and difference in the field, whilst possibly involving participants more in decision-making processes (postmodern).

The potential, nevertheless, for social work is considerable, especially if access is gained and the researcher is able to explore the many different worlds and experiences of the 'service user' as resident in a nursing home, or the practitioner based in a hospital. Inevitably, spending time with people and perhaps engaging in aspects of their role (a common tradition in most forms of ethnography) can potentially tell us much more than the typical one hour interview alone.

Practical concerns

Grills (1998) presents us with basic practical questions that ethnographers attempt to address. Study questions may include:

- Identifying the *perspectives* of people researched. Or how social actors interpret, understand and, most significantly, *make sense* of their world. As part of this process we may be able to uncover common attitudes, beliefs or habits and roles missed by earlier and less engaged studies.
- Exploring *relationships*. Or how human beings interact with one another within their group 'sub-culture': for example, how members

of an organised carers' group communicate inside and outside monthly group meetings at a local church. This may also include exploring loyalties, empathy, difference and points of conflict, power dynamics based around class, status, charisma, and so forth.

- Recognising and analysing social *action*. What is it that people chose not to do as well as do; how are such actions articulated and what do particular actions mean to participants? The researcher should try to identify and unpack the complex nature of social actions, roles or habits.
- Analysing continuity and change over *time*. The researcher should be able to grasp implicit and explicit trends and outcomes as they gradually emerge over a period of time. For example, how relationships with service users or colleagues develop from a practitioner's viewpoint, or the different ways in which people interpret and apply policy or organise their tasks or role.
- *Contextualising* our findings. This includes linking up individual or group attitudes, beliefs and actions with wider cultural and social trends (for example, relating to tradition, expectations, policy or organisational norms, etc.).

The first practical step in ethnographic research is to establish a provisional research question or problem that relates to your topic of enquiry. As stated earlier in chapter two, this should ideally be a brief statement of one or two sentences which encompasses what it is your research hopes to explore and address. Although this question or problem may be revised or adapted once in the field, it is still worth constructing an interim question/problem which helps to focus your activities and plans. You can also create a brief list of related core objectives that you hope to achieve whilst in the field. As always, you will need to be as clear as possible how your ethnography links with any research topic. To begin with, try to be as unambiguous as possible about what is it you are likely to be observing. For example, will it be particular people fulfilling a certain role or specific dynamics that link to an aspect of social work practice or values? Try to be realistic about what can be achieved throughout your project, rather than simply attempt to do everything in a relatively short space of time.

The next key decision relates to the intended site of research. In practice, it is likely that the types of possible fields in which to undertake an ethnographic study will be somewhat restricted for a social work student or practitioner. Commonly three possibilities persist for students – a practice placement or previous or current work environment or a voluntary sector organisation. In all of these environments it is likely that your research will be open and explicit (overt) to all participants, although 'boundaries' of study can change: for example, the research may move outside a voluntary sector organisation and into other institutions or environments used by service users (for example, a day centre or sheltered housing, etc.). Ethnographers need to utilise their professional discretion and must abide by ethical rules of conduct (see chapter eight).

Regarding time, Wolcott (1999) argues that a thorough and full ethnography should last for at least a year. As this is unlikely to be possible as part of a social work course or many research studies a less ambitious form of ethnography, also known as 'micro-ethnography', is more likely to be feasible. A micro-ethnography takes place over a shorter time period, from several weeks to a few months, and as a consequence tends to be much more focused and somewhat less ambitious regarding what is explored (see also Bryman, 2004: 293). For example, one or two themes or issues in relation to a specific culture might be investigated, such as forms of communication or types of relationships between people. As Wolcott (1999: 29) highlights, most ethnography seeks to study only a few aspects of their setting and people:

> No ethnographer wants or can ever be expected to take responsibility for providing the full and complete account of some group of people. Such a goal is unattainable. We do well to capture some of the relevant detail, and do even better when we can capture some of the more elusive spirit of those among whom we study.

It is then important to decide how data will be collected within any research field. Who will you observe and also where, when and how? You may wish to distinguish between different social groups in a place of study: for example, health or social care professionals, different service users according to gender and/or age or different roles undertaken by staff (for example managers, social workers and administrative staff). In which setting will you base your research and is this likely to change over time? Some of these points are difficult to predict and are contingent, yet some planning and foresight always helps. At what times are you hoping to undertake your research (for example, early morning, evening, weekends, etc., so as to encourage consistency) and how will you record your data? It normally helps to keep written notes, such as within a diary (Fetterman, 1998). More generally, research notes also have a number of advantages, most notably to remind you of observations, key events, and also allowing a record of contacts and relations with other people to be kept. It is worth remembering that sections of such notes are also admissible as 'evidence' in the final write-up of your dissertation (typically the findings and analysis sections).

The length and detail of ethnographic notes will differ from topic to topic, but in general you should aim to be clear and concise about what you have observed. Typically, diary notes should also contain early attempts at analysis – whereby your observations merge with, and respond to, themes identified in the literature review; or other themes you have already recognised as being important to your study. Perhaps inevitably, it will also be of benefit to be imaginative and creative regarding how data is uncovered and explored – for example, consider what possible sources of data might be suitable beyond observation of behaviour and talk. Are there any written documents or tasks that are completed by staff that might give a clue regarding attempts to explore your research question? Perhaps it would help to maintain a record of your emotional responses to the new world around you as well as the concrete 'real world' activities and events that you witness. Essentially, ethnography is a broad church, and as with other methodologies it typically demands both a sense of pragmatic realism alongside creative flair.

Access is typically a crucial obstacle to overcome for the budding ethnographer. You will need to consider how access to your intended population and field might be achieved. Do you already have access to the organisation or group you intend to study? Where might you attain permission to undertake your study? Knowing people typically helps. Indeed, as Marvasti (2004: 47) concedes, 'it helps to know someone who can give you access to the particular places and the information you need'. However, you might also need to gain formal permission, such as through a 'gatekeeper' and/or ethics committee. As noted earlier, undertaking qualitative social work research is never straightforward, and as stressed in chapter eight advanced planning for ethical dilemmas and permission mean that you will often need to plan well in advance. Potentially at least, access can undermine a whole project so try to organise your location and receive formal permission (such as from a senior member of staff or formal committee) as soon as possible.

Field relations are another aspect of ethnographic research that requires particular attention. Although each topic and research field will generate different demands, there are some general rules that can be applied to most studies. In a detailed discussion of field relations, Hammersley and Atkinson (1995: 80–123) draw from a number of previous ethnographies undertaken by different researchers to offer general guidelines on what is often a delicate and highly skilled set of techniques and aptitudes. Typically, research participants:

- are initially suspicious or uncomfortable with an ethnographer's presence but early scepticism tends to 'quickly dissipate as contact increases';

- are also often more interested in the researcher's *personality* rather than the research project or aims, and are often looking for evidence of trust and empathy.

Ethnographers should try to:

- be tactful and avoid confrontation or difficult and/or inappropriate questions throughout their fieldwork;
- shun appearing aloof, distant and obsessed with only the research project being investigated;
- avoid asking too many questions and try to be subtle and discreet. It is possible that you may appear 'very threatening to hosts if one pumps them constantly about matters relating to research interests';
- engage in small talk if and when appropriate, and formal and informal rituals if necessary (for example, going to the pub with staff or attending other social events);
- take a sincere interest in research participants' lives and role without prying or appearing to snoop at every given opportunity;
- be careful with personal appearance and dress code. For example, avoid dressing in an overtly formal style in an informal social setting (and vice versa);
- be as honest and open as possible;
- recognise possible difficulties, such as the possible impact of your gender, age, class, etc., including if such personal or cultural traits contrast with research participants. Consider how you might accommodate any differences;
- be critically reflexive and avoid relying upon preconceived and culturally constructed stereotypes or 'misleading preconceptions about the setting and the people in it';
- be open and empathetic to unique and possibly very different work or other organisational or group cultures and processes;
- avoid drawing undue attention to yourself such as by using complex language or by discussing personal interests or hobbies that a social group may find threatening or odd;
- avoid generalisation or condemning seemingly 'alien' practices and beliefs;
- avoid *complete* integration, especially to the point that sympathy with observed organisations and people means that your ethnographic gaze becomes blurred and/or loses focus;
- avoid developing intimate relations with research participants.

The emphasis then is very much upon subtlety and a careful degree of conformity to group norms and values.

The writing up of ethnography usually takes place in two stages. First, detailed notes or a diary (chapter thirteen) within the field ensure that as much information relating to core events, relations and themes are captured. Usually these will be recorded on site or away from the field each day or evening. Fetterman (1998: 116) suggests holding field-notes in a loose-leaf folder 'with tabs to identify each section'. Typically, notes or diary accounts are often assumed to be descriptive; however, for a dissertation or report it is best to begin the analysis as soon as possible due to time restrictions, and therefore also keep more analytic notes alongside or beside any descriptive notes.

The second part of writing relates to later stage analysis and the final writing of the dissertation or report itself. In relationto this, Denscombe (2007: 72, my emphasis) discerns two traditions in ethnography:

> At one end of the spectrum there are those who regard the main purpose of ethnography as *providing rich and detailed descriptions of real-life situations as they really are*. At the other end ... there are those who see the role of ethnographic fieldwork as *a test-bed for theories – a means of developing theories by checking them out in small-scale scenarios*.

For a social work dissertation or research project detailed descriptions alone are unlikely to suffice. Part of the reasons for this relates to any expectations of students at Post-Qualification, Masters or Bachelor degree level; not least including the need to show evidence of a capacity to analyse and critically assess during the research process. For such reason it is likely that you will need to undertake any ethnography alongside some reference to established or emerging theory or theories.

In recognising the centrality of reading before and alongside ethnographic fieldwork, Hammersley and Atkinson (1995: 241) note that ethnographers 'write, certainly; but their writing is shaped by what they have read ... The good ethnographer cannot hope to succeed without a habit of wide reading'. As well as reading and awareness of theories that link to your research topic other priorities include:

- being focused and succinct and trying not to wander away from your original intentions;
- avoiding over-description and articulating unnecessary details;
- developing your own writing style and especially the capacity to put into words your key findings, and how they compare or contrast with previous empirical research or theoretical assumptions.

Ethnographic research is sometimes criticised for being narrowly focused and failing to permit generalisation. In relation to this, it is still the case that the contents of any dissertation or report will have to show evidence of an awareness of wider events. These may include historical trends, more recent social policy, pivotal legislation or emerging social trends. As Fetterman (1998: 19) summarises, contextualising data throughout ethnographic research 'involves placing observations into a larger perspective'. Indeed, as Skeggs (2001: 433) adds:

> Ethnography is probably the only methodology that is able to take into account the multifaceted ways in which subjects are produced through the historical categories and context in which they are placed and which they precariously inhabit.

This point also relates to the role of personal reflexivity. Here the researcher as ethnographer reflects upon their subjectivity or preconceived norms, values or beliefs about participants present within a research field. A researcher can persevere to consider at regular intervals how their beliefs, interests, gender, 'race', prior work experience, class or culturally conditioned assumptions impact upon how they perceive a social group or organisation and its people inside.

Regarding interviews within ethnographic research, Hammersley and Atkinson (1995: 112) stress the importance of listening and being attentive. They also note that some idea of what you plan to discuss needs to be identified in advance. It is unlikely, however, that you will undertake long structured interviews, in contrast more informal 'chats' are often more suitable. In theory such informal interviews can proceed throughout a study or be combined with more formal one-to-one interviews. Marvasti (2004: 57) also highlights the significance of ethics and the context of place:

> The principles of doing ethnographic interviews ... are not fundamentally different from the principles of doing ethnographic research in general: build rapport, be sensitive to your ethical obligations, and continually consider how the social context influences the meaning of everything that you learn in the field.

Indeed, a vital concern also remains potential ethical issues relating to gaining permission from a tutor, ethics committee or organisational representative. You should also think carefully about your accountability, and make all participants aware of your research aims and objectives; and ensure that data is secure and that the respect and privacy of participants are guaranteed at all times.

Case study: An ethnographic study of the use of evaluation skills by approved social workers within a community mental health team

David wanted to examine the role of the (social work) approved mental health practitioner (AMHPs) based in a community mental health team within an inner city. To begin with, he unearthed, compared and contextualised prior empirical studies undertaken into the responsibilities of the AMHP, and also began to critically explore academic papers and other publications relating to a role that first emerged following the recommendations of the Mental Health Act 2007 and subsequent revision of the Mental Health Act 1983. He also looked at discussions and studies of the AMHP predecessor, the Approved Social Worker.

Following extensive reading around a relatively broad topic, David began to form his research question and related objectives; in particular he decided to concentrate upon AMHP's personal attitudes regarding their use of evaluation skills within practice. Having gained approval from his tutor, and senior management within the local authority at which his practice placement was based, David began his ethnographic study at a local community mental health team. Throughout his practice placement over a six-month period he maintained a detailed diary, to which he added notes each evening on his return from the placement. As well as meet and chat to people, attend meetings and 'shadow' different staff, David also took some notes at the placement setting itself. He also took the time to formally interview health and social care practitioners and patients about their opinions on the AMHP role towards the end of his placement.

The observations, experience, diary notes and interviews all provided a wealth of data, and David was able to explore key themes within his study and final write-up. In particular, he discovered that AMHPs utilise evaluation skills throughout their work, but many such professional skills are restricted and sometimes compromised by agency procedure and norms. Some health professionals also implicitly attempted to undermine the evaluative role of the social worker.

Some problems and criticism of ethnography

A customary criticism made against ethnography is its alleged lack of commitment to researcher objectivity – any long-term contact with research participants is seemingly more likely to encourage subjective accounts that may undermine the likelihood of achieving unbiased research findings. One possible risk of this tendency is that the researcher may also 'take sides' with research participants and subsequently fail to acknowledge other factors that impact upon the objectives of the project. A good example of this would be if a student who studied the role of social work practitioners for a period failed to take into account the views of service users or informal carers. In this instance, limited contact with other groups may lead to a narrow focus upon one group's agenda and interests.

There may also be a tendency on behalf of a researcher to over-describe any organisation, events or people's behaviour, and subsequently neglect analytical or theoretical concerns. Ethnography may also be problematic for ethical reasons – especially regarding attempts to guarantee the privacy and consent of all participants involved. Finally, some researchers may struggle with an understanding of how to *apply* ethnography. This is because ethnography is such a diverse and varied approach that continues to develop and expand (Coffey, 1999; Pink, 2001). As previously stressed, success with this methodology should be built upon the foundations of a clear research question, focused and realistic aims and objectives, and a confident plan regarding methods of collecting, interpreting, recording and detailing data. If you intend to undertake ethnographic research for the first time, then it is always advisable to maintain close contact with a tutor and also invest time to undertake adequate reading around the methodology. There is a wealth of published information available regarding ethnographic research (and related forms of participant observation), and some of the best books are listed at the end of this chapter.

Auto-ethnography

Related to, yet distinct from ethnography, remains auto-ethnography. This methodology emphasises the adaptive role of the researcher, especially their experiences, reflections, learning, changing attitudes and emotional engagement within a research field. Central to auto-ethnography is reflexivity and self-observation, through which the researcher reflects upon their values and beliefs prior to their research beginning, and then carefully considers any changes throughout a project. Research becomes a voyage of sorts and there is little if any attempt made by the researcher to objectively study participants from a distance. Instead, the *authenticity* of the researcher is privileged, including our emotional attachments, honesty, empathy and commitment to people in the field (Ellis, 2004). However, there is still a privileging of the self and, ironically perhaps, in some projects at least, participants can become *almost* a residual concern as it is the experiences of the researcher as much as the people held within the field of practice that remains the raison d'*être* of this methodology. Perhaps the best way to view this approach is part ethnography and part-self-observation, a mixture of viewing the changing field and its people *alongside* the fluid or adapting self.

Although distinct in its reflexive study of the self, the auto-ethnographer still utilises many of the same techniques and skills which are used within ethnography. For example, the researcher enters a largely unknown field, may keep a detailed diary and converse with and perhaps interview people, take notes, and more. Importantly, the researcher aims to also connect with the wider culture or organisation, both in a physical and emotional sense, internalising if possible its history and the traditions of people. We may look to also link the personal with the political (Dominelli, 2002), or view ourselves as researcher as agent connecting with wider structures such as established norms, languages or inherited cultures. Auto-ethnography often demands passion and the fulfilment of the researcher: again, it is part of a deliberate strategy to remove the seemingly cold mask of the objective researcher from their gaze into the lives of 'others' and the self. The researcher's feelings, experiences and wider sense of change become as much data as other observations and conversations in the field, if not more so.

Auto-ethnography has particular relevance to social work. This is for many reasons, but in particular the emotional engagement that is typically such a central part of the role. As an obvious example we may look critically at our role as social work practitioners, concentrate upon our learning or engagement with social problems, discuss and detail our own experience of discrimination alongside our service users or carers, and so forth. Many other potential examples and possibilities persist. It may be an ideal way to explore mental health needs or the experiences of a woman with a particular disability, and so on. Auto-ethnography has faced the usual criticisms of lacking objectivity and of being highly subjective, and some commentators propose that the approach can be somewhat pretentious. Auto-ethnography links to biographical research, discussed in the next chapter.

Conclusion

This chapter has explored ethnography. This methodology is distinct and has unique attributes which include its intimate and close and thorough examination of people's lives, experiences and values, especially those held or expressed within specific 'sub-cultural' settings and context. This methodology also tends to take place over a protracted period of time and as a consequence will tend to make greater demands on our skills as researchers than other more formal methods. Ethnographic research also looks to explore group relations, dynamics, meaning and understanding: for many anthropologists the core of 'true' social research. In practice, it can also be used to examine in great detail and depth an aspect of social work practice, experience or the values and belief systems of practitioners or other people. There are also different theoretical approaches which are applied to ethnography, with a much greater emphasis now drawn to developing critical analysis and personal reflexivity whilst recognising fluidity and change in the field.

Further reading

Coffey, A. (1999). *The Ethnographic Self – Fieldwork and the Representation of Data*. London, Sage

Davies, C.A. (1999). *Reflexive Ethnography*. London, Routledge

Ellis, Carolyn (2004). 'The Ethnographic I: A methodological novel about autoethnography'. Walnut Creek: AltaMira Press

Emerson, R.M., Fretz, R.L., Shaw, L.L. (1995). *Writing Ethnographic Fieldnotes*. Chicago, University of Chicago Press

Fetterman, D, M. (1998). *Ethnography – Step by Step*. London, Sage

Hammersley, M., and Atkinson, P. (1995). *Ethnography – Principles in Practice*. London, Routledge

Humphries, B. (2008). *Social Work Research for Social Justice*. Basingstoke, Palgrave Macmillan. Chapter 9 – Ethnographic Research

Taylor, S. (2002). *Ethnographic Research: A Reader*. London, Sage

Tedlock, B. (2000). 'Ethnography and ethnographic representation'. In N.K. Denzin and Y.S. Lincoln (eds), *Handbook of qualitative research* (2nd edn, pp. 455–84). Thousand Oaks, CA: Sage

13 Life Histories and Biographical Research

Introduction

This chapter looks at two alternative historical methodologies commonly identified as life history and biographical approaches. Each attempts to detail and examine extended periods of time and draw from the usually rich lived experiences of research participants. We first look at life history research, which investigates the recounted *experiences* of a person's life. Then we will look at the related yet distinct biographical approaches that emphasise the discussion and *narrating* of life. We also discuss the use of a diary by the researcher or sometimes even participants, a method that can also be used alongside other methods such as the interview.

Life Histories

Life history approaches, as with biographical research, draw from the tradition of historical research in which:

- current data (gathered through conversation) is drawn upon to help explain and understand the past;
- solutions to contemporary issues or problems are sought from the past;
- new light from the past is utilised to help explain present and future trends;
- cultural interactions (for example, around age, disability, race, gender, and so on) are drawn upon through the relative voices of participants;
- data is re-evaluated according to generalisations held in the past.

Such historical approaches also link to case study and narrative research in their search for deeper understanding or meaning from participants' themselves. However, they also have distinct qualities; including a tendency to grasp the historical and the holistic. They may represent a sincere recollection of the past, but also recognise some of the difficulties in achieving any holistic representation due to difficulties in acquiring more specific details from interviews.

Through life history research, interviewees will be encouraged to talk in general about their past. We may, however, not draw simply upon interviews with participants, but also can engage in observation or talks with relatives, friends and colleagues in order to gradually build up a picture of a person's life. Other evidence may include diary notes, letters and other documents such as photographs or more general informal conversations. We can also look to explore what happened to the participant as their own 'eye witness', a process which takes place alongside attempts to discover the inner experience of individuals, [and] how they interpret, understand, and define the world around them. As a consequence, the most common and perhaps ideally suited method used for life history research remains the unstructured interview. This method allows more discretion on the part of the participant and is perhaps, therefore, more authentic, but it can also be time consuming. Researchers with less available time may therefore still draw from this methodology but instead utilise semi-structured questions in which more specific questions may be asked.

As part of any preparation for a life history the researcher looks at what possible topics may suit this methodology. Might you wish to explore a volunteer's career or a person's time spent in foster care? The researcher might then consider the selection of a research question or social problem, and related decisions regarding likely participant(s), questions to ask, methods to deploy, location of interviews, and so on. A good working relationship between participant(s) and any researcher are a priority for this methodology. This is because as with other more intimate and close methodologies, such as ethnography, we need to project empathy and gain trust so that we can form a general bond. Again, this attachment and bond the life history method from the realist privileging of objectivity and the maintenance of a formal 'professional distance' and space or gap between researcher and the passive participant (see chapter six).

Many life history interviews stress the importance of allowing participants space and adequate time to talk about their past. As with the narrative interview tradition (chapter fourteen), there is also a tendency to avoid interruption from the interviewer. Participants are usually also allowed more control and, as Plummer (1983) notes, there is an emphasis placed upon the associate use of alternative methods such as the 'self-interview' or diary keeping and personal reflection. Nevertheless, life history interviews can be flexible and draw upon 'a variety of interview techniques' which may, depending upon circumstance and the topic of inquiry, include the use of structured interviews or, instead, much less formal unstructured approaches (Cohen et al., 2007: 191). Central, however, in Plummer's (1983) vision, remains the presence of genuine warmth from the interviewer felt towards the participant(s). A not uncommon technique also includes a combination of participant observation, casual or unprompted chatting and selective note-taking. As can be seen, the life history method of data collection can neither be standardised nor reduced to a predictable series of 'scientific' tasks.

The collection of extensive data is often inevitable for most life history approaches. Diversity amongst data collection methods does not mean, however, that rigour is not a priority. Indeed, analysis represents the next phase of the research process and this involves priority being given to representativeness, rigour and validity (see chapter three). Here the researcher seeks to bridge interviewees' personal experience with a wider population and events. As well as people that link directly to the chosen population, there is also often an attempt to bridge participants with the historic, the cultural and/or the political. In social work we may wish to link practitioner's or service user's experiences with wider long-term historical or demographic trends – such as in relation to community care initiatives or newer developments such as 'personalisation' – or more specific themes that link to the ethnicity or social class origin of participants, among other possibilities.

Plummer (2001: 39) maintains that life histories seek to explore a personal life with regard to 'how it is lived over phases, careers, cycles, stages; and with time outside the life – of how the "historical moment" plays its role in any life's shape'. Here, the researcher tries to bridge the micro (personal) with the macro (cultural, institutional, political, etc.), and *contextualise* the talk of participants. As Payne and Payne (2004: 24) suggest, the participant presents us 'with *both* a perception of self and the social world'. Plummer (1983) also highlights how life histories should look to reduce bias within a methodology, or increase the *reliability* of a project. Bias can emerge from the researcher or the interviewee or the nature of any association between both camps. Although many feminists argue that bias may never be eradicated from qualitative research, Plummer recognises ways by which to reduce its overall impact. These include:

- Allowing participants to read interview transcripts and findings to check what has been discussed. This includes with a view to potentially changing inappropriate material.
- The researcher comparing their findings with other sources, including official documents.
- Comparing interviewees' data with one another, again for similarities and differences.

Cohen et al. (2007: 200) stress that the validity of any life history 'lies in its ability to represent the informant's subjective reality, that is to say, his or her definition of the situation'. As well as exploring the findings held within interview extracts, life history researchers will also seek to delve into associated sources of 'evidence' so as to develop a thesis. This may include historical records, journals, monographs, newspaper articles, television archives, magazines, or letters, among other relevant sources. It is not unusual for a disparity to emerge between seemingly 'official' reports – such as those presented in media outlets or even academic sources – and accounts given by research participants. Inevitably, it is the researcher's job to scrutinise any discovered 'gaps' between the micro and the macro, or contextualise and try to understand and explain disparities between participants' accounts and more formal reports. In relation to this, Clifford (1994) highlights the potential of life history approaches to allow excluded or seemingly 'invisible' people within social care (notably service users, carers and members of minority groups) to be recognised and given a voice. This process might also help us to draw attention to forms of discrimination or abuse experienced in the past (and possibly still present today). Similarly, D'Cruz and Jones (2004: 120) argue that life history approaches are effective for critical social work research: and are suitable in attempts to 'restore lost voices and knowledge', including 'about colonised societies and peoples'. Inevitably, life history approaches are especially relevant with regard to research that deals with service users and carer-related needs (see case example below), although research with practitioners may also be relevant. Questions of access and the nature of the topic being explored, alongside possible ethical dilemmas and processes, may affect a project; if unclear seek some professional advice.

For some smaller social work projects such as a dissertation a single yet extensive life story interview with one interviewee may suffice regarding data collection. For example, a practitioner or manager with many years' experience in social work may be asked to reflect upon their work experience, or more specifically an aspect of their practice (such as changing relations with different service users). There are, nevertheless, some limitations if we do simply rely upon one interview, such as a lack of opportunity to compare different cases and experience, as well as the possibility of generating too much bias. Research participants will tend to vary, and may include health or social care professionals or unqualified 'personal (care) assistants' that work alongside social workers, and it can support understanding to be able to compare different perspectives. As each individual life history can demand extensive time, commitment and energy it helps not to be too ambitious: four participants are likely to be enough for a dissertation or small project.

Plummer (1983) distinguishes between a 'retrospective' and 'contemporaneous' life history. The former stresses past events and comparing each to present feelings whilst the latter explores in great detail daily life today. A life history methodology will usually concentrate upon one of three possible models:

- individual recollection
- themes to explore which have been identified by the participant
- themes presented by any participant and which have then been distilled and interpreted by the researcher.

It is not, however, enough to explore a person's previous life experiences or general attitudes: the narrowing of any focus and clarity about what it is you intend to explore is always of benefit. It is again vital to construct a clear definition of the research question or problem in advance (as stressed in chapter two) of any interviews taking place. Broad questions may lead to an excess of data being collected and this can mean a struggle to develop any analysis relating to a topic at a later period. Although this problem is evident within all qualitative research, it is more of a hazard within many types of life history research because of the longer periods of time spent with participants, the reduced structure often apparent as part of interviews, and the extensive amount of data subsequently collected in relation to a participant's life experiences.

Case study: Recounting personal life histories of psychiatric treatment within an institution

Paul is an ex-community nurse and current social work practitioner working with people with mental health needs. He wanted to look at patients' previous experiences of therapeutic care within an institutional setting. After much deliberation and reading, he decided to utilise a life history approach and to interview people with a mental health condition who had previously been detained in a long-stay hospital in the North West of England.

After gaining permission from a relevant ethics committee within his local authority, Paul interviewed some of his current service users living in the local community. He interviewed three people who had previously been detained for therapeutic support during the 1970s and built up his life histories with two men and one woman, all of whom were more than sixty years of age. Paul discovered some startling findings, some of which were also deeply moving or upsetting. He noticed contrasting treatments, including the use of drugs and surgery as well as a contrast in the attitudes of psychiatrists, nurses and social workers in the delivery of care. Whereas nursing support was often viewed positively, psychiatric care tended to receive more mixed opinions by those interviewed, ranging from the 'reserved and detached' personality of the typical psychiatrist to the occasionally more empathetic. However, all respondents felt that their views were rarely taken seriously by any of the professionals, and such often angry opinions were articulated throughout the deeply moving and articulate life history accounts (see also Rogers et al., 1993).

Plummer (1983) suggests three priorities for the presentation of findings. These include:

- Being clear about what you wish to accomplish and who it is you are writing about.
- Be careful regarding interpretation and editing, as making false claims from collected data always remains a possible hazard. Always check and confirm with a participant, if possible, before formally writing up any research, as authentic meaning from a participant remains imperative as part of life history research.
- Always begin your writing early and practise any writing wherever possible prior to a final write up.

Critical (especially feminist) alongside interpretive theory (chapter five) fit closely with and support the core principles of life history research. These theories emphasise and allow participants' vocal accounts to take precedence, whilst also contextualising and framing perspectives within an empathetic framework. Life history approaches have, however, been criticised for potentially being too subjective and also of limiting our understanding by concentrating on only a small handful of personal accounts. Once again, this methodology is able to accommodate other approaches as part of a project, such as ethnography or the focus group and individual interview, among others.

Biographical research

Perhaps somewhat confusingly, biographical and life history research are related yet distinct approaches. Rosenthal (1993) recognises biographical stories as '*narrating* life' whereas a life history will instead stress 'recollections of life *experience*'. Over recent years, the biographical method has encouraged a tendency to emphasise narrative-based research (detailed in chapter fourteen) and related forms of 'social construction'. Both draw from the post-modern tradition in which comments made by participants are treated or codified as a 'text' which can be investigated regarding its *structure* and *context* or *meaning*. Again, there is a tendency to link individual narratives with wider social and cultural dynamics, including historical events or policies or traditions. As Fischer-Rosenthal (1995; cited in Stroobants, 2005: 48) propose:

> The notion of biography does not reproduce the split between individual and society, but rather structures both spheres. In its manifestations of life history, life story and institutional biographical patterns, biography bridges the theoretically constructed gap between inner and outer spheres. Thus, biography has a double meaning. It refers to social structure by providing agents with various socially patterned life courses to be transferred in the course of their life histories. It also refers to the story which the individual is able to – and indeed – must tell.

The biography becomes not merely a set of statements about the world, but instead is viewed as a deeply personal *interpretation* of a life *within* a world. Other approaches and techniques used in biographical research will typically include:

- Scepticism towards conventional approaches to the interview (structured and semi-structured) that may undermine the ability of the interviewer to understand the participant's viewpoint or truly explore a research question.
- It is assumed that traditional interviews often ignore the complex and reflexive nature of biographical encounters.
- That the interviewer should be a good and attentive listener.
- The participant is recognised as an active and vibrant teller of stories rather than a passive and docile respondent.
- A researcher should concentrate upon the stories generated by the participant and, particularly, the *significance* and *meaning* of the *content* of responses.
- Any initial agenda on behalf of the researcher is open to change, especially if the participant decides to discuss other topics that *matter to them.*
- Recognition that participants may organise their experiences into meaningful episodes that call upon culturally defined forms of thinking and representation.
- Acknowledgement that wider organisational and cultural traditions often restrict the capacity of people to fulfil their aspirations. For example, formal conventions and rituals or institutional procedures and norms.

The researcher will carefully consider transcripts from interviews and attempt to assess core themes, such as the use of rhetoric, emotional stances, strong opinions expressed alongside more subtle viewpoints, reflections, evidence of self-identity or change, beliefs, self-esteem, and so on. In the tradition of post-modernism as an eclectic sociological and cultural theory, the interview is also interpreted as fluid and unstable, always open to change or multiple interpretations. Such interpretations can refocus attention back to biographical voice of excluded people.

Biography takes as its premise a laid-back pluralism of styles and a concomitant celebration of the worth of a diverse range of social beliefs and cultures. Of significance for social work has been the post-modern stress (chapter six) upon the need to appreciate previously excluded voices and opinions, which includes those of people with a disability, black and ethnic minority groups, older people and disadvantaged women and gay people, amongst others. Research themes inherent in transcripts are considered from the perspective of their cultural meanings and interpretation, especially regarding the topic being researched. Because of the complex relationship between societal structure (for example an institution, language or culture) and agency (a person), it is imperative that thorough background research and reading take place prior to any analysis of research transcripts. This should help the researcher to better understand the context of any participant's response.

A second tradition within biographical research draws significantly from feminist research. Although drawing upon core biographical techniques – such as avoiding a strict interview structure and allowing participant(s) to largely self-control the process – feminist biographies seek to:

- take a sincere interest in some of the many issues that affect women;
- allow participants to express personal experiences of gender inequality and exclusion, discrimination or subjugation;
- acknowledge the concomitant impact of class, disability, age and ethnicity if and when appropriate;
- emancipate and empower women, again by allowing previously invisible or unheard people to express themselves in open spaces;
- actively utilise empirical and theoretical methodology to highlight the experiences of women;
- contextualise the personal biographies of participants and link these with political and social issues;
- include women participants in decision-making processes relating to research;
- seek to undermine male-dominated research methodologies, including the search for objective and science-based truth and avoid traditional patriarchal 'top down' hierarchies of social research;
- encourage a self-critical 'reflexive' approach to research.

(adapted from Stanley and Wise, 1983; 1993)

The biographical method permits many of the ambitions inherent within feminist research and life history approaches. This is due to related factors, such as the centrality of participant involvement as a key aspect of the interview.

There is also usually a general anti-scientific stance utilised throughout, with emphasis upon participant discretion rather than researcher control. In essence, feminist biographical research should be able to provide a platform for participants to talk openly about their personal gender or disability, and so on, whilst the researcher will attempt to theoretically contextualise any such discussion by critically examining open talk about the past alongside the scrutiny of established literature and other documents.

Again, it helps to remember the perennial issues of limited time and resources. As a social work student, practitioner or volunteer, etc., you may wish to isolate specific themes to address over the participant(s) life course, or instead concentrate on more recent themes inherent within a biography. Try to be realistic about what can be achieved within the available time, especially regarding the numbers of participants approached and interviewed and also the issues to be explored. In general, biographical research, like the life history approach, tends to collect extensive data from long interviews with a small sample (between one to eight people). Alongside many of the approaches discussed in this book, personal experiences – around topics such as disability, mental or physical health, foster care or motherhood, poverty, identity, and more – can also be explored in great detail and depth through the reflexive lens of the biographical method. A thorough literature review prior to any interviews again remains a priority, especially to help us understand our findings, as does the establishment of a clear and focused topic, social problem or research question.

Use of diaries

Another possible means to collect data remains the use of a diary or diaries to supplement other research approaches such as the interview or biographical method. Here a researcher may keep regular notes about participant behaviour or attitudes and/or maintain details about key events or occurrences that link to any topic of investigation. Such notes can then be used by the researcher to supplement other data collected. In particular diary notes may allow the researcher to supplement other findings which may otherwise be missed or forgotten. You may decide to maintain a diary that reflects personal general experiences throughout a project or decide to be more structured and specific, such as by only detailing observations that link to one or two research objectives (Elliot, 1997). A researcher may also wish to detail their biographical experiences of undertaking research: such as regarding difficulties faced, times of pleasure or anxiety and notable experiences (see also auto-ethnography in chapter twelve).

Another possibility is to encourage participants to keep a diary, such as social work practitioners at work or carer's supporting a relative. It is likely that you will need to provide a diary for each participant (which may prove expensive) and also offer clear instructions or brief training regarding which specific details or observations you require. For example, you may wish to ask practitioners to detail their personal experiences of supervision, relations with colleagues or contact with specific professionals or service users. Inevitably diaries kept by each member of a sample may collect extensive data so be careful to limit this if possible, such as by reducing the sample size or by clearly focusing the accounts of each diary keeper.

Conclusion

This chapter has explored two of the more creative and indeed younger research methodologies. Within both life history and biographical methodologies there is a tendency to allow the participant much more discretion and say what it is they wish to detail and discuss. There is also a tendency to encourage empathy and warmth from the interviewer, reader or observer. Inevitably, both approaches sit well with the emancipatory traditions of critical social work and for this reason they are especially well suited to exploring social problems and issues, as well as disadvantaged or marginalised social groups.

Further reading

Giele, J.Z., and Elder, G.H. (eds) (1998). *Methods of Life Course Research: Qualitative and Quantitative Approaches*. London, Sage

Millar, R.L. (2000). *Researching Life Stories and Family Histories*. London, Sage

Mishler, E.G. (1986). *Research Interviewing: Context and Narrative*. Cambridge, MA; Harvard University Press

Perks, R., and Thompson, A. (eds) (2006). *The Oral History Reader*. Oxford, Routledge

Plummer, K. (1983). *Documents of Life: An Introduction to the Problems and Literature of a Humanistic Method*. London, Allen and Unwin

Plummer, K. (2001). *Documents of Life, 2: An Invitation to Critical Humanism*. London, Sage

Roberts, B. (2002). *Biographical Research*. Buckingham, Open University Press

Rosenthal, G. (1993). 'Reconstruction of Life Stories. Principle of Selection in Generating Stories for Narrative Biographical Interviews', in Josselson, R., Lieblich, A. (eds). *The Narrative Study Lives*. London, Newbury Park

Scott, J. (1990) *A Matter of Record*. Cambridge, Polity

14 Narrative and Discourse Analysis

Introduction

This chapter looks at two newer methodologies which, like life histories or biographical research, are more in-depth and thorough yet also more nuanced in their organisation and application. Narrative and Discourse analysis look to explore the use of language in great detail, including its cultural and political meaning. Such approaches also involve a thorough yet typically fascinating exploration of personal experience. In general, these methodologies are more varied and complex than, say, the typical research interview, so careful planning and pre-reading prior to their application may be required. For example, if possible it may help to consider at least a cursory read of some of the literature cited at the end of the chapter. The chapter defines and explains each approach and also details some of the ways that each methodology can be used in practice.

Narrative analysis

Narrative analysis (NA) looks to evaluate the different ways by which people use and make stories to understand and interpret their present and the past. Reissman and Quinney (2005: 392) note that the explosion of interest in narrative within the social and human sciences over the past two decades has not, until recently, been echoed within social work. This is something of a paradox as narrative is central to all forms of social work, even the many types increasingly undertaken as part of the growth of social work call-centres. However, although NA is difficult to define we can still assume that:

> All talk and text are not narrative …. Missing for the narrative scholar is analytic attention to how the facts got assembled *that* way. For whom was *this* story constructed, how was it made, and for what purpose? What cultural resources

does it draw upon – take for granted? What does it accomplish? Are there gaps and inconsistencies that might suggest alternative counter-narratives? In popular usage a 'story' seems to speak for itself, not requiring interpretation – an indefensible position for serious scholarship [through narrative analysis].

NA does not see stories are simply transmitting information or hard facts. For example, a social work assessment undertaken over the telephone by a call centre 'professional' – gathering facts, figures and hard details to consider the eligibility for support of the passive 'user' on the end of the line – is not a form of narrative unless we address the cultural context and political implications of this event. In this instance following an interview with a client we might highlight the political implications of call-centre 'social work', such as the limited power possibly held by service users unable to express their true feelings to a telephone operator rather than professional as 'real person' in their living room. Narrative is viewed as a set of social constructs that represent particular locations and environments and are determined or moulded by specific political, cultural and social experiences, places and events. Narrative may also be about how people represent themselves to people around them and how they understand and interpret themselves. It is such dynamics and themes that the NA researcher is interested in; much like the social anthropologist in the 'field' it can be seen as a 'search for and analysis of the stories that people employ to understand their lives and the world around them. It is a thorough yet delicate methodology which is able through talk to connect the participant with their past, their roles, surroundings or workplaces, and other possible ties.

Lawler (2002: 242) interprets narrative as 'storied accounts' or 'interpretive devices' that embody a person's sense of belonging or understanding of themselves: it can permit reflection and analysis by participants' themselves. NA seeks to connect the individual to their local community or groups of friends and family: a cultural tradition that is widely claimed to be a proud tenet and practice of social work.

Life history approaches (chapter thirteen) provide but one example of NA. Narrative approaches draw significantly from constructivist (chapter three) and interpretive theories (chapter six) that stress the importance of interpretation, choices, meaning and understanding, culture, location and context from the perspective of the participant (or 'agent'). Narrative or story-telling becomes a social or cultural product created by people, yet it also remains strongly influenced by factors such as a person's identity (for example how a 'professional' or 'service user' understands themselves), their past experiences, or the influence of institutions, peers and community, or dynamics such as tradition and norms (for example, wider pressures or expectations placed upon mothers or carers to fulfil a particular role).

Lawler (2002) highlights that narrative theory tends to make certain assumptions about people and the interview process which include that people will be able to openly express their feelings, attitudes and values through their (typically uninterrupted) stories or narratives. At least part of an interview is likely to contain stories and such tales may be able to link the present experiences of people to, more commonly, the past, but also in some instances to the future. There is, however, no such thing as any 'unbiased' account and stories are more likely to be subjective and therefore biased. Characters and actions detailed by participants may contain some fantasy (including exaggeration, digression or factual inaccuracies due to time) and like a play, stories will usually contain actors and characters, a plot and events. Narratives also have a temporal dimension, an underlying point from the perspective of the story-teller and a story will detail change over time which, like the plot and actors, may draw the attention of the interviewer during analysis.

Another distinguishing feature of NA remains its strong inter-disciplinary perspective; which prevents it from being introspective and reductive. Indeed, as Andrews et al. (2004: 103) suggest

> Narrative analysis, as an interdisciplinary practice that cuts across the arts, humanities, sciences and social sciences, is also a useful corrective to the reductive tendencies that other analyses, rooted in individual disciplines, can manifest. It opens up some very exciting possibilities for thinking about creativity in relation to research and it provides a very rich source for theory building.

Typically – as in life history approaches and so much qualitative research – semi-structured and unstructured interviews are likely to be the main methods drawn upon. The researcher will tend to play a relatively passive role, allowing the participant to speak freely and openly. Interruption may occur if silences persist or if the participant has wandered away for some time from the original question or core intentions of the study. There can, however, be problems with openness, especially considering the cultural and other disadvantages often faced by users of social work services. For example, Harlow (2005) notes her own difficulties in trying to encourage teenage parents to open up about their personal experiences, factors which have led other researchers to abandon narrative in other social work projects dealing with 'difficult' subject-matter. Clearly, discussing sensitive issues in an alien environment, typically with a previously unknown researcher, is likely to take time, especially to build mutual empathy and trust.

Reissman and Quinney (2005) offer four rules for good quality narrative research, which include:

1. *Maintaining detailed transcripts*: try to accumulate as much detail as possible from interviews and ensure that you have adequate source material available.
2. *Focusing upon language and the context of its production*: the crux of NA in which the stories of participants become paramount, how each person describes characters, a plot and change, etc. Discussion of 'real world' events and practices may then be linked to possible influences such as policy developments, legal practices, a person's role or identity.
3. *Acknowledge dialogic characteristics and use a comparative approach (if appropriate)*: make notes where possible about any participant's emotional responses within discussions (are they calm, upset, etc., at specific times). Comparing the findings from different interviews may assist analysis.
4. *Give attention to structural features*: do not concentrate entirely upon the meaning and use of language from the perspective of participants themselves. Instead, stories should be evaluated where possible according to wider cultural and structural influences. In particular, how do contingent external influences shape the narratives produced. It is typically helpful to carefully and not intrusively ask questions regarding the participants' background: how many years have they engaged in social work practice or been a user of services, what is their status and background and for what reasons did they enter social work or become a user?

Fraser (2004: 181–4) again stresses NA's relevance to social work research. This includes by providing a way 'to make sense of language' and permit a 'plurality of truths to be known', as well as allowing the researcher a chance to better appreciate 'interactions that occur among individuals, groups and societies'. NA also encourages less superficial discussions to prevail between the interviewer and researcher and instead engage more intimately with 'social phenomenon' and 'cross cultural work', especially with people from different backgrounds. NA can also allow 'excluded voices' to be heard and thus encourage anti-discrimination and social justice through a series of 'inclusive narratives'. The researcher should ideally look to studying the socio-historical contexts of participants' lives, their locality and background, ethnicity, status, etc. We should also avoid interrogation where possible or the cross-examination style of interviews. Generally, interviewees should be allowed to dictate the pace of their conversations and the researcher should aim to create a 'climate of trust' and be sensitive (such as to the timing of questions and avoid interruptions). We should also try to allow participants to ask questions of their own and be transparent and make clear our intentions for undertaking the research. Finally (as with the life history approach), we should share with participants some of our interpretations made about participants' attitudes and experiences and integrate where possible their responses into our analysis.

As with any other interview, NA interviews again generate the problem of access to a suitable sample. There may also be longer periods of time spent involved in this less formal approach – as with life history research and more generally social work, getting to know participants is often crucial so that we can build up trust and mutual understanding. More time may also be needed to transcribe and analyse our detailed and extensive findings. Narrative interviews tend to involve more detailed exploration of variables (such as participant's body language and emotional responses) and this may be demanding and time consuming. NA has also received some criticism, which includes that it may be more prone to bias and misrepresentation of participant perspectives. It has also been interpreted as more conservative than many other critical approaches due to its reliance upon interpretive and post-modern theories Some researchers have, however, successfully bridged NA with more critical and grounded approaches (for example, Andrews et al., 2004).

Case study: Reflections upon the different lives within a community day-centre for older people

Karen wanted to use narrative analysis to represent the ways by which a day-centre specialising in support for local people diagnosed with depression was experienced and run. She decided to interview two residents (75-year-old man and 84-year-old woman) and a long-term member of staff who was a colleague of Karen's. The interviews took place over the course of a month and lasted around one hour. Each participant was involved in at least three interviews as part of the research, in which each discussed their childhood, present living and viewpoints, career, and so forth. Large sections of the interview also involved discussing time spent at the centre, including relationships with other attendees, activities, coping with a support role, and so forth.

Karen recorded the interviews and took notes after each interview but only partially transcribed her findings. As part of her analysis for a dissertation as part of her social work course, Karen was able to detail how each person as attendee or member of staff had come to arrive at the centre and what 'being there' meant to them. As well as evaluating the centre, Karen was also able to learn much more about her colleague and also of the residents through their own vocal accounts. Karen drew significantly from health and social care literature that had depicted lives and evaluated services within institutional and community settings.

There are different ways that narrative approaches can be used to analyse transcribed interviews. Each of these is discussed in chapter seventeen, such as thematic or comparative analysis. However, you may also wish to summarise, compare and present case studies from each interview, such as by identifying key events in a person's life or career or citing quotes that reflect common opinions expressed by any participant. Opinions can then be better understood by comparing them to other research findings.

Many social care and social work related topics are suitable for this methodology: from the personal experiences of practising social work over many years and in different setting for women to the different ways that three or four people have lived with their disability or exploring how and why two men became homeless, and so forth. Because of the small sample sizes often used any findings from this approach are unlikely to be representative of a wider sample.

Discourse analysis

As with narrative research, Discourse Analysis (DA) seeks to meticulously investigate the use of language – or more particularly discourse (written or spoken communication and a coherent order of beliefs, ideas, traditions and practices which relate) – within a social and cultural context. D'Cruz and Jones (2004: 156) define discourse as a means by which 'language is used to produce versions of knowledge that then *gain legitimacy* in a political, social, cultural and professional sense'. For example, within a medical discourse, certain practices, traditions and knowledge emerge that help to shape and determine appropriate behaviour, beliefs, relations and practices within settings such as a hospital or clinic. Through careful scrutiny and investigation by the intrepid researcher, DA seeks to reveal the use of or concealed meaning and political intentions behind the use of language as presented in a specific *context*. DA draws from different theories and there are varied methodologies now used, but, significantly, many draw upon social constructivist and 'post-modern' theories (chapter's three and six) which again highlight the ambivalent, fragmented and fluid nature of social and cultural life. Indeed, 'reality' itself is seen as often representing a text with meaning being expressed through language. Texts and speech acts are held within specific discourses and the language that we use every day has a profound impact in shaping our meaning of events and experiences.

Humphries (2008: 120) notes how DA interprets language in a very different way to conventional theory:

DA research rejects a view of language as only a way of transmitting meaning from one person to another, as a transparent, neutral, information-carrying vehicle. Rather DA sees language as *constitutive* – as actually creating, negotiating and changing meaning. It is not a static system but is located in ongoing interaction involving competing attempts to fix meaning and pin it down once and for all. The study of discourse, therefore, confronts debates about what constitutes reality and 'truth', what are social problems and solutions and what is 'real', and about the very nature of meaning.

Through discourse, language translates into a variety of formats: from theories to discussions and ideas or acts of legislation, reports, traditions or procedures, and so forth. A common example of a discourse in action relates to professional practices. Medicine is the most successful because it offers legitimacy, power of influence and financial gain, high status and other related rewards to those who qualify to practise under its rules and laws. Although always altering shape and open to change over time, a medical discourse is still founded upon linguistic forms such as its core theories, codes of practice, 'expert' knowledge, belief systems, procedures, traditions, ideas and forms of guidance, which help to constitute its shape and parameters. Together, these linguistic devices offer not merely a means by which medical practitioners maintain their power and interests but also, relatedly, a way by which the views, actions and choices made by patients or other professionals are influenced or subjugated by the dependent 'other', such as the patient.

Jupp (1996) argues that different discourses compete against one another at any given time and are also likely to be arranged socially in a hierarchy. For example, medicine and law as dominant professions stand against 'quasi' or semi-professions, such as nursing, physiotherapy, midwifery or social work. There can also be conflicting interpretations regarding how to explain and understand a social issue such as poverty or unemployment or how particular human needs, such as dementia care, should be provided. For example, influential figures within medicine are unlikely to prioritise the structural causes of ill health and poverty as such critical interpretations contradict the interests of a medical profession reliant upon extensive public funding from governments as well as the need to encourage reliance of the general public upon individual and clinical medical support. More dominate voices emerge across and between discourses: for example, the more legitimate and socially organised opinions of a doctor in contrast to an apparently less knowledgeable patient. Competing views can also emerge within a discourse, such as differing views of how social work should be understood and practised depending upon different ideologies, theories or policies.

Distinctions and tensions regarding power can be explained within DA through an analysis of power and the ways by which facts or reality is presented through language in reports, articles and conversations or meetings between people. In these instances, documents, papers or attendance at meetings, etc., all provide data as evidence for the researcher as critical interpreter to scrutinise. Discourse, however, is not always consciously organised and applied by *individual* actors, however: instead it tends to be more subtle, nuanced, sometimes unconscious and embedded within learnt behaviour or traditions as well as individual interpretations that are open to change. As Crossley (2005: 61) notes:

> Those who partake in [a discourse] are largely unaware of the system of conventions they habitually use and are perhaps also unaware of specific consequences that their way of speaking may have, such that an analysis which unearths and 'deconstructs' that system has a potentially liberatory value. Social agents are able, reflexively, to recognise that their way of seeing and thinking about the world is derived from a social structure (a discourse) that they have learnt and that they habitually rely upon.

Despite the emphasis placed upon ambivalence and uncertainty, there have been numerous attempts to pin down a more concrete set of rules and approaches for DA. Humphries (2008: 121–6) draws from Taylor (2010) and offers, among others, three examples of applying DA research. These include looking at:

1. *The structure, patterns and functions of language*   This approach is used in socio-linguistic research and explores the patterns, functions and structures of language as well as the use and meaning of vocabulary. The researcher considers the stability or organisation of language within what are otherwise imperfect or unstable linguistic systems. Also what function does language provide to those who use it?

2. *Social interaction and the use of language*   This approach is commonly referred to as conversation analysis (CA) and offers a greater link to social work research. It looks at the different ways that people use conversation and are influenced by its structure and patterns within an institutional setting (such as a hospital or social work department) or more generally in conversation (such as in meetings, interviews or informal conversations, etc.). This approach is influenced by ethnomethodology (see chapter five) and looks at how social actors use phrases, words, utterances or periods of silence or evasiveness as methodological strategies to achieve order and control in their lives. The most common arena for this type of research is the study of people's behaviour in institutions and their interpretations of what is going on around them. Since influenced by an interpretive methodology (chapter five), this approach commonly uses interviews to collect data.

CA begins by asking a research question or looking at a problem or social issue. Data is then collected, such as from interviews or the taping of a series of conversations in a room or office. Detailed transcripts are then created which represent the canvas upon which the researcher works. The researcher looks for recurring trends or themes (such as explored in chapter seventeen in thematic or content analysis) relating to the conversations, in particular the search for patterns of language use. Finally, the researcher may build a theory from their findings or additionally analyse their findings by comparing them to other people's findings in a final report or dissertation.

The CA approach has been criticised for concentrating upon interpretation and neglecting the influence of power and discourse upon the roles and understandings of research participants. As discourse is usually unseen and ambivalent questions remain as to how reliable some topics may be to explore using this approach. Despite this, the methodology is extremely valid for some social work research topics and it fits closely to practice-related themes that link with official published documents such as assessments of need, or legal documentation and court reports, and so forth.

3. Social and cultural context   This research is more political and utilises an approach known as Critical Discourse Analysis (CDA). It stresses the analysis of language use and discourse to maintain power or control on behalf of dominant minorities. Jupp (2006: 75) identifies some of the main questions asked when looking at a document (such as a policy, legal or practice related document) as part of a CDA. These include asking:

- *Under what circumstances has a text emerged?* For example, what are the historical, cultural or political conditions that have made this text possible?
- *How coherent or contradictory is the text?* Are the arguments coherent and do they give equal attention to all opinions? For example, in a report, are all minority ethnic groups recognised as important? If not, what motivations might have influenced this?
- *What traces of other text(s) are evident in the document?* How might this relationship be explored? What references do the author(s) cite and are authors and ideas presented in a balanced way. Why might references be emphasised or distorted and what possible interests might be encouraged or suppressed?
- *How are people, events or thought categorized?* Who or what are included or omitted? Are there notable omissions within a text and is priority given to some people, arguments or sectors that may not be justified?
- *Who and what are viewed as normal or naturally occurring?* Does the nature of the text and style of writing assume too much?

- *What are the likely cultural, social or political effects of the text?*
- *What alternative readings of facts or arguments presented might be made by different social groups?*
- Are there any silences or 'absent presences' within the text?

Practically, it would not be possible to achieve all of Jupp's identified aims, so a researcher will concentrate upon one or two of the questions asked. As part of this approach the researcher looks to carefully read, reread and evaluate published documentation relating to an identified topic or research problem. Within social work, this might be in relation to legislation and policy documents detailing carer's needs or published empirical research that explains older people's experience of receiving domiciliary care. As with CA above, CDA uses thematic, content or comparative analysis to look for emerging trends within the literature but will also be especially keen to identify and understand social power and disadvantage. CDA typically assumes that certain groups tend to promote their interests through legal and policy documents and other publications, in particular governments, professionals or managers, often to the detriment of service users, disadvantaged parents or other minority groups. The researcher will often look carefully for evidence of exaggeration or distortion within a series of texts and the subsequent promotion of particular interests. Findings will then be presented in a final report or dissertation, often combining evidence such as quotes from the analysed literature with arguments presented by other researchers, or comparing rhetorical claims in policy documents within empirical evidence that contradicts this.

Some further questions to ask as part of a CDA might include:

- *Identifying obstacles that hinder the reduction of social problems:* for example, the role that ideology or dominant discourse plays in *maintaining* social problems such as poverty, neglect or homelessness. Here we ask 'how does the problem arise and how is it rooted in the way that social life is organised?' A response may include analysing documentation relating to a wider social policy initiative, or other rhetorical devices including business interests. The researcher asks how rhetoric devices reveal themselves and how might it differ to the reality embodied in empirical evidence or the experience of the researcher?
- *Asking whether politically dominant groups would benefit from a social problem being resolved, and what possible interests the problem may serve:* The researcher asks whose interests are promoted when social life is organised under a particular discourse (for example a bio-medical or social model) and why do aspects of discourse maintain the problem.
- *Identifying the rhetorical or argumentative organisation of talk and text:* this might consider how the carefully constructed details and claims made

in official reports or documents contrast with key elements of social work practice.

- *Examining potential ways that obstacles relating to a social problem might be overcome*: this may include by providing resistance to dominant ideas and practices, such as the counter-arguments or evidence provided by a service user advocacy group or a series of papers provided by a radical social worker.

(Fairclough 1995; 2003)

Perhaps inevitably, DA is not a precise or exact methodology because by its very nature and rationale the interpretation of texts and events are seen as being open to multiple translations. This may undermine the legitimacy of DA in comparison to more 'stable' approaches, such as are embodied within a realist methodology (see chapter three) that rely upon more exact and rational approaches, such as the questionnaire or interview. Although there is no precise way to approach the DA methodology, the potential benefits to a researcher are many because of the flexibility of the approach and variety of social issues or research questions that may be addressed. Also, despite a variety of formats, clearer methodologies and approaches have emerged such as those relating to CD and CDA discussed above.

Applying the DA or CDA approach can be an especially useful methodological device for considering non-traditional or alternative viewpoints or evaluating arguments and claims raised by competing social groups. They are also especially effective for looking with a critical gaze at policy or law or some other historical trends or cultural occurrences within social work (such as the development of anti-oppressive practice) that relate to social work. Each methodology can also be used as part of a wider life history or biographical method if interviews are involved. In practice, it will not prove helpful to simply criticise anything and everything, instead it is advisable to carefully consider document(s) and then gradually reflect upon and identify trends and other findings whilst introducing other arguments or ideas to develop a general thesis. As with any methodology, DA or CDA takes time to learn and develop, and you are also free to adapt this approach to your own particular needs or blend it with components of another methodology: for example by combining DA with some interviews and analysing both published documents and interview transcripts.

Conclusion

This chapter has detailed the two admittedly complex methodologies of narrative and discourse analysis. Each inductive approach seeks to explore in great detail the use of language whilst also offering a systematic means to explore social work-related issues. Narrative research helps us to investigate people's past, their experiences, thoughts and viewpoints, whilst trying to better understand and place each in context. As in so many more recent qualitative approaches, discourse analysis again shares a desire to scratch below surface 'realities' as well as to scrutinise everyday appearances or rhetorical claims. There are also important distinctions with each methodology: such as narrative analysis's capacity to draw from personal experience whilst discourse analysis does not necessarily require interviews and fresh data.

Further reading

Elliott, J. (2005). *Using Narrative in Social Research*. Sage, London

Fairclough, N. (1995). *Critical Discourse Analysis*. Longman

Fairclough, N. (2003). *Analysing Discourse: Textual Analysis for Social Research*. Oxford, Routledge

Hall, C., and White, S. (2005). 'Looking Inside Professional Practice: Discourse, Narrative and Ethnographic Approaches to Social Work and Counselling', *Qualitative Social Work*, 4: 379–390

May, T. (ed.) (2002), 'Qualitative Research in Action'. London, Sage. Chapter 11: Lawler, S. 'Narrative in Social Research'

Reissman, C.K. (1993). *Narrative Analysis*. Sage, London

Reissman, C.K., and Quinney, L. (2005). 'Narrative in Social Work: A Critical Review'. *Qualitative Social Work*, 4(4): 391–412

Wetherall, M., Taylor, S., and Yates, S.J. (eds) (2001). *Discourse as Data: A Guide for Analysis*. London, Sage

15 Participative Research

Introduction

This chapter explores participative forms of qualitative social work research. Participation and inclusion are a relatively new development in qualitative research and typically translate into participants being actively involved in a research project to varying degrees. As we have seen earlier, theoretical schools such as feminist or critical approaches (chapter six) are often highly critical of realist approaches that stress a formal distance between the 'expert' researcher and 'submissive' participant. The chapter begins by giving a critical overview of participation, including its different interpretations, applications and some of the recognised pros and cons of the approach. The chapter then looks at how qualitative participation approaches can be applied in practice. Finally, we look at some of the complex ethical issues that relate to participative research.

We begin by looking briefly at some of the types of approach and active debates that have taken place around participatory methodologies.

Participative research in context

Participative research now draws from a wide variety of political and theoretical frameworks, including realist, constructivist (chapter three) or 'emancipatory' approaches. At heart, however, the variety of participatory methods seek to practically involve and draw from research participants' experience and knowledge in order to support a research project. Participation can mean the involvement of many different groups of people, including service users, patients, practitioners, students, carers, and so on, in activities such as a the setting of a research question, the development of a questionnaire, the asking of interview questions or the presentation and writing up of research findings, among other examples. Usually, only one group such as service users or carers will be drawn upon, yet the extent to which such participants are involved in activities will vary according to several factors. These can include the age or status of participants, the nature and intentions of the project in hand, the methodology being drawn upon and the time available to any participants. Despite this, more realist orientated projects (chapter three) will tend to limit and control participation, such as by consulting with participants during certain 'low level' stages of a project, whereas many feminist models (chapter six) will be keen to encourage the active involvement of participants at different if not all stages (for example, Whitmore, 2001). However, even many types of constructivist or critical research can still regularly ignore or relegate the involvement of research participants. Such a political stance has been criticised for sometimes reflecting the arrogance of the professional researcher and also as failing to draw fully from the typically rich experiential knowledge that service users and others can offer many projects. It is recognized that that in practice there tends to emerge a continuum or hierarchy of participation in which involvement in decision-making and processes is contingent on different factors (Arnstein, 1969; Banks, 2012: 149). From the bottom upwards four levels of involvement include those which accommodate:

1. Full decision-making powers on behalf of users or carers
2. More explicit joint involvement with professionals in decision-making
3. Permitting a degree of direct involvement in decision-making processes
4. Informing, listening to or consulting with service users and carers.

For research purposes the financial cost, knowledge, adept skills and time required of the principal investigator will increase, often significantly, as we move up each level. Again some projects and users are more suited to different levels of participation although few are likely to reach level one for practical and/or political reasons.

Although participation research draws significantly from core ideas developed within feminist and other critical approaches, there are, nevertheless, other models of involvement that have emerged. Indeed, as Braye (2000: 9) suggests, despite an 'apparent consensus that participation is a good thing' this assumption 'masks mayor differences of ideology between different interest groups'. In particular, Braye (ibid.: 18–21) notes the tensions that persist between 'consumer' and 'democratic' models of participation. The former 'accompanies the ideology of welfare markets, in which [service user] needs and [support] services are commodities to be traded'. Critics also argue that this model limits the involvement of participants to a point where it becomes 'tokenistic' and avoids attempts to recognise or address social inequalities, disadvantage or forms of 'citizenship'. In contrast, democratic models of participation allegedly seek to encourage the direct involvement of users within most, if not all, key stages of the research project. In addition, they may also aim to be more collective from both the researcher(s) and participants' perspective.

More importantly, however, democratic models at least aim to encourage aspirations towards achieving positive social goals that reach beyond the seemingly narrow consumer-led drives to achieve improvements in welfare service delivery (within health, housing, education and social care sectors, among others). Such 'emancipatory' goals include attempts to use research and associated 'conscious raising' to draw attention to and confront discrimination and redistribute power imbalances and types of economic inequality. Braye (2000: 19), however, points out that the two models tend to share a bond which can itself cause problems:

> Because the models can and do co-exist ... they risk overlap and confusion. Whilst both demand change to the status quo, the consumerist model often has a stronger presence – it is more tangible and may appear easier to achieve – thus giving the illusion of participation without the substance

In relation to this Carey (2009) draws attention to some of the benefits and drawbacks of participatory forms of qualitative research within social work. In particular, participation may:

- enhance the quality and reliability of research findings;
- improve the knowledge and skills of participants and researchers;
- increase opportunities for participants, as well as bridge any power gap between the researcher and participants;
- require significant time, effort and possible financial cost on behalf of the researcher, including necessary training and other forms of support required for any 'new researchers';
- prioritise research *process*, especially data collection, above research *outcomes*, or the end product (findings, dissemination, emancipatory benefits, etc.) of any project. This tendency means that many of the benefits claimed by democratic models may also prove difficult to achieve in the long term.
- be interpreted as being too ideological and therefore lack objectivity and therefore lack legitimacy, especially among powerful professional groups.

McLaughlin (2006) draws from personal experience of undertaking participatory social work research with children. He notes the benefits of increased focus gained with young participants as well as the richer data gathered and the potentially increased employment opportunities for his 'lay' researchers. Also, the quality of social work support services, such as residential care, may also improve as a result of any lay participation. Despite this, difficulties can also quickly emerge which may include the recruitment of participants and the likely need for provision of regular support and training. Also, other problems can emerge, such as the researcher having to accommodate the need for schooling or other activities typically pursued by teenagers, such as football or friendships. In relation, maintaining motivation among younger researchers may prove especially challenging for the researcher, as can support with core tasks such as writing or presenting research findings to an audience.

The extent to which benefits and drawbacks impact upon a project will of course largely depend upon the size and scale of any research undertaken, and the likely social groups who participate. In general, smaller projects should be much easier to manage, and also whichever user group is involved (for example, participants with mental health needs, a disability or older participants or children) will demand different degrees of support. Some research projects will also be more suited to participative research than others. For example, more obvious projects that are likely to benefit from involvement may include those that seek to investigate the attitudes of users of a social work service, including opinions on how this service might be improved, or which look to investigate personal experiences of social exclusion or discrimination. Less suitable projects may include those that seek to investigate delicate topics and 'hard to reach' or even 'invisible' groups such as illicit drug users or young men who suffer from depression. Whatever the related difficulties or resource demands, it is likely that participative research will continue to expand: this is not merely due to the ways by which this often practically and emotionally difficult approach can lead to more reliable findings or increase its legitimacy but also due to some of the other positive social and political benefits identified with the feminist and/or democratic approaches.

Research question, training, literature review and data collection

As in all research projects, the first obstacle to overcome is the framing and development of an idea or project to pursue. As discussed earlier in chapter two, any researcher needs to decide what it is they wish to investigate. For participation, the conception of the project might well emerge from or be influenced by participants themselves: for example, a group of service users who access a particular service might wish to evaluate how effective this service is for users and how it might be improved.

If participants are not already involved from the beginning, then once a suitable topic has been identified the second task will usually involve the recruitment of research participants. McLaughlin (2009: 91) suggests that the researcher will need to decide as early as possible 'both the number of co-researchers required and the type of activities they are required to do'. Three possible strategies are then available for recruitment, which include:

- Working with an already established group of service users, carers or practitioners.
- Placing an advert in a location attended by the target group or within a relevant publication such as a local newsletter.
- Utilising a 'snowball' effect (chapter three) whereby one participant leads the researcher to another, and so on.

McLaughlin (2009: 92–3) notes the problem of 'representativeness' or how best to fit your 'sample' of participants within the wider population of users or practitioners, etc. By and large, recruiting a representative sample is not possible and is not normally a priority for most smaller-scale qualitative projects. However, there is criticism that 'the usual suspects' can be selected or sometimes even 'cherry picked' by researchers: that is seemingly 'ideal' users who will not 'rock the boat' or who will be easier to integrate into a project because of their pleasant personalities, reputation or cultural background (for example, white middle class carers or professionals, etc.). We should always endeavour to avoid such bias in our recruitment, not simply because it is unfair or discriminatory but also because it will limit our capacity to fulfil our research objectives. On a practical level, however, there is often likely to be a tension between ideal criteria for participants and the finite available time and resources we have to complete any project.

Once participants have been recruited, the researcher then needs to arrange a suitable meeting with those involved in order to explain the intentions of the project, the likely extent of any involvement and the roles to be fulfilled by participants. Padgett (2008: 37) suggests that qualitative participation research in social work nearly always demands great time, energy and resources, and that researchers should try to be realistic about their intended outcomes and commitment. In general, the less ambitious a project from an early stage the much more likely it will achieve its intended aims. Although this rule of thumb can be applied to most models of research, it is especially true for participation: this is because so much more is outside of the researcher's direct control, especially if involving a group of people who we wish to have a tangible influence on the project.

We may then be faced with the potentially thorny problem of training. The big question being: do I provide some form of training for my eager participants? Leamy and Clough (2006) offer some sound advice which suggests that the researcher should:

- Decide as early as possible if formal training is a necessity or whether the researcher can 'teach' the budding co-researchers 'the ropes' as the project moves on.
- Try to avoid patronising users whilst also offering clear and sound training or advice that will maintain their interest and capability.
- Use discretion so as to decide what level of training is required and how best to provide this.
- Bear in mind the potential high cost of training as well as the time commitment.
- Participant interest may wane if the training is perceived as dull or boring (perhaps too many 'power-point' slides used. Too much emphasis placed upon the use of computers, etc.). If this is the case then regular breaks, relatively short periods of teaching and a variety of learning techniques (for example, combining power-point with discussion and film or other 'fun' activities such as role play, etc.) can help.
- Remember that a distinction can be drawn between the theory and practice of qualitative social work research and that participants are likely to benefit from some grounding in both.

Typically, any project will then be encapsulated within a research question that neatly summarises what it is we wish to investigate. As discussed earlier in chapter two, we should endeavour to capture our question or problem in one or two sentences and also aim for a clear and crisp question that can be realistically addressed with the available resources. As principal researcher, you will need to decide whether or not participants are to be involved in the design of the research question, and if so to what extent. For example, might you wish to develop an initial question by yourself and then bring participants in for advice at a later stage? Alternatively, you might instead decide to allow participants to offer advice from the beginning or to take control of the process. These questions depend upon the type of participants involved in the research: for example, users with no research experience are likely to require at least some support in the development of a research question. There is also unlikely to be a scenario where a researcher can simply leave participants alone to construct a research question by themselves. More likely, however, some degree of mutual consultation will be beneficial.

Once we have an idea of the research question (and related aims and objectives discussed further in chapter two), we then need to consider the literature review. Although the principal researcher will need to follow the processes set out earlier in chapters four and five, they will also need to consider carefully if and how participants might become involved in this crucial stage in the research process. For example, might participative co-researchers read and evaluate some, many or all sources of information? In practice, this is likely to be a difficult task for lay researchers, especially if they have no formal academic training. Support may be provided, as evaluation and analysis of literature sources tends to be a complex task that may take many months or even years to develop. More realistic alternatives include allowing some or more participants to offer their opinions on any written literature review or instead evaluating the less challenging documents and previous research findings. The researchers can also summarise many or all documents for co-researchers or possibly discuss the overall findings from any literature review at planned meetings. An accessible presentation of previous literature and findings for co-researchers might also be possible. The opinions from participants can then be integrated into the next stage of the research.

We then need to consider our likely types of data collection (or research methods to apply). If we are to involve participants in this key stage of a project then some formal training will almost certainly be required. This can range from personal advice or discussions to regular planned meetings between the principal researcher and co-researchers. Alternatively, formal courses specifically set up for participants, or applicable to the needs of the participant group, may be beneficial. Ultimately, participants may struggle to undertake interviews or focus group meetings or whatever methods are drawn upon without some form of regular support. If such provision proves too challenging, time consuming or expensive then you may wish to consider on-going consultation with co-researchers as you undertake the data collection. Padgett (2008: 37) highlights that if collecting data with participants in a community setting then any methods used (interviews, focus groups, ethnography, etc.) will usually need to be brief and focused:

> Because time and resources are almost always limited, a premium is put on abbreviated and focused methods that can yield findings in a short turnaround time (sometimes six months or less) and with wide impact on improving community health and mental health.

Such a pragmatic response takes account of the limited knowledge base or skills that users, practitioners and professionals may hold about formal research processes. However, there are further additional alternatives available to help support inexperienced co-researchers. For example, in some instances it may be possible for co-researchers to complete interviews in pairs, a process that can offer mutual support during a potentially stressful encounter (McLaughlin, 2009). Foster (2007) has also offered other examples of alternative data collection (and analysis) that can be more meaningful and engaging for participants: such as the use of drama or pictures to convey meaning and understanding through 'arts based qualitative research'. Such initiatives – as well as related innovative ideas generated by the researcher or participants themselves – can again assist the difficult process of data collection for those without formal experience or knowledge.

Analysis, writing up and dissemination

As with data collection, analysis is likely to be a part of qualitative social work research that is challenging to many 'lay' researchers. This is because analysis is arguably the most demanding and traditionally 'academic' element of all qualitative research. As we shall explore further in chapter seventeen, analysis seeks to identify core trends, themes, and/or patterns amongst a sample of people or amidst relevant literature. We then compare any such patterns to findings from other related studies in order to understand or contextualise what it is we have discovered. Although often assumed to take place towards the end of a project, more often than not analysis starts early within qualitative research and continues throughout.

Detailed analysis may be beyond the scope of many participants. Thus, although not compulsory, alternative approaches that still involve participation may instead be favoured. For example, as with the literature review the researcher may wish to summarise her findings and allow participants to offer their opinions or suggestions. This might take place in a series of formal group or individual meetings. A verbal summary of findings could be provided or again pictures might be used to convey meaning in a more accessible format, assuming this is not too patronising. Flipcharts can be used as an alternative, or power-point slides. The crucial intention, however, must be that participants involved in a study are allowed to offer their opinion on the research findings. McLaughlin (2009: 117) views the participant as a 'critical friend' through the process of analysis and also suggests beginning in pairs and then meeting as part of a gradually larger group to discuss findings. Co-researchers should be able to offer another angle from which to interpret any findings, which are likely to then increase the quality of our interpretations and findings. It is possible, however, that participants may wish to be engaged in more sophisticated processes of analysis, such as the use of coding (explored in chapter seventeen) or even the use of computer technology such as QSR NUD*IST that sorts and evaluates collected data.

In general, conclusions should draw directly from any data collected or other findings, and participants again have a right to contribute to this aspect of any project. They are also likely to extend any recommendations in their 'critical friend' capacity. Indeed, as McLaughlin (2009: 119) stresses:

Recommendations for change are often a major motivating factor why service users get involved in research in the first place. Service users or co-researchers are often critical of current service provision and want to see change.

How this is achieved remains up to the researcher but certainly individual and group meetings are likely to be a good way to facilitate this process. Again, alternative methods such as drama, role play or pictures to convey meaning and interpretation may support and extend this role for participants. The critical imagination of both the researcher and participant can so often be crucial resources to be drawn upon within participative research.

For writing there are again different possible scenarios, that may include:

- a partial contribution from some participants
- concentration by co-researchers upon one chapter or sector
- evaluating and making recommendations from a final report
- co-authorship with the principal researcher.

Once again, alternative means of communication to support the process of communication and writing may aid participation: for example, participants recording, drawing or selecting pictures to convey their interpretations. In some instances, an interview with participant(s) filmed on DVD and which represents research findings, recommendations or conclusions might be suitable and submitted alongside the final report. Of course, the internet and a relevant website might also provide a suitable resource.

A dissemination strategy can be forged along with participants at a meeting and can then take a variety of forms, which might include a group presentation at a conference or an academic paper jointly written with participants or revised by each at a later date. Foster (2007) again used drama – and in particular a pantomime full of satire, irony and humour – to present her research findings along with participants to an audience of parents and welfare professionals at a local *Sure Start* centre. We can see here then that within participation and involvement the emphasis may often very much be upon creativity and the use of imagination as much as hard work or drive; sometimes to challenge the limits of 'reductive' or essentialist scientific approaches favoured in many more traditional forms of research.

Ethics of participation

Although many of the rules relating to ethical research translate instantly to participation research – most notably the importance of anonymity, safe storage of data, informed consent, confidentiality and voluntary involvement, and so on – there are some distinctions to those set out earlier in chapter eight. In particular, any lead researcher will have to consider carefully the issue of consent as well as how they intend to provide both relevant training and support to participants alongside the usual priority given to anonymity, safety, and so forth. Think carefully about how you intend to recruit participants: do you intend to recruit through a formal institution or known contacts or via a snowball sample? If so, might the latter challenge ethical norms and expectations? Do you have any plans to offer additional support if participants are involved in data collection and become upset during this formal and likely alien routine? Do you intend to offer training to accommodate the typically greater learning needs of participants? Inevitably, if participants have a specific medical condition or disability or are children, then you will have to consider how you will provide additional support throughout the research project, assuming this is required. These types of questions need to be considered very carefully but most importantly any ethics committee will want to see evidence that you have made plans to accommodate the specific needs of your intended or recruited co-researchers.

Shaw (2005) has critically assessed some of the possible problems that may present in attempts to involve service user participants in research. He draws examples from a wide range of social groups that social work has worked alongside, including adults who are homeless, experience issues around drug misuse, mental health problems, have a disability or are HIV positive, or young people with problems relating to truancy or family breakdown. The author highlights the difficulty of locating and recruiting participants 'with problem experiences', since they are more likely to move around localities, and are less likely to be in regular employment or a stable relationship. In addition, such service users do not always 'live by a set agenda or a planned time scale' from day to day. Perhaps more controversially, Shaw argues that due to personal and cultural disadvantage, service user participants are more likely to exaggerate or lie in conversation, be 'emotionally incontinent' and unpredictable, or withhold critical facts that can hinder and potentially jeopardise any research (ibid.: 843–5). Although such personal attributes will not be present for the majority of service users – and indeed some of these attributes persist for people in all socio-economic classes – they *may*, however, be present for at least a small number of user participants, and this needs to be recognised. Consequentially, such potential hazards to a project may have to be considered and placed in an ethical and practical context prior to and after recruitment. As an example, you may wish to ask whether it is really sensible or fair to involve users with emotional or mental health needs in your project, especially if we are researching sensitive topics such as abuse or neglect. Potentially at least, this could be construed as exploitation. Possibly, however, with careful planning, organisation and sheer hard work, your project might again be rewarding and indeed 'therapeutic' for some participants, as indeed Foster (2007) discovered. Again, and as with many of the more complex methodologies discussed in this book, such as discourse analysis or ethnography, personal discretion and careful decision-making needs to take place alongside careful advice given by colleagues tutors or whoever.

Conclusion

This chapter has looked at one of the more creative yet often challenging forms of qualitative social work research: that of participative approaches. We have seen that participation raises many political and ethical questions that more traditional approaches such as the interview or questionnaire are able to sometimes limit. For example, consumer or feminist/critical types of participation seek different political goals that range from improving services to challenging discrimination and making a wider cultural and socio-economic difference for participants. Similarly, participation often creates much greater demands for the researcher: it tends to generate more work regarding the provision of support or education but is also equally rewarding and can offer more focused, accurate and detailed findings. It has been suggested that the key to good participation remains not merely hard work but also the use of a strong sense of imagination and creativity, both on behalf of the researcher and lay experts.

Further reading

Kemshall, H., and Littlechild, R. (eds) (2000). *User Involvement and Participation in Social Care: Research Informing Practice*. London, Jessica Kingsley

Leamy, M., and Clough, R. (2006). 'How Older People Became Researchers: Training, Guidance and Practice in Action'. York, Joseph Rowntree Foundation

McLaughlin, H. (2009). *Service User Research in Health and Social Care.* London, Sage

Nolan, M., Hanson, E., Grant, G., and Keady, J. (eds) (2007). *User Participation in Health and Social Care: Voices, Values and Evaluation.* Maidenhead, Open University Press

16 Internet Research

Introduction

In this chapter we explore the use of the internet to undertake qualitative social work research. The internet can now be used to facilitate a significant proportion of literature-based research, including with support from methodologies such as the systemic review or a critical interpretive synthesis (chapter five). This chapter builds upon such recent developments by exploring two other key forms of internet-based research methods: the questionnaire and the interview. The chapter also looks at some additional advantages that online research provides as well as some of the potential problems that may become apparent, such as bias or ethical hazards and dilemmas. Finally, a list of some helpful sites is presented, alongside a case study which illustrates how the internet can been used to undertake qualitative research.

We begin with a brief overview of the internet and internet research.

Internet research in context

The internet was developed by the US Department of Defence in the late 1960s to support communication for the military via computer networking. Initially it developed the ARPANET (Advanced Research Projects Agency Network) system which had facilitated the linking of 23 host computers by 1971. Email emerged one year later and very basic international connections were established by 1973. A commercial form of ARPANET emerged in 1974.

Additional networks such as USENET (1979) and BITMET (1981) were created, and in 1982 a simple version of what we now widely refer to as the 'internet' was born. By 1984, more than one thousand computers were connected through the internet, which then grew rapidly to over ten thousand by 1987, a million by 1992, 3.2 million by 1994 and 56 million by 1999. As Hewson, et al. (2003: 4–5) declare:

This growth in the number of hosts is mind-boggling, particularly when considering that the individual hosts can serve many more individual users. 'World Wide Web' and 'Internet' have now become household terms; everyday more and more people are accessing the Internet through academic, private, military, government, and commercial interests, primarily through networked computer systems.

As a highly sophisticated communication network the internet can also provide us with an invaluable resource for social research. As Jones (1999: xii-xiii) suggests, much of this has tended to be administrative, commercial and quantitative. However, the net can also be used to undertake a variety of forms of qualitative research. This reflects not only the greater opportunities available for potential access to research participants across time and space (including in other parts of the country or internationally), but also stronger links now persist between our increasingly blurred 'on-' and 'off-line' worlds:

> The Internet does not exist in isolation. To study it as if it was somehow apart from the 'off-line' world that brought it into being would be a gross mistake. Internet users are as much a part of physical space as they are of cyberspace (more so, really, insofar as users' choices regarding place, identity, etc. are far more limited in physical space). As a result the notion that our research should be 'grounded' takes on even greater significance when it comes to Internet research. That makes Internet research particularly interesting – and demanding. Not only is it important to be aware of and attuned to the diversity of on-line experience, it is important to recognise that on-line experience is at all times tethered in some fashion to off-line experience.

O Dochartaigh (2002: 7–18) highlights some of the implications of using the internet within social research. Among others, these include that there has occurred a possible tendency for 'information overload' regarding many disciplines (academic included), which potentially can make it difficult to attain an adequate overview of any one subject area (including within a literature review). This partially helps to explain the hunt for more precise search methodologies, such as the systematic review. Despite this, other benefits remain, such as that contacts are easier to make with other people, and inevitably this allows more options to the researcher. Primary sources such as newspapers, magazines or official reports produced by Universities, or other organisations and governments are now also easier to access. There has also occurred the development of online journals, some of which are grounded in social work and are free to access (for example, the *Social Work and Society* or *Critical Social Work* Journals). Public affairs or policy and law documents have now become much more widely available.

A researcher's location is also now less important since the 'internationalisation' of information has been promoted. For example, studies of other countries – including regards policy, law, social work practice and theory development internationally, etc. – have, again, become easier. Potentially, at least, excluded groups (geographically, politically, economically, culturally etc.) now have more access to information than ever before through the internet, although direct and regular access to the internet is notoriously class-specific and is still largely dominated by more privileged groups. Also, for academics, pressures created by the internet have encouraged researchers to further 'micro-specialise' within most subjects, which has resulted in already somewhat tenuous bonds being further broken with local communities. Despite this, more ties have tended to form with other people internationally, whilst local links (paradoxically) can recede or even break down. Thanks to the internet you may have more regular and closer day-to-day contact with someone on another side of world in comparison to people sat in the office next door (O Dochartaigh, 2002: 7–18).

Some helpful questions to consider relating to internet based research include:

- Thinking carefully about whether or not your potential research topic is viable for this method? For example, will any gender or class bias regarding access to internet technology obscure any findings, such as if access to the net for participants may be difficult?
- Can any type of workable sample be found via the internet? If so, how might you gather the information that you require from this sample?
- How might you limit or reduce any possible forms of bias relating to gender, class and/or the ethnic background of possible participants? For example, could you target emails to specific people or specialist sites and voluntary organisations to encourage more engagement from internet minority groups?
- What might the pros and cons of applying this unique method be, such as regarding the need to answer your research question? Do the former outweigh the latter?
- Might there be any outstanding ethical problems generated by this method? If so, how might they be overcome?

In general, if you intend to undertake interviews or distribute questionnaires it is important to consider the extent to which your potential sample may or may not have regular access to the internet. Also some of the possible ethical issues that may be generated by this approach will need to be considered.

We now look at two of the key forms of empirical research on the internet before turning our attention to the ethics of internet social work research.

Online interviews

Interviews on the internet can provide a cheap and quick source of data collection that might also help you gain relatively easy access to a reliable sample of research participants. The potential scope is promising but this also very much depends upon mitigating factors such as your topic of inquiry and the types of research participants that you wish to gain access to and interview. First it helps to ask if the people you wish to interview are likely to have access to email technology or if they are likely to enter internet chat rooms? Also, are 'faceless' online interviews the best way to engage with your intended participants and unpack the research question that your study intends to answer? Think carefully or in consultation with a tutor about the reliability (chapter three) of this method or any possible ethical implications (chapter eight). These are the types of question to ask before committing to any method. For example, some older people who receive domiciliary care are likely to be more suitable for online interviews than children in care – especially regarding research ethics – yet their likely access to, or use of, the internet may be limited. In contrast, many more social work practitioners now have access to the internet as part of their work, and some are likely to access website chat rooms, such as on the *Community Care* website based in the UK. In general it helps to ask:

- What level of access to computer technology do your potential research participants have?
- Are you likely to be able to gain consistent access to such participants through the net?
- Are there any ethical dilemmas or questions which might hinder this type of research?

Since social work research so often engages with sensitive topics relating to human need, emotions, neglect, and so on, the internet may at least potentially provide some 'hidden' protection to participants and can also facilitate the investigation of more delicate matters. This is because, crucially, participants may remain anonymous in chat rooms or through email. However, as Hewson et al. (2003: 45) note:

> Interviewer and interviewee need not know anything about each other's identity or biosocial attributes. This makes the Internet unique as a tool for conducting

interviews and opens up new possibilities. On the other hand, the flexibility of an Internet interview, as well as the scope for making use of body language and other non-verbal information, is reduced.

However, the internet interview is ideal if looking at people who are difficult to locate or access. For example, practitioners living abroad or who are based in another part of the country. LeBesco (2004: 63) labels possible participants 'online discourse communities' and points out that researchers potentially now have 'interpretive access to participants and conversations that might be otherwise restricted in the real world'. Once again, there are ethical questions to consider depending on *the type of research* and especially *subject areas* you intend to investigate.

Despite lacking the spontaneity or intimacy of a real interview, email still remains the simplest and cheapest way to undertake an ongoing interview. Another notable advantage remains that suitable times to communicate are more flexible and increase in comparison to a face-to-face interview. In addition, both interviewer and interviewee are more likely to have time to consider potential questions and responses. Typically, following an introduction and brief outline of your study and aims (which might be pre-prepared in a word document) one or two initial 'tester' questions may be asked. Following a successful reply from an interviewee, further questions may then follow. The types of question asked will tend to follow the basic rules explored for face-to-face interviews outlined earlier in chapter nine. Overall, however, it is more likely that an interview email (with set questions) will be returned, complete with useful data, if it is brief, clear and unambiguous, focused and easy to follow (again, chapter nine provides further detail on constructing questions).

Ongoing discussions can occur based around the initial two to five set questions and any uncertainties or ambiguities regarding a participant's responses – or participants own questions regarding the topic – may mean that numerous email exchanges occur. Potentially at least, each participant may also offer advice regarding, and access to, further research interviewees (such as work colleagues or fellow carers) and this may help you to build up a reliable 'convenience' sample. As suggested earlier, one notable concern is the possible bias inherent within internet-based empirical research. As Coomber (1997, cited in Payne and Payne, 2004: 125) highlights, people who have access to the internet are 'more likely to be white, male, first world residents, relatively affluent and relatively well educated'. Inevitably in a profession such as social work that deals for the most part with poverty and disadvantage there may be problems of suitable access to some participant groups. However, Hewson et al. (2003: 27) suggest that this once widespread assumption is now being increasingly challenged. In particular, both 'the number and diversity of Internet users are increasing, facilitated by the availability of cheap Internet-capable computers'. Many social groups that enter into the remit of social work research (practitioners, volunteers, carers, etc.) are also ever more likely to now have at least some access to the internet.

Additional technology such as Skype.com can also facilitate a cheap and direct face-to-face interview, despite being somewhat delayed. With Skype you will probably need to again prepare a word-document that outlines your research objectives and introduces you to interviewees. Arranging suitable times to 'meet' and talk are also essential. Again, this allows former barriers of time and location to be overcome. Another viable option remains internet chat rooms, where communication can be ongoing and continue as part of a group of internet loggers. This type of 'online focus group' meeting may be more suitable for topics which benefit from open debate and group insight: such as regarding opinions about new policy initiatives or the effectiveness of innovative available support services within social care. More sensitive topics may be explored but, again, tact and discretion will need to be prioritised alongside any other ethical concerns. If uncertain, then consult with your tutor or a senior member of staff or contact a relevant association such as the Social Care Institute for Excellence or a local University social work department.

The construction of questions asked for such empirical research will be much the same as in a normal interview, questionnaire or focus group meeting. Often, however, you will need to be more succinct and ask fewer questions since people may have limited available time, cannot be seen and may leave the internet at any stage without warning, especially if the discussion becomes boring or difficult. It is also a priority to plan any sessions well in advance and if you intend to generate a debate think carefully of how best to construct any questions. With generally fewer possible questions to ask they will need to be focused yet sensitive to the people on the site. You will also need to decide how you intend to collect and quantify your data. Will you tape-record Skype interviews, or store or print off transcripts from an online chat or interview? Be careful about storage of any such data, ensuring that it is safe and secure. Analysis of such data follows the same rules as those set out in chapter seventeen.

Internet surveys

Social surveys remain a distinct approach more commonly used in quantitative research yet often adapted for smaller qualitative projects. Surveys traditionally draw from a realist perspective (chapter three) that seeks to make more general and broad observations about a larger population. In practice, this typically consists of distributing a relatively brief questionnaire attached to an email or linked to a specific website. As Gaiser and Schreiner (2009: 68) note, surveys on the net appear to be everywhere; especially consumer surveys distributed through email, following purchases online or linked to 'pop ups'.

Surveys may often lack the rich insight or thorough analysis usually apparent with more in-depth qualitative approaches such as an interview but there are still notable advantages with such methods. Among others, these include that surveys:

- reduce cost and save time
- allow a large population and sample to be accessed
- permit otherwise difficult groups to be reached
- enable respondents to complete a questionnaire in their own time
- permit more options for the researcher: such as in designing a questionnaire due to ever-more word package graphics
- do not intimidate participants in comparison to other approaches, such as the telephone interview.

In general, it is better to keep an internet questionnaire simple, focused and as brief as possible: such attributes will not only increase response rates but will also often lead to better data being collected that is easier to analyse. Dillman et al. (1999) offer some further helpful advice on the design of internet questionnaires. These include to:

- Begin with a welcome screen and brief and succinct introduction (stating who you are and what it is you are researching).
- Be especially careful with the first question as if this is confusing it may put respondents off.
- Try to keep to a paper style format as respondents are likely to be more familiar with this.
- Try to allow a gradual flow from one question to the next so respondents do not have to go back and forth or jump across to questions on different pages.
- Keep the questionnaire as brief and uncomplicated as possible.
- Use larger and bolder fonts that can be helpful to highlight instructions.
- Ensure consistency and readability: in particular avoid over-colourful formats and/or complex structures.
- Spread instructions throughout the questionnaire rather than listing too many at the beginning.
- Offer a support contact, such as your own mobile number or email address.

- Restrict or avoid adding caveats, attachments or drop-down boxes, etc. Again, such additions have a tendency to confuse or annoy people.
- Try to keep multiple choice questions to a single screen.
- Avoid too many open-ended questions as these are time consuming and may be difficult to analyse.

Gaiser and Schreiner (2009: 68) add that making research topics 'interesting and engaging' for potential participants always helps to increase response rates. Bear in mind also that responses to net surveys tend to be poor, possibly a consequence of their omnipresence, so be careful to consider all of the guidance above.

Case study: Online survey of the working relationship between social work practitioners and disabled service users

The case study below provides an example of a questionnaire distributed to social work practitioners via email. The topic explored personal relationships built between practitioners and service users with a physical disability. In particular, it asked what extenuating factors might impinge upon this relationship (including factors outside of the control of individual practitioners).

As can be seen, the questionnaire begins with a brief introduction setting out the purpose of the survey. There are then four simple questions that seek to discover some general information about each participant whilst still maintaining their anonymity. The next section then presents core 'scaled' questions (chapter nine) that seek to quantify the opinions of each practitioner. In particular, the questions are asking practitioners their views on the overall quality of any relationship they have with users, and also to what extent factors such as policy, legislation, resources, available time, and so on, may influence this. There is an additional question which permits further comments to be made. Towards the very end, there is also a section that allows each respondent to detail any additional factors that they believe may impact upon their relationship with service users, and which is not able to be detailed elsewhere on the questionnaire.

Although this questionnaire does not allow for more in-depth insight regarding any findings (such as might be gained in an interview), it is still cheap, saves time and is likely to collect a great deal of data from many participants. Indeed, as stated on the form this type of questionnaire can be completed in less than 10 minutes, as opposed to an hour for many interviews.

The working relationship between social work practitioners and service users with a disability

Thank you for agreeing to participate in this study which is part of our research project at the University of West Kirkby. Your participation will help us explore ways to evaluate the working relationship between social workers and disabled service users. This survey should take between 5-10 minutes of your time. We will only report summarised results, so your identity will be unknown. The information will only be used in connection with our project at the University of West Kirby that seeks to identify the factors which may influence the relationship between practitioners and disabled users of social services.

1. Age:

☐ 18-25
☐ 25-30
☐ 30-40
☐ 40-50
☐ 50+

2. Gender:

☐   Male
☐   Female
☐   Other

3. Ethnicity

White:	Black/Black British:
☐ White British	☐ Caribbean
☐ White Irish	☐ African
☐ White Other (please specify)	☐ Black Other (please specify)
....	....
Mixed Heritage:	Asian/Asian British:
☐ White and Black Caribbean	☐ Indian
☐ White and Black African	☐ Pakistani
☐ White and Asian	☐ Bangladeshi
☐ Mixed Other (please specify)	☐ Asian Other (please specify)
....	....
Chinese or Other Ethnic Group:	
☐ Chinese	
☐ Any Other (please specify)	
....	

From standard classifications for presenting ethnic groups.
Office for National Statistics (2001)

4. Period of practice as a qualified social worker:
☐   0–12 months
☐   1–5 years
☐   5–10 years
☐   10 years plus

Please click in the circle that represents how you feel about the following statements.

5. I have a good working relationship with a majority of my service users

	1	2	3	4	5	
Strongly Disagree	○	○	○	○	○	Strongly Agree

Any further
comments:_____
_____
_____
_____
_____
_____

6. My knowledge of specialist legislation and policy affects the quality of my relationship with service users who have a disability

	1	2	3	4	5	
Strongly Disagree	○	○	○	○	○	Strongly Agree

Any further
comments:_____
_____
_____
_____
_____
_____

7. Available time to spend with service users affects the quality of my relationship with service users who have a disability

	1	2	3	4	5	
Strongly Disagree	○	○	○	○	○	Strongly Agree

Any further
comments:_____

_____
_____
_____
_____
_____
_____

8. Available resources and a subsequent capacity to provide support services can affect the quality of my relationship with service users who have a disability

	1	2	3	4	5	
Strongly Disagree	○	○	○	○	○	Strongly Agree

Any further
comments:_____

_____
_____
_____
_____
_____
_____

9. Establishing a good relationship with informal carers or the relatives/friends of service users affects the quality of my relationship with service users who have a disability

	1	2	3	4	5	
Strongly Disagree	○	○	○	○	○	Strongly Agree

Any further
comments:_____

_____
_____
_____
_____
_____
_____

10. A good relationship with other professionals affects the quality of my relationship with service users who have a disability

	1	2	3	4	5	
Strongly Disagree	○	○	○	○	○	Strongly Agree

Any further
comments:_____
_____
_____
_____
_____
_____
_____

11. A good working relationship with immediate colleagues affects the quality of my relationship with service users who have a disability

	1	2	3	4	5	
Strongly Disagree	○	○	○	○	○	Strongly Agree

Any further
comments:_____
_____
_____
_____
_____
_____
_____

12. What additional factors (if any) not listed above might improve your relationship with disabled service users (please list and briefly explain)

_____
_____
_____
_____
_____
_____
_____

Thank you very much for your participation.

A final note relates to validity and reliability, as explored earlier in chapter three. A questionnaire normally has higher validity (findings respond to 'reality') if it is able to accurately measure what the study intended to explore. In this instance, the questionnaire is touching upon and exploring themes that prior research has indicated may influence the relationship between a practitioner and service users (for example, available time or resources). The researcher should be able to get a reasonably accurate measure of the impact of each theme from each respondent, which can then be compared with other findings isolated in associate questions. Generally the larger the size of the sample the higher the rate of validity. Nevertheless although difficult to plan or organize the validity of this study would increase further if brief interviews accompanied the completion of the questionnaire. This is because the researcher would be able to collect further details and address any uncertainties that link to the questionnaire being completed.

Reliability relates to whether the same method will generate the same results elsewhere, thus indicating that the questionnaire is an accurate instrument for quantifying a particular set of social opinions or attitudes. As stated in chapter three, this is rarely the priority within qualitative social work research where the depth of analysis and wealth of insight are more likely to be prioritised rather than the accuracy of measurement. Despite this, as the questionnaire detailed in the example above predominately relies upon opinion scales, it is likely that the reliability of the instrument and method will again be relatively high.

Many of the general rules and advice offered in chapter nine regarding appropriate interview and questionnaire questions and structure are also relevant for online surveys.

Ethics

By and large, research on the internet should always conform to the same guidelines and rules for ethical practices as any other type of qualitative research. For example, the researcher should seek to maintain the privacy of participants or avoid coercion, disrespect or the telling of lies, alongside other criteria detailed in chapter eight. However, for practical reasons some of these rules can be more difficult to fulfil due to the intricate nature of technology and communication on the internet.

Hewson et al. (2003: 51–3) identify three areas of potential concern which can make internet research ethics more difficult to fulfil. These include informed consent, confidentiality or security and, finally, debriefing. First, informed consent is usually acquired by asking research participants to read and sign a consent form prior to any interviews. Unfortunately, as internet users are typically anonymous, it may prove impossible to know if they are old enough (i.e. 18 years old) to participate and they may sign an attached form despite being under age. However, as Hewson et al. (2003: 52) state, this type of fraudulence 'may in practice be both rare and easily detected (depending upon the nature of the research question and procedure)' In addition, passwords may be set up which allow a filter system to be in place or instead email questionnaires can be targeted at specific groups of people already known to be suitable to the research. Also, it is possible to allow participants to leave a study if a 'withdraw' button is attached to a document alongside a 'submit data' button.

Second, confidentiality and security of information can be more difficult to guarantee when collecting data through the internet. For example, an email may be sent to the wrong address by mistake or hackers might obtain access to your files if stored on a hard drive. The types of sensitive issues dealt with within social work research make confidentiality and security especially important. Confidentiality can be ensured by maintaining anonymity during data presentation.. Also, the simplest way to guard against security threats remains to avoid storing data on a hard drive and to place 'pegs' or other external devices in a safe place. Obviously, activities such as 'hacking' into specific websites in order to obtain illegal sources of data remain unethical. Potentially, there are numerous other ways to guarantee confidentiality or further increase security. Technology is also changing fast and new or more reliable methods are likely to emerge. The key point, as is often the case with research ethics, is to make plans in advance and consider potential risks, as well as how to best reduce or avoid the compromising of ethical research processes.

Finally, the issue of debriefing may be more difficult to sustain when participants are not known or will never be met or spoken to in person. Debriefing typically consists of a verbal summary provided to participants by the researcher after an interview or other method: for example, an outline of the intentions of the study as well as explanation of what will happen to the findings alongside an opportunity for participants to ask questions. A solution to this usually translates into the researcher sending a 'debriefing text' that summarises the intentions of the study as well as allowing participants the opportunity to respond via email to any queries. Alternatively, the debriefing may be attached to a questionnaire, as in the case example presented above. Ethical concerns still remain, however,, because the researcher is not able to guarantee that such a debriefing text has been read. Nevertheless, Hewson et al. (2003: 53) insist that:

> While this is an issue it is not specific to internet mediated research .... In our view, ensuring that a debriefing note is sent immediately after the study, which is clearly visible/accessible to participants, and which includes a contact address, is enough.

As is apparent then, the unique context of the internet as a means of mass communication generates some different questions for the researcher regarding how best to apply ethical principles and regulations. More often than not, however, ethical codes are not so much compromised as adapted and reformed. Indeed, in some instances, with rigour and creative imagination, internet-based research may be more ethically sound than some traditional 'face-to-face' methods.

Useful social research and social work related websites

There are a number of websites which are likely to help support a social work dissertation or research project, especially any literature-based searches. Some of the best include:

www.socscidiss.bham.ac.uk/s1.html: an excellent site that provides information on research methodology, methods, and all the key stages of any dissertation.

www.radstat.org.uk: the radical statistics group (Radstats) was established in 1975 and aims to critically assess and question the government and institutional representation of official statistics; especially for political purpose. The site is invaluable, providing free access to a journal and other resources, often with contributions from leading experts in a range of academic and practice-based fields.

http://www.lwbooks.co.uk/journals/soundings/contents.html: the *Soundings* journal offers critical analysis regarding many issues relating to social work and social policy research. Some articles are free to access.

http://scholar.google.co.uk/: his search engine is an excellent resource that will find and retrieve relevant articles and books which relate to any dissertation or research project. The more specific words searched for the better; although numerous individual searches may be instigated.

http://www.webofknowledge.com: the web of science database offers a search engine that is able to identify relevant articles which link to a specific topic.

http://www.scopus.com/home.url: This is the largest abstract and citation database of research literature and quality web sources and covers nearly 18,000 titles from more than 5,000 publishers.

http://www.socwork.net/: this site, which links to the *Social Work and Society* online Journal, deals specifically with critical research relating to social work and is free to access. This is an essential resource for students and practitioners.

http://www.socialworkfuture.org/: the social work action network (SWAN) is a collective of academics, alongside some students, practitioners, managers and service users within social work. The website offers articles, general information and provides a forum for critical and political debate, and principal members also have their own manifesto!

http://www.scie.org.uk/: the Social Care Institute for Excellence offers a database of social care related articles, books and other publications that link to social work and social care. The site also contains films and other helpful learning material yet is a government initiative that is strongly influenced by the politically conservative 'what works' agenda and evidenced-based practice. Some of the material, such as the films, should, therefore, be treated with a healthy degree of critical scepticism.

www.communitycare.co.uk: the weekly social care magazine has its own website which is continuously updated and includes weekly articles. It also has an archive article search section which is extremely useful for researchers.

http://www.jiscmail.ac.uk: intends to 'facilitate knowledge sharing within the UK-centred academic community'. Resources include forums for discussion (including social work and social welfare).

www.vts.rdn.ac.uk: among other facilities, the virtual training suite offers advice on social work resources and free online tutorials for undertaking research in different subject areas.

www.vts.intute.ac.uk/he/tutorial/social-worker: part of the Virtual Training Suite, this site includes forums for discussion around social work related issues. This is also a possible site to gain access to participants for empirical research.

www.sosig.ac.uk: offers a comprehensive and precise search engine in specialist subjects, including social policy and social work.

www.bubl.ac.uk: a wide catalogue of academic links and resources is on offer, including a section dedicated to social work research.

www.loc.gov/: the American Library of Congress claims to be the largest library in the World. Among other resources, this site offers a powerful search engine that scours books and manuscripts published in every country in the World.

www.bl.uk/: the British Library website boasts a catalogue of over 13 million books and 920,000 journal and newspaper titles. This is particularly useful for gaining access to obscure or out-of-date publications.

www.ilo.org: the International Labour Organisation is a tripartite United Nations agency that 'brings together governments, employers and workers ... to promote decent work throughout the world'. Among other things, this site offers annual reports and working papers related to work, industry and employment.

http://europa.eu.int/comm/eurostat/: the main gateway to statistical data regarding the European Union; it also accommodates policy and legislation. May be of particular use if engaging in a comparative study of two European countries.

www.data-archive.ac.uk/: again, this site offers a rich source of statistical information across Europe and also provides other resources, such as online learning and teaching programmes.

www.essex.ac.uk/qualidata/index.htm: this site – based at Essex University – offers a richsource of primary data gathered from qualitative social research undertaken over the years. Potentially, some of this data could be used to undertake secondary analysis as part of a social work dissertation.

www.mimas.ac.uk: this site, which is based at the University of Manchester, provides data and information resources 'to support teaching, learning and research across a wide range of disciplines'. It also provides staff contact details for help and assistance.

http://qb.soc.surrey.ac.uk/: the question bank is an information resource geared towards quantitative research and questionnaire surveys and structures. The guidelines and examples from prior questionnaire designs can offer extremely useful pointers to designing your qualitative research questionnaire and may also be a good guide for appropriate interview questions. A number of topics related to social work research are covered.

www.natcen.ac.uk/: the National Centre for Social Research is the 'largest independent social research Institute in Britain', which carries out and 'analyse[s] research studies in the fields of social and public policy'. This site is excellent for examples of qualitative methodology that link to social work.

www.publist.com/: this site offers a database of over 150,000 magazines, journals, newsletters and other periodicals.

www.lse.ac.uk/IBSS/: the International Bibliography of the Social Sciences offers access to articles, papers, abstracts, books and reviews, and also offers tips for using the site for dissertations and an online thesaurus, among other resources.

www.oclc.org/firstsearch/: among other services, this site offers access to multidisciplinary databases.

www.lib.gla.ac.uk: Proceedings First is based at Glasgow University and offers access to e-journals, newspapers, exam papers, etc.

(adapted from Carey, 2009; Menabney, 2003)

Conclusion

This chapter has explored some of the methods used as part of internet-mediated research. It has proposed that the internet offers great potential for qualitative social work research. In particular, access to difficult-to-reach social groups, the overcoming of traditional barriers regarding time and place and the saving of time and money all remain notable advances gained through this new technology. Despite this, there are also potential hazards attached to the use of this ever-changing technology, the majority of which are either practical or ethical. Although saving time and money, extra care is required to ensure that factors such as the safety of participants and the security of information are not compromised.

Further reading

Fink, A. (2005). *Conducting Research Literature Reviews – From the Internet to Paper*. London, Sage

Gaiser, T.J. and Schreiner, A.E. (2009). *A Guide to Conducting On-Line Research*. London, Sage

Hewson, C., Yule, P., Laurent, D., and Vogel, C. (2003). *Internet Research Methods: A Practical Guide for the Social and Behavioural Sciences*. London, Sage

Hine, C. (2005). *Virtual Methods: Issues in Social Research on the Internet*. London, Berg

O Dochartaigh, N. (2001). *The Internet Research Handbook: An Introductory Guide for the Social Sciences*. London, Sage

Spence, G. (2001). *A Simple Guide to Internet Research*. Harlow, Prentice Hall

Part 3

Analysis, Writing and Dissemination

The second part of the book looks at some of the principal methodologies and methods used as part of any qualitative research project. As detailed earlier, methodology can be viewed as a 'recipe' that guides and holds together our project. It may be theoretically informed or instead might be driven by clear plans based around a research question or problem and objectives. Methods are techniques which are held within the walls of a methodology, and are represented by skills, tasks and procedures that help us to gather information and data so to address our research question or problem. In this part of the book we present different research methodologies and methods. Importantly, however, different methodologies or methods can link or overlap. For example, interviews may also offer a form of case study research and ethnographic research can also contain interviews or case studies, etc. We now take a look closer at the variety of different methodologies and methods open to the qualitative social work researcher.

17 Analysis

Introduction

This chapter discusses analysis, which in qualitative research is a significant skill that is employed from an early stage of any project. We take a look at some of the *general* forms of qualitative analysis, including some of the skills and tasks that are applied. It will be shown that there are different ways to undertake analysis, and present some of the general rules or guidelines intended to assist this process. We also then look in more detail at specific forms of qualitative analysis: including thematic, comparative, and documentary analysis. Finally, we then look at possible alternatives to more traditional methods.

Qualitative Analysis

As part of analysis, the researcher is essentially attempting to better *explain* and *understand* their findings, and also extract *meaning*. Blaxter et al. (1996: 185), for example, identify four inter-related tasks which remain at the heart of qualitative analysis. They include:

- *Understanding*: our 'perception of the meaning of something'.
- *Explanation*: statements that clarify and help explain 'why things are the way they are'.
- *Concepts*: abstract or general ideas that help determine how we consider and critically assess subjects or ideas.
- *Theories*: suppositions that seek or help to explain something.

In general, we seek to encourage understanding of our topic through explanation and with the support of concepts and theories. The researcher looks for patterns or trends following interviews with their participants or their overview of relevant literature and from these practices they seek better understanding and explanation with a view to eventually building concepts and theories that reflect their data.

Qualitative research is also recognised as being distinct from quantitative methods regarding the process of analysis. The important difference remains that with quantitative approaches data has to be collected before analysis can begin. In contrast, qualitative research is less straightforward and is more nuanced. Analysis tends to be *ongoing* and takes place *alongside* data collection: the task is also likely to change in response to data collection. In effect, data collection and analysis intertwine with one another. Finally, in practice qualitative research is usually subjective and personal, reflecting the emotional engagement, prior experiences and different perceptions of individual researchers who not unusually differ in their interpretations and understanding of any research findings.

Qualitative analysis within social work tends to demand that the researcher thinks 'creatively and conceptually' and is able to place *into context* what has been discovered (Padgett, 1998: 72). Meaning and understanding emerge and grow during analysis, such as following the identification of trends, patterns or general occurrences in research findings and then comparing these to other people's research. Qualitative analysis draws from a variety of source material but commonly finds and explores data in people's use of words and language. We also study people's behavior, such as through ethnography or during interviews, and, of course, analysis takes place during our literature search. Also for a literature based project we tend to be looking for nuanced details, patterns or trends that emerge from other peoples findings. Partly because of the ambivalent and disparate nature of language (and behaviour or experience), analysis is not exact, precise or 'scientific'. We are instead looking to analyse themes, trends and issues and draw conclusions that can be presented as part of a thesis; yet we are often trying to make sense of findings that may appear raw or uncertain or unclear to begin with (such as following a long interview or after reading a complex series of academic papers).

Analysis at its most basic level will typically begin with transcribing interviews and then reading and re-reading our transcripts to look for emerging trends, especially those that link to our research question and objectives. We might also scour notes taken from a focus group meeting or in relation to literature we read and again note trends, regular occurrences, themes, patterns, etc., that emerge from our reading. From any such trends (such as a number of informal carers repeatedly discussing their financial difficulties) we may then decide to create 'codes' that reflect chunks of conversation from the transcripts, notes or reading which can represent the key findings from our study. Following the further gathering of data, codes may 'wither away' reflecting a lack of importance, or merge into others (two or more collapse into one) or alternatively may be split to create two or more codes. Each established code is then allocated a representative number or letter, and eventually codes that occur often enough emerge as a 'research theme' that helps us to answer or better understand our initial research question. We can, of course, avoid the use of codes and instead look for general occurrences, themes and trends from available data or literature as it emerges.

The range of activities that can be understood as offering types of analysis may include to:

- interpret
- discover patterns
- generate themes
- summarise
- portray
- describe
- understand individuals and/or groups (and related norms, patterns, etc.)
- raise issues
- prove or demonstrate
- explain and seek causality
- explore or test
- discover commonalities, differences and similarities
- examine the application and operation of the same issues in different contexts.

There are also different scales of qualitative analysis. In particular, there are types which are highly qualitative and which rely upon on-going intuition and reflexivity rather than measurement, counting or codes. For example, the researcher may carefully consider their findings from one or two interviews, and subsequently refine their research aims or decide to alter their method. At the other end of the spectrum remains analysis that is more through or partially scientific and which will stress the use of careful procedures, codes and possibly computer packages. A notable example of this approach remains content analysis (discussed further below). A position between both extremes – in which both reflexivity and codes are drawn upon – remains with approaches such as discourse or conversation analysis.

Although qualitative analysis may never be truly 'scientific', and will always accommodate 'diverse pursuits and methods' (because of the wide range of social trends and patterns that are dealt with), some researchers have provided suggestions for more elaborate rules to follow. For example, Bromley (1986: 26) provides a list of stages to adhere to when undertaking qualitative analysis. In order, these include:

- Stating clearly the research question or problem.
- Collecting background information in order to better understand the context, concepts and theories that relate to the question/problem (literature review).

- Identifying different answers, interpretations or responses to the research question or issues from past studies/evidence.
- Using this past evidence to influence your own research strategy in your attempt to answer the research question/problem.
- Continuing to look for further evidence and gradually eliminating interpretations that lack relevance.
- Carefully examining data and new evidence(from interviews or other studies and literature) for accuracy and consistency.
- Carefully checking the logic and validity of any arguments that are built from data and which are used to construct a thesis.
- If more than one case can be made from findings or interpretations, choosing the strongest case which will be represented as part of any thesis.
- Preparing the final report based on the findings.

Miles and Huberman (1994: 9) again suggest processes to follow as part of ideal forms of qualitative analysis. These will include:

- identifying similar *phrases* or *relationships* between topic-related patterns and themes or distinct *differences* and common *trends* within research data;
- gradually constructing a small set of *generalisations* that cover the *consistencies* recognised in the data;
- confronting such generalisations with a formalised body of knowledge in the form of *theories, constructs* or *models.*

As part of this inductive process (content analysis), there is also a continued attempt to *manage* and *reduce* data (Miles and Huberman, 1994). In most cases, data reduction continues from an early stage, whereby 'the potential universe of data is reduced in an anticipatory way as the researcher chooses a conceptual framework, research questions, cases, and instruments'. Then, once 'field notes, interviews, tapes, or other data are available', we continue to collect and to reduce data and create 'data summaries, coding, finding themes, clustering, and writing stories' (Marvasti, 2004: 89). More often than not, far more data (or other information from literary sources) is collected than can be analysed in a final write-up. As a consequence, the researcher will continue to refine their research question and reduce their data whilst also excavating and 'pulling out' key themes: in particular, those that directly link with the research question or issue(s) being explored. Again, initial 'codes' from transcripts may be revised, such as because they have lost their significance or we decide to merge several codes into one or split one to create two.

As well as identifying trends or themes, the unpacking of research findings also represents an important aspect of analysis. This can include methods such as attaching meanings to new data, evaluating or assessing it, critically engaging with such findings, or trying to understand and culturally or politically locate identified patterns. This may also include a capacity to articulate and relate your findings to social work theory, historical trends, and policy or practice. Not unusually, an established theory may be criticised and revised following analysis, or new recommendations may be made regarding how policy or practice might be improved. For example, you may feel, following interviews with social work practitioners working with children, that systems theory does not adequately explain family dynamics within their role, based on the new information that you have gained. This is all part of the process of drawing conclusions from research findings. Here, the researcher seeks to create *meaningful statements* that draw from their data (observations, transcripts, notes, etc.) and related findings (Marvasti, 2004: 88–90). Below, in Table 17.1, is an example of meaningful statements drawn from some collected data.

Table 17.1   Codes and meaningful statements drawn from interview data with a social work practitioner

Statement from interviewee(data)	Meaningful statement (codes)
…I didn't wish to upset her but she just kept pestering me and asking the same questions time and time again. I had no choice but to answer in the most direct way that I could. It was only afterwards that I realised that this was not a good way to respond to the situation.	Sincere and emotional regret for unplanned verbal response to informal carer requests
I apologised that no more could be done for her daughter and made it quite clear that in future I would argue the case for more support than what is currently provided. I have always argued the case for my most needy 'clients' and will continue to do so.	Apology and insistence on practising altruistically despite extenuating difficulties

(Adapted from Marvasti, 2004: 88; Carey, 2009)

The next key stage relates to how any data might be displayed. Typically, qualitative data for a social work dissertation will be represented by textual information – such as verbal quotes from a practitioner interviewed or written observational notes made by the researcher when in the field or during reading. This will normally need to be highlighted, reduced and then organised – such as within a file of written notes – so as to make it easier to access and understand.

There are again no concrete or scientific formats for this process, and most will be influenced by your own interpretation, findings and objectives. Analysis is a means by which to locate, gather, manage, reduce, display and evaluate data and general findings which will then be utilised to draw conclusions, which may include a discussion of their relationship to service user need, theory, policy or legislation.

Boundaries are often blurred within most if not all forms of qualitative analysis: this is because of the unpredictable and diverse nature of qualitative data itself, as well as the movement back and forth between different research stages, which includes a 'repetitive interplay between the collection and analysis of data'. This is commonly known as an 'iterative' approach, in which cyclical movements back and forth between research stages leads to the development of ideas, and the transcending of raw information or data.

We shall now look at two core examples of analysis, thematic and comparative analysis, before exploring documentary approaches.

Thematic analysis

Thematic analysis focuses on identifying themes and patterns regarding individual or, more often, group attitudes, behaviour or values. This approach looks to again combine data collection and analysis together. The essence of the approach is to collect data and then allow patterns of experience/attitudes to emerge from this new data. We then seek to combine and catalogue patterns to create themes or sub-themes, most often specific sections drawn from extracts of conversation by interviewees that relate directly to our research question and objectives.

Themes may be represented by recurring actions undertaken by participants or common values or unusual practices or how types of relationships form between social workers and service users or carers, etc. They emerge and develop from the patterns of experience/attitudes identified at an earlier stage during interviews or the reading of transcriptions, etc. Themes are then collected together and used as evidence to support or adapt your thesis. You can, of course, adapt this approach and introduce a number of codes or simply concentrate upon one or two key themes.

Aronson (1994) offers a clear and brief summary of the core stages followed within thematic analysis. Six processes are followed, and each is adapted to social work research below:

1. *Collect data*: such as from interviews, focus group meetings, and so on.
2. *Transcribe conversations*: a written record of any conversations, full transcripts are common yet a selective transcript will suffice for many projects.
3. *Identify themes from patterns within the transcriptions*: this may include research participants' experiences or opinions, etc. May include fragments of ideas or experiences that otherwise might appear meaningless if viewed alone.
4. *We then 'pieced together' our themes to create a 'comprehensive picture of ... [participants'] collective experience'*: The researcher can identify themes as an interview progresses and then decide to adapt some questions to explore each further.
5. *Build a valid argument for developing any themes, such as by using each 'to develop a storyline'*: This involves reading relevant literature and formulating thematic statements that link to our findings.
6. *Apply findings to practice*: Here we may relate our findings to social work practices or aspects of policy, legislation, etc., as part of analysis.

As part of participation research (chapter sixteen), it is possible to ask research participants to be involved in thematic analysis, such as by asking them if they agree with the chosen themes and conclusions drawn. As noted earlier in chapter sixteen, we may choose to use pictures or symbols to illustrate in a clear form what we mean, assuming that participants have had only limited training in research methods. Before writing up, you will need to be able to justify your choice of themes and related conclusions: this may be supported by 'evidence' drawn from the viewpoints of participants and past relevant empirical studies drawn from the literature. Thematic analysis can be applied to topics that involve either empirical research or documentary research. It represents a core technique and one that is the most popular in qualitative forms of research (Carey, 2009). Not unusually, it can also be used alongside our next approach, that of comparative analysis.

Comparative analysis

Comparative analysis involves the researcher assessing, evaluating and contextualising the contrast, differences and similarities between two or more theories, types of practice, support services, user needs or social policies, and so on. Comparative analysis may also be used alongside thematic analysis, such as if comparing the outcomes and findings of two or more separate interviews. In general, if compared with another single theory, practice, or interview, etc., each will typically be viewed as a 'case' with its own characteristics. Analysis of cases will seek to:

- *Be clear regarding what it is that is being compared and why.* For what reason(s) are two or more cases being compared, how does this link to your research objectives and how might each case be compared?
- *Identify one or more themes upon which comparison will be based.* This may include a problem, theory or specific area of interest to the researcher. Any identified theme(s) should hold together a thesis and provide a focal point for discussion and analysis.
- *Begin to arrange a thesis that relates to the cases explored.* What is the relationship between each case and is there a clear theory or set of arguments that link? A unifying thesis should help to avoid the risk of *separation* between cases within analysis.
- *Provide basic details regarding each case but avoid merely describing any cases.* The reader will also need to be made aware of background information relating to each case so that any analysis which then takes place is better understood.
- *Explore similarities and/or differences relating to each case.* By its very nature, comparison should stimulate us to consider links and parallel attributes or differences and disparities regarding each case. Potentially, this task can be exhaustive so try to narrow the focus as comparison proceeds.
- *Aim for firm conclusions and recommendations relating to the findings.* Have we learnt anything specific from the comparison and how might findings assist our understanding of each related case?

In addition, there are alternatives ways to apply a comparative analysis. For example, Walk (1998: 1) discusses the benefits of a 'lens' or 'keyhole' comparison. Here the method of comparing two cases equally is replaced by an attempt to place greater emphasis upon one above the other. That is, 'weight A less heavily than B' whilst also 'us[ing] A as a lens through which to view B'. Essentially, one case is presented and used to explore another in more detail and depth. Overall, many types of comparative analysis will proceed *point-by-point,* in which a different issue relating to each case is discussed and analysed, followed by the next (Carey, 2009).

Case study: Comparative analysis of privatisation policy within social work in England and Canada

Carey (2008) relied upon published accounts that looked at the influence of privatisation within social work policy in both England and Canada. By looking at two different systems of organising welfare, and countries with distinct localities, histories and demographic trends, he was able Case study: Comparative analysis of privatisation policy within social work in England and Canada
Carey (2008) relied upon published accounts that looked at the influence of privatisation within social work policy in both England and Canada. By looking at two different systems of organising welfare, and countries with distinct localities, histories and demographic trends, he was able to better understand how the now extensive and increasingly 'global' process of privatisation works.

For example, Canadian provinces with their own distinct powers developed a welfare state relatively late in the 1970s. This tended to be less idealistic than the English (and British) version and also relied heavily upon a culture of volunteering. The English welfare state which developed in the latter half of the 1940s relied extensively upon the state sector yet also proceeded to embrace marketisation and privatisation from the 1980s onwards, most prominently and aggressively within social work. The extent and speed of this process caused considerable structural problems for local authorities and also, therefore, for service users, informal carers and practitioners.

By looking at a case example of radical policy initiatives (England) and a more subtle process of reform (Canadian provinces), Carey was able to use comparative analysis to better understand both the development of the privatisation policy initiative and its direct impact upon service users or practitioners as 'subjects'.

Documentary analysis

Documentary Analysis (DA) is now increasingly popular due not least to greater access now being gained to documents previously inaccessible or unavailable. This is largely thanks to new technology, such as the internet. Whittaker (2009: 77), however, notes that some students can confuse a more common literature review with documentary analysis (DA) and provides us with a useful distinction:

A literature review is a critical summary of what other researchers have found, i.e., *their* analysis of *their* data. So, in your literature review, you are reporting what other people have found. A documentary analysis is *your* analysis of *your own data* in which you are reporting what you have found.

Silverman (2005: 160) highlights how qualitative researchers seek to analyse small numbers of texts and documents to understand categories and 'the process through which texts depict "reality" than with whether such texts contain true or false statements'. We first need to decide what we mean by a document. Documents can include newspapers, reports, minutes of meetings, books and even photographs or television programmes, among others. Whittaker (2009: 76) adds that documents 'are central to the everyday realities of working in the health and social care field and serve many purposes'. Such social work related documents include official reports, assessment documentation, diary or contact forms, court reports and policy related legislation, among others. More often however we are likely to use secondary sources not constructed by ourselves but which already exist. These sources are interrogated and drawn upon to gain knowledge and insight into the phenomenon under study. Style of writing or specific forms of expression may subsequently be scrutinised for meaning and context. In essence documents replace the traditional interview or observation as the researcher's source of datum.

Many documents also contain significant amounts of rhetoric or implicit meaning – or may draw from limited or suspect evidence to make rather strong claims. In the tradition of critical discourse analysis, discussed earlier in chapter fourteen, it is such nuances and implicit meanings or power dynamics that are often the interest of the documentary analyst. We may decide to look at the context (i.e. historical, political) at which the document(s) were created, by whom and in accordance with what conventions, and what remains the purpose or implications of the document(s), and how were they received within social work? Some or all of these questions are likely to generate enough material to sustain a dissertation or small project.

Whittaker (2009: 79–85) outlines three stages to DA, which include:

- *Deciding your research question and designing your research*: often content or thematic analysis is used to scrutinise a sample of documents. The research question is likely to change and become more focused as more documents are read and evaluated.
- *Deciding which documents to analyse and what to include in your sample*: an inclusion criterion allows the researcher to find a 'sample' of documents with which to undertake analysis. Might you use a sample of newspapers from a specific year or perhaps specific papers or articles relating to your topic? You will need to be careful that you do not select too many documents which may make the task in hand unrealistic.

- *Collecting and analysing your data*: This is the crux of the approach and you will need to think carefully about factors such as what will be used as a unit of analysis (or code). Will specific words, phrases or whole articles be evaluated? Might you analyse the emotions expressed (optimistic, damning, uncertain, etc.) within a series of texts that address a specific topic, such as neglect, poverty or safeguarding? Or instead the political perspectives or models of disability supported or criticised in specific journals. You may then create a 'recording sheet' or diary to detail your analysis of identified codes. The types of theme that analysts typically look for include *frequency* (of words, phrases, etc.), *context* (for example, how were words used and what meaning did they transmit), *prominence* (for example, how often did words or phrases appear in articles and where) and *intensity* (or how powerful was the message, etc.). Data is then evaluated and used to present your findings within a thesis or report. You may wish to ask towards the end of the analysis if the statements and conclusions of any authors remain credible or not.

Alongside these stages there are a range of skills which fit within the remit of DA. These include looking within documents for:

- *why* the document was produced and whether this could have influenced any content and findings;
- how convincing are the arguments?;
- assessing any underlying assumptions and arguments presented;
- possible inconsistencies or paradoxes held within a debate or thesis;
- types of possible bias;
- any personal interests that may be held by the author(s) and which may have influenced the findings;
- any notable strengths and weaknesses of the document, such as those relating to the methodology, general arguments, conclusions, etc.;
- whether the findings contrast with your own experience and views;
- the circumstances under which the document emerged and what impact this may have had on the content;
- who the document was produced *by* and *for*, and how this might have affected the subject-matter and stance of the author(s);
- whether there is sufficient evidence provided to support the claims;
- how the findings compare to or differ from arguments presented by other authors and research.

Deciding which tasks fit with your objectives and then investigating each – especially those that link to your initial research question – will help to extend the process of DA. Taylor (1989, cited in Blaxter et al., 1996: 217–18) also draws attention to the most common responses to published documentation within a critical tradition. They include one or more of the following:

- defending or confirming a particular view;
- revising a personal stance in the face of new evidence or arguments;
- criticising yet reformulating a particular view in order to improve the argument;
- dismissing arguments due to 'inadequacy, irrelevance, incoherence or by recourse to other appropriate criteria';
- reconciling two positions and proposing a compromise;
- proposing something different and original.

There remains a wealth of possible topics within social work that can be drawn upon from a DA perspective. For example, you may wish to analyse legislation or policy-related documentation regarding social care or more generally professional social work practice, scrutinise critically academic literature, such as regarding the relevance or otherwise of a particular theory, evaluate prior empirical research regarding specific outcomes, or compare official rhetorical claims with empirical findings in government publications, and so on. The internet now also offers a cheap and reliable gateway to so much documentation, including government reports, official statistics, the reports of charities, and so on.

Some additional types of analysis

Although much emphasis within qualitative social work research is placed upon emergent themes, comparison and codes, there also remain alternative approaches to draw upon, present or utilise alongside these traditional techniques and cultures. You may, for example, feel that your findings are not best represented by themes or comparisons, or may indeed have found that an original plan to use code-centred research has not been possible. At another extreme, some traditional anthropologists or postmodernists claim that formal research method training, and subsequent rational approaches, take away some of the mystique of the field or more generally research. We instead need to immerse ourselves in an organisation or sub-culture to truly understand it from the inside (such as through ethnographic analysis). Also if we prioritise meaning and understanding, and have an altruistic recourse to critical engagement (chapter four), surely that is enough? We don't after all wish to make research mechanical or tedious. This may be a valid attitude for your research or dissertation, but, if not, possible alternatives to use alone or alongside traditional approaches exist. Indeed there is now extensive choice regarding how to analyse qualitative data. Among others these can include:

Organisation charts   such diagrams can be used to display the relationship between different types of variables, data or people and relationships. For example, the hierarchies of status or role within a hospital and how social workers or patients fit into this matrix. A diagram might be used to create a discussion that draws upon supporting literature and your own experiences or interviews.

Flow charts   these tend to explore and represent processes or procedures and may be used to examine and gain a better understanding of research concepts. For example, a study and representation of the assessment processes followed by employees in a social work organisation, and the different people that might be drawn into this formal ritual.

Tree diagrams   such as a 'dendrogram' or 'taxonomy' aims to depict the relationships and links that hold together different parts or elements and might be used to better understand concepts, people, family networks or the workings of groups. Such a diagram depicts the roots and branches of relations and networks.

Cognitive maps   this approach looks more at the world from an individual's point of view and in particular their way of thinking about something that is important to them or different ways that they behave. Among other options this may be useful in examining some casework, represent a life history or present comparisons of different people, such as a small group of advocacy workers.

There are also four general skills which can be identified within qualitative analysis for social work. Briefly, they include:

Context   The placing of research findings *into context* represents a core component of any research project. Here we locate arguments, raise points, state and unpack issues addressed, etc., especially regarding attendant priorities. To contextualise means to place an argument, point raised, interview theme, etc., into perspective by evaluating it from a historical, political or social and cultural perspective. Context also draws upon comparison or to contrast different experiences, attitudes, forms of organisation, theories, and so on.

Use of theory   Theoretical stances help to avoid pure description and encourage the researcher to critically understand their findings, rather than passively accept information without careful consideration (Holloway and Jefferson, 2000). It also helps to provide a *framework* around which to support our research. Potentially, there are dangers inherent in any over-reliance upon established theory. These include that such theory may limit any analysis by encouraging a restricted view of any findings (Holloway and Todres, 2003).

Reflexivity　this remains a core skill used by many qualitative researchers. Reflexivity is critical engagement and personal introspection through which the impact of any preconceived or culturally defined beliefs, values and possible prejudices are identified, considered and confronted by the researcher. The researcher may also contemplate how the research process may impact upon any findings, results or conclusions.

Critique　this approach seeks to question normative practices and values. For example, if a care home or set of practices is identified as not meeting the needs of its users, then critical analysis may include an attempt to understand and explain this outcome, as well as suggest possible new ways in which such needs might be better met. Recommendations regarding how we might move to more ethical practices, and towards ideal outcomes for participants who engage with our research, may also represent an aspect of our analysis.

Since qualitative approaches have few set traditions or rules of analysis, there are potentially at least an even wider variety of alternative techniques to draw upon. For example, if undertaking a Master degree in social work, you may wish to utilise or adapt an approach more commonly used in your first degree. This might be developed alongside your tutor.

Summarising analysis for social work

To summarise, the most common approaches typically involved in analysis for any social work project will include an ability to engage with many of the following processes:

- unpack, investigate and present arguments and debates linked to an individual topic (such as those proposed by academics, policy makers, advocacy groups, practitioners, etc.) and related themes;
- identify, decipher and critically engage with emergent themes, tendencies, processes and issues embedded within a chosen area of researchreduce, distil and refine your data;

- present data and other findings as meaningful statements;
- scrutinise meaningful statements and draw conclusions;
- construct codes and consider each carefully to eventually dismiss, extend their significance or increase their number based upon personal analysis;
- compare and contrast differing viewpoints and arguments;
- question and critically assess dominant and 'taken for granted' assumptions, values, and practices, such as those presented by policymakers, legal discourse, organisational routines, or research participants themselves;
- develop or reform a theoretical framework(s) or model(s) that relates to a research topic and which may be applied to theory, policy or a form of social work practice;
- construct diagrams, taxonomies or maps to represent and discuss findings.

Conclusion

This chapter has detailed qualitative analysis. It has been shown that there are many different types of qualitative analysis but all share some similar attributes. Analysis is distinct in qualitative approaches because it emerges early – typically alongside the collection of data and information – and also encourages the researcher to 'move backwards and forwards' between the stages of any research process. Specific types of analysis may be used for qualitative social work research, including content, thematic, comparative or alternative approaches. In general, there are attempts made to unearth and locate relevant themes and critically engage with each to extend meaning and understanding.

Further reading

Boeije, H. (2009) *Analysis in Qualitative Research* London, Sage

Bryman, A. (2004). *Social Research Methods.* Oxford, Oxford University Press. Chapter 19: Qualitative Data Analysis

Ezzy, D, (2002) *Qualitative Analysis: Practice and Innovation* London, Routledge.

Marvasti, A.B. (2004). *Qualitative Research in Sociology.* London, Sage. Chapter 5 – Data Analysis

Padgett, D.K. (1998). *Qualitative Methods in Social Work Research – Challenges and Rewards*. London, Sage. Chapter 7: Data Management and Analysis

Ramazanoglu, C., and Holland, J. (2002). *Feminist Methodology: Challenges and Choices*. Sage, London. Chapter 8: Choices and Decisions: Doing a Feminist Research Project

Wertz, F.J., Charmaz, K, McMullen, L.M., and Josselson, R. (2011) *Five Ways of Doing Qualitative Analysis: Phenomenological Psychology, Grounded Theory, Discourse Analysis, Narrative Research and Intuitive Inquiry* London, Guilford Press

18 Writing Up and Dissemination

Introduction

This chapter looks at the process of writing for a report or dissertation. The chapter considers when to begin writing and the different writing styles and structures.

This includes differences in structure between a literature-based and an empirical dissertation. There are also suggestions made on how to revise and improve the content and presentation of any final document. Finally, ways in which research findings might be disseminated are also presented.

Writing Up

As with analysis, writing should begin early in a research project. For example, sections including the literature review and methodology can be completed in draft form relatively early on. Other tasks, such as data collection, demand that writing remains a key part of both the collection and analysis of data. Some research methods also demand periods of writing throughout. For example, much ethnographic fieldwork will include the researcher keeping a diary of their observations and findings.

There are clear advantages to beginning the task of writing as early as possible. Most notably these include avoiding any need to write up a long report or dissertation in a relatively brief time towards the end. Inevitably, anxiety and stress all remain possible symptoms of starting to write up late, and also beginning early is likely to increase the quality of the final document since you will have more time to complete and reflect on the work. Any final report may also be the only outcome of your research that most other people view, so making plans and a general strategy for this important document again makes sense.

Perhaps most importantly, however, starting early offers an opportunity to develop and enhance any writing skills, since like many things in life writing improves with practice. Qualitative research writing and data analysis are inevitably linked and there are risks in leaving the core of writing to the end of your project. Regular writing will help us to remain focused and also stay on track, in particular to maintain a good link between what we are doing and our initial and/or changing research objectives.

For a literature-based project or dissertation, writing progresses as you further your reading, and key ideas and themes begin to emerge and develop. Again, starting as early as possible will nearly always improve the quality (and grade if it is a dissertation or long essay). Another option that this approach permits is to be able to show this initial work to a tutor, colleague or friend for critical feedback. Writing for most research tends to also be a cyclical process, with the researcher drafting a chapter and then moving to another activity such as interviewing or reading and then returning to redraft the original version. This iterative journey back and forth occurs due to the impact of new findings or further reading and reflection and can also support and promote analysis (Carey, 2009).

Finally, we also need to think carefully about research ethics prior to beginning any final report or dissertation. All of the points discussed in chapter eight will need to be considered carefully, such as the importance of confidentiality, anonymity, safety, and so forth. For example, it is rarely wise or indeed safe to name any participants interviewed as part of a project, and indeed the use of pseudonyms tends to be widespread in qualitative research writing, especially when difficult or sensitive topics are explored or discussed. We also need to think carefully about the use of direct quotes: for example. is it appropriate or fair to present a statement from a participant made during an intimate interview? Again, if uncertain you should seek further advice from a tutor or senior member of staff or call a relevant number (through, for example, the Social Care Institute for Excellence in the UK).

Style

Writing styles tend to differ according to personality, approach, flair, style, the topic being explored, whether the research is empirical or literature based and also the nature of any findings. Despite differences and a lack of rigid formats for writing within qualitative research, there are general guidelines regarding style. For example, focus and clarity are typically appreciated by readers, as is engagement with the material being presented. For dissertations, examiners and supervisors will nearly always prioritise precision, detail, rigour, and coherence with academic work, as well as use of appropriate reference to other people's work and originality. Academic writing styles need to aim to be detached and passive and it is advisable to avoid strongly opinionated, polemical (and usually highly subjective) stances or rants. Over-complex ideas or convoluted sentence structures are also best avoided unless perhaps this has shown to be rewarding in the past. Nevertheless, deliberately complex or convoluted arguments and ideas may appear confusing and annoying to the reader, and for some, at least, suggest a lack of creativity and ideas. We may look at samples of writing styles within previously published qualitative literature, including in journals, books or previous reports or dissertations (Carey, 2009).

Despite the lack of standardisation, Padgett (2008: 210–11) still notes the distinct 'rhetorical devices' embodied within qualitative research. These include a tendency to:

- debunk or refute cherished notions, such as stereotypes and outdated beliefs;
- probe beneath carefully constructed facades and come up with findings that challenge the status quo;
- give a voice to excluded people;
- articulate emotions and often express passion through our writing (within reason);
- take risks and be open minded about saying something different.

Dawson (2007: 132–4) offers a more sober stance and highlights that students on taught courses should always check the 'strict rules and guidelines' regarding dissertations or long essays, such as may be available in module or dissertation handbooks. Universities, colleges and tutors also typically provide clear guidelines regarding essential criteria, such as referencing, style and presentation. Again, if available, it is also worth looking at some previous dissertations in the library to see how relevant work has been structured and presented. Always remember, however, that your own style is likely to come through and there's little point in trying to precisely emulate other people's styles: it may simply have some influence and improve the quality, if only a little. The same rules apply for research reports, including those presented on relevant websites (government, voluntary sector such as the Joseph Rowntree Foundation or Mind, etc.). More generally, for writing Dawson (ibid.: 134–5) also stresses consideration for the audience. In particular:

- What styles would your audience prefer? Should language used present 'complex terminology' or be kept simple?

- Will the audience understand complex statistics or should you 'keep it simple'?
- Might the audience only be interested in conclusions and recommendations (unlikely for academic material but possible for some reports)?
- Do you need to carefully consider the methodology?

Regarding style, most reports and dissertations should *use the third person* (avoiding the use of 'I', 'my', and 'we') wherever possible and *write in the past tense*. The example below is written in the first person and present tense:

I was a little surprised to have just found out in my research that many men living in residential care prefer having more time to spend with their social worker. I have also just discovered through my interviews that ….

The example below is written in the more appropriate third person and past tense style:

The research findings suggest that men in residential care prefer having more time to spend in the company of their social worker. It was also discovered that….

There should also be a coherent 'flow' to arguments and debate with the presentation of any findings. Arguments or themes should proceed one after another and each argument – or author's work cited – should be adequately explored and unpacked. Critical engagement with previous related research is essential within qualitative research and should be sustained, especially in key sections such as the literature review or findings and 'discussion' stage. Often this will mean trying to avoid passively agreeing with each other author – an outcome that seems unlikely with the wide range of conflicting opinions held within most publications and debates. Denscombe (2007: 318) suggests the importance of:

- *Being selective about what is included and presented in the final document.*
- *Avoiding bias but at the same time trying to be positive about your findings.*
- *Recognising the impact of your own norms and values upon any research.*

Taylor (1989) also provides possible responses to academic material on behalf of researchers that may include:

- Agreeing with or confirming a stance.
- Accepting many of the argument(s) presented by author(s) but suggesting additional points and/or disagreeing with some issues raised.

- Revising a general point of view and thereby improving the argument(s), ideally with a rationale for any such revision.
- Dismissing argument(s) or a thesis and underlining the weaknesses inherent in the work.
- Accepting much within two opposing ideas or theories but offering an alternative stance that accommodates the best aspects of both viewpoints.
- Acknowledging the weaknesses of your own research or arguments and identifying ways in which this may be revised.

There are also relatively common techniques used as part of academic writing styles. A relatively common stance is to encourage the reader to re-evaluate or *reconsider* an accepted belief or practice. If questioning traditional and established viewpoints, beliefs or practice, it is important to provide clear *evidence* to support any critical stances made. Such evidence may also come from your own empirical findings, alternative research sources or a combination of the two.

Structure

For the structure of a research dissertation or report there are usually six major sections that need to be covered in any dissertation or report. The questions you will need to address include:

1. *Explaining the purpose of the research*: for example, why did you undertake this piece of research and what was the research question or social problem being explored? What were your research aims and objectives and to what extent have these been achieved? Usually a brief and succinct section.
2. *Describing how the research was done*: for example, how did your research objectives guide your work? What research methods were applied as a consequence? Were there theoretical influences that influenced the research process? Did they help you analyse, understand and explain the findings? Again a brief and succinct section.
3. *Presenting the findings from the research*: the reader will be keen to know exactly what you have discovered. Although a core section, this is still likely to be a condensed version of your findings and will also need to be presented with at least some contrast to previous research findings relating to the topic. Perhaps inevitably this is a larger section of most reports and dissertations.

4. *Discussing and analysing the findings*: this will usually represent an attempt to contextualise your findings by comparing them with previous research and factors that might impact upon findings (historical influences, prior legislation, etc.). You will also be expected to critically extract meaning and ways by which such findings can be linked to social work practice. This section should be closely linked to the original research question. Again, this is a moderate-to-large section.

5. *Reaching conclusions:*_this section deals with questions such as what have you discovered and also learnt from the research that you have completed. Also, what improvements or revisions might be made regarding social work practice. This section will tend to be brief to moderate.

6. *Making recommendations*: how might your findings influence your future practice and might policy, legislation or general practices needs to be revised? What advice might you wish to give to the reader regarding practice or teaching relating to your topic? This is usually a relatively brief yet succinct section.

Although there remains an almost limitless number of ways to present research within a report or dissertation, there are still established and proven ways by which to structure research findings. We now look at a typical example for both a literature-based and an empirical piece of research. To begin with, literature-based reports or dissertations are often structured as follows:

Typical structure of a literature-based dissertation/report

Introduction   this is usually represented with a brief outline. The chapter introduces the reader to your topic of inquiry as well as some possible trends or recent legislation. The chapter offers a summary of initial information and also possibly reasons you may have had for choosing to research this topic. This chapter also offers an opportunity to 'sell' the research to the reader; especially why you believe it is important to current and future social work practice. This section is typically brief and succinct.

Methodology   this section explains to the reader what it is you have been trying to achieve, and *how* the information relating to the literature search on which your work is founded was *collected, processed* and *analysed*. For example, the reader may be presented with your research question and aims and objectives as well the methodology that you drew upon. For example, did you undertake a systematic review, and if so how did that develop? Did you also use any theory as part of your methodology and if so what were your main motives for this choice? This section is again typically brief and succinct.

Literature review   this is a crucial section of a literature-based report or dissertation. It presents your findings, including a summary of what other research has discovered and concluded. You can then compare your own findings and pull out and unpack any key themes that relate. As part of this process, you are also seeking to analyse evidence in relation to your research question and aims and objectives. This section should also seek to present any notable points of contention in other research and your findings. These sections are generally of a moderate to large size.

Analysis and discussion   Although analysis occurs throughout the write-up, there may be themes that require specific attention in this chapter. You may identify and unpack important themes from the previous literature review chapter(s) and perhaps also discuss unclear or ambiguous themes discovered. Although a discussion section is not compulsory, this can help to prioritise and better contextualise your core findings. This chapter will typically be a moderate size.

Conclusion and recommendations   this chapter will tie together and summarise your findings. It is also a good stage to make recommendations such as regarding future social work policy and/or practice. This chapter will often be brief and succinct.

In contrast a dissertation or report that draws upon empirical findings will normally be presented as follows (Carey, 2009).

Typical structure of an empirical dissertation/report

Introduction   again, this is a foreword with introductory information such as:

- A brief outline and introduction to the topic, including with some reference to other people's research.
- Some possible related trends or recent legislation.
- An opportunity to 'sell' the research to the reader; including why you believe it is important to current and future social work practice.
- This section may also be used to introduce the research question, including what is it that you are trying to find out and why?

Again, this section is typically brief and succinct.

Literature review this is typically briefer than a literature-based report simply because you have empirical findings to present. It is a briefer overview of your *background* research or sources of literature such as academic papers, text books, and relevant reports, etc., that link to a topic. Usually a literature review will begin with a wide gaze and then narrow in focus closer to a specific topic as it proceeds. There is an attempt to make the reader more:

- Aware of the range of opinions and debates relating to the topic you are presenting.
- Aware of key pertinent themes and issues that have been identified as linking to a research question.
- The literature review offers an opportunity to summarise your reading and research undertaken prior to empirical research and also allows you to reveal to the reader the key debates that link to later empirical research.

This section is normally of a moderate size.

Methodology this section is especially important because you are identifying, describing and trying to justify your methodology and subsequent methods utilised to collect and analyse data. You may also wish to present any theories which were part of your methodology. This section can also include reference to any problems encountered in collecting or analysing data. This chapter is brief but needs to be carefully presented and checked by a supervisor or peer.

Findings and analysis   in this section you will present exactly what it is you have discovered. This may include details of issues you explored, such as when participants have responded to and addressed questions during interviews. You may wish to present your findings in tables and graphs, but generally most findings are presented in written form for most qualitative research.

It is important to be detailed, succinct and selective when presenting core findings. Only material that connects with the research aims or objectives should generally be included. Try not to cram too much information into this chapter as an avalanche of findings may confound the reader. Try to decide what takes priority and think carefully about what to include and how this links to your research ambitions.

Overall, you are seeking to compare and contrast your findings with other research; looking at the theoretical implications of your data; considering your findings in relation to past or current social work practice or policy; or more generally contextualising what you have discovered regarding how it links with wider trends.

The presentation of analysis is also likely to present a summary of the results of one of the key forms of analysis that you have applied. That is thematic or comparative analysis, and so on. This chapter will typically be moderate to large in size.

Discussion   for empirical research, a discussion section is not compulsory yet it may help to unpack and better explore certain pertinent themes that have emerged from the research. This may include points that are especially important to social work practice. This chapter will usually be brief and succinct.

Conclusions and Recommendations   again, this chapter will bring together and summarise your findings. You should be able to draw from your research and make clear statements regarding what you have learnt and also how this might influence future policy and practice. This chapter will usually be brief and succinct (Carey, 2009).

Dissemination and writing for publication

Dissemination represents the distribution or 'spreading out' of research findings. Regarding official research, this may be a duty as part of a contract but for others, such as feminist researchers and theorists, dissemination remains a crucial stage of the research process because it helps to draw attention to social injustice or forms of disadvantage. We could, of course, make similar arguments about the role of the social worker, that we have an ethical duty to disseminate our research findings, including through better practices or values.

Dissemination helps to draw attention to our work and may also influence our practice or the lives of other people that we come into regular contact with, including service users or colleagues. Dissemination may take many forms, that include:

- Simply handing in your dissertation to be marked!
- Allowing friends or colleagues to read it.
- Making our research available such as in a library or on the internet.
- Allowing research findings to directly influence our beliefs and those of other people.
- Allowing findings to influence our social work practice.

- The discussion of research findings with social work colleagues or service users and carers.
- Writing an article for a social work magazine or an academic journal.
- Presenting an oral paper at a conference.
- Integrating any findings in future research, such as for an MPhil or PhD.

Matthews and Ross (2010: 473–4) suggest that there are two main stages to dissemination, which include:

- *Deciding on an audience for your work*. This may include through the media (radio, television, newspapers, etc.), the internet (blog, wikipedia, voluntary sector site, etc.), through a poster or report. It may also include a presentation at a conference or as part of a seminar or group meeting. We can also include the general public, policy-makers, a manager or boss and peers, colleagues, carers and service users.
- *How and where to publish*. This includes the obvious examples, such as books, journals, magazines such as *Community Care*, or through the internet.

The authors add that an important component of dissemination remains indicating if more future research is required on the topic and why. Dissemination may also help us to bridge the gap between theory and practice and allow us to communicate with policy-makers, practitioners and other policy researchers. Dissemination can begin early, such as within a practice placement or by discussing aspects of any research with friends or in a seminar, and so on. Of course, dissemination may have an impact many years after a dissertation module or course has ended, and can prove to be the most tangible and lasting component of a social work dissertation, report or publication within a suitable journal, etc.

There may be an opportunity to write up your findings for publication. The best place to present your work for publication remains academic journals, of which there are now many different types, including some which are solely online. Many of the best journals for social work and related disciplines are cited in chapter four (table 4.2). Each journal tends to have its own objectives and will tend to reflect particular disciplines. However, if you are preparing a manuscript for submission, most tend to be between the 4,000–7,000 word length so clarity and focus in your writing style remains a priority. Try to plan your ideas as clearly as possible and avoid being too ambitious. Ask yourself, is there something different you have to say and detail which has not been discussed before? This is what most editors of journals tend to be looking for, and they are usually happy to answer questions from budding authors via email or over the telephone. Next, have a look at previous articles that have been published in your journal of choice, and consider carefully the styles of writings, referencing and the structure of a few. Most articles have a similar structure which includes an:

Abstract: summarising the objectives, findings and conclusions of the paper.

Introduction: Giving a pithy insight into any background information and previous research, also clarifying the topic and what is achieved within the paper.

Methodology: briefly clarifying how the research was undertaken, what the objectives were and methods used, and how the data was analysed.

Findings: the crux of any article, which presents the key findings along with analysis, usually including critical reference to other people's findings.

Conclusion or discussion: a summary of the findings, often within social work or social policy, with recommendations for policy or practice.

Ideas for an article can emerge during your data collection or reading or whilst you write or present your findings at a conference. Ask yourself if there is something that has not been said before or which you have discovered and that is not as yet realised by the academic community. Or do your findings contrast with other people's research? Alternatively, your findings may add some flesh to already-established theoretical bones or bring in a new perspective, such as regarding the ethics of research or the politics of social work practice. Material that links to and which may influence policy or practice is especially popular with journals and audiences within social work. Ask yourself if there is something you have detailed and analysed which would interest your social work colleagues or influence provisions of need for service users?

You can, of course, just try to edit your report or final dissertation and structure it more like a paper. A more common approach, however, is to pick out one or two key themes from your research findings and then build them up into a paper by adding theory or a wider discussion. Generally, less is more with a journal article and if you have more to say then other articles can proceed over time.

Try to show another person your final paper before sending it off to the journal – a service user, friend, relative or colleague perhaps – for feedback.

This will help ensure that your ideas are clearly written, focused and understood by your critical friend. You may have a writing partner in mind who has already published. Finally, don't be upset if your work is rejected or requires revision, this is the most common response and typically comes with positive suggestions for revision. It is important to follow any such advice as it nearly always improves the quality of the final work.

What becomes of research findings after a report is completed or a dissertation is submitted is typically at the discretion of each student. As critical and especially feminist researchers have stressed, dissemination can also be a way of raising consciousness and awareness in readers, audience members, service users, practitioners and even members of the general public. This includes regarding issues or topics for which there is currently little available information for practitioners to draw from, or for which there is only one or two, possibly politically biased, perspectives. Therefore, there also remain potential ethical or political benefits attached to the process of dissemination, including its capacity to confront discrimination or support service users through increased knowledge and understanding, including ways to question established, conservative or normative values and behaviour.

Further reading

Becker, H.S. (1986). *Writing for Social Scientists: How to Start and Finish Your Thesis Book or Article.* Chicago, Chicago University Press

Blaxter, L., Hughes, C., Tight, M. (2006). *How to Research.* Berkshire, Open University Press. Chapter 8: Writing Up

Marvasti, A.B. (2004). *Qualitative Research in Sociology.* London, Sage. Chapter 6 – Writing

Padgett, D.K. (2008). *Qualitative Methods in Social Work Research – Challenges and Rewards,* 2nd edn. London, Sage. Chapter 9: Telling the Story: Writing Up the Qualitative Story

Royse, D. (1991). *Research Methods in Social Work.* Chicago, Nelson-Hall Publishers. Chapter 13: Writing Research Reports and Journal Articles

Glossary

Action research: approach in which the researcher and participant(s) collaborate in defining research objectives and any diagnosis and seek to solve subsequent problems through collaborative research, sometimes with a political purpose

Analysis: the interpretation of research findings which aims to achieving better understanding of a problem, often with the use of theory and comparison. Fundamental to qualitative social work research

Anonymity: when the participant's identity is deliberately unknown for ethical purpose

Auto-ethnography: an approach to research strongly influenced by feminism and postmodern theory in which the researcher critically draws from their own attitudes, experiences and subjective reflexive changes whilst studying participants in the field

Case study: research design which encourages the detailed exploration of a single case, such as a person's identity or experience, organisation, support service, and so on

Comparative analysis: research design which compares attributes relating to two or more cases to better understand each

Confidentiality: precautions taken to protect the identity of research participants for ethical purpose.

Constructivism: influential philosophical school that stresses how human culture and practices construct 'reality' for people. Often compared to realism

Content analysis: systematic approach to the understanding of research findings that involves the search for patterns and trends through the use of codes

Convenience sample: type of sampling which is built around research participants that are known to the researcher or who are easily accessible. Widely used in qualitative research but not reliable for generalisation

Critical realism: philosophy which assumes that the study of society should be based upon exploring the structures which generate the social world. Can look to challenge such structures through research and accepts, unlike positivism, that social structures are not always accurately evaluated by the senses

Critical theory: an approach which looks to question 'normal' practices and tradition and draws attention to disadvantage whilst seeking to promote social justice. Such diverse theories are strongly influenced by feminism, Marxism and to some extent postmodernism

Data: the building block of all research, which is categorised by information which can be measured, notably words. Data is used to answer a research question

Data reduction: to reduce data into manageable portions, a process followed during analysis

Deductive reasoning: the movement from theory to observation and from the more general to the more specific. Utilised within quantitative research and contrary to inductive reasoning

Discourse: how we organise and understand the world, especially through language and traditions that are often imposed, such as within institutional practices and ideological beliefs

Discourse analysis: the critical study of discourse, especially with a view to unearthing rhetoric and the partisan interests of powerful groups

Ethnography: one of the oldest and most profound research methodologies, which entails living among and studying people and their cultures from their perspective. A core of anthropology, yet now adapted by different disciplines

Epistemology: a theory of knowledge within qualitative research, represented by realism, positivism, interpretivism and critical approaches

Feminism: influential theory or movement within qualitative research that seeks to draw attention to the disadvantages experienced by women as well as the exploitation of research 'subjects' within the established traditions of 'scientific' research

Field: the main place of study for the researcher, such as an office or wider community

Focus group: a group interview comprising a collection of research participants often unknown to one another. Typically, members are brought together by the researcher into a small group to discuss topic(s) of mutual relevance or interest

Grounded theory: a research approach that aims to build theory from data by maintaining a close link between the two. A sample is built until 'saturation' point, when findings begin to repeat

Hypothesis: an educated guess or statement that is subsequently tested by the researcher. Rejected, accepted or revised following data collection and analysis

Inductive reasoning: the movement from observation to theory and specific findings to generalisation. Common within qualitative research and contrary to deductive reasoning

Interpretivism: a theory commonly used in qualitative research that seeks to discover participants' understanding and meaning of their subjective experiences

Interview: the collection of information by asking questions of participants face to face or over the telephone or internet. The most popular qualitative research method

Informed consent: verbal or written description which informs participants about the purpose of a research project and its potential benefits or risks

Methodology: the orientation and philosophy of how a research project is organised and applied

Methods: techniques and skills used to undertake research

Narrative analysis: an approach to research that carefully explores the use of language by participants, especially when recollecting their life experience

Narrative review: a traditional survey of literature 'by hand' that does not claim to be precise or scientific

Participation: varying degrees of direct involvement by research participants in a research project

Population: the total group or collection of people from which a sample is drawn

Positivism: a theory which advocates the application of natural scientific methods to the study of people and social reality

Post-modernism: a theory which questions 'grand' theories such as Marxism and instead stresses the importance of difference and change whilst questioning single interpretations of 'truth' or events

Praxis: the link between theory and practice, or in social work how our research findings link directly to practice. Positivism, for example, is more likely to separate theory from practice

Purposive sampling: participants are chosen because of their relevance to the study. This will encourage relevant rather than reliable results

Quantitative research: a culture of research which emphasises data collection, measurement and the use of statistics to generalise and predict

Qualitative research: a culture of research that privileges meaning and understanding rather than a search for truth or generalisation. This approach also relies upon observation or the use of spoken and written words by participants, with whom a closer relationship is often forged

Realism: a commonsense philosophy which assumes that there is a reality independent of our senses and one that the researcher can account for

Reflexivity: popular within feminist and critical research, an approach that promotes the researcher being reflective about their possible prejudices and changing values and norms as a project progresses. We may also consider the implications of our findings upon participants

Reliability: the extent to which our research findings can be replicated by others and over time, not always the priority of much qualitative research

Rigour: the extent to which our research is thorough and meticulous in its organisation and application. Not always a priority for some qualitative research but certainly a sustained objective

Sample: a segment of a larger population which is the priority of the researcher

Snowball sample: a non-representative sample which gradually grows around a small group of initial participants sometimes known to the researcher

Social work: the assessment and support of vulnerable people in need, including children and adults, which may also involve subtle or more direct forms of social control. Despite deskilling it is increasingly identified as a formal professional activity complete with relevant training and qualifications

Semi-Structured interview: the most common form of interview in qualitative research which includes pre-planned questions for participants to answer alongside the spontaneous

Structured interview: a research method which involves the formal asking of pre-planned questions by the researcher of participants

Systematic review: a scientific approach to any search for literature linked to a research topic which is influenced by evidenced-based practice

Theoretical sampling: an initial sample is selected and grows on the basis of its capacity to support the development of theory. Part of grounded theory in which the sample size is checked once our data repeats and we reach 'saturation point'

Unstructured interview: questions for participants in which there is no or limited set questions yet some planning is normal. Popular in narrative research including life histories and also part of biographical methodology

Validity: whether what we are measuring is what we think we are measuring

Variables: attributes of participants that can be measured and may change throughout a study, such as attitudes, behaviour, beliefs, experiences, and so forth.

References

Alston, M., and Bowles, W. (1998). *Research for Social Workers: An Introduction to Methods*. Australia, Allen and Unwin

Alvesson, M., and Skoldberg, K. (2000). *Reflexive Methodology*. London, Sage

Alvesson, M. (2002). *Postmodernism and Social Research*. Buckingham, Open University Press

Andrews, M., Day Sclater, S., Squire, C., and Tamboukou, M. (2004). 'Narrative Research'. in Seale, C., Gobo, G., Gubrium, J., and Silverman, D. (eds). *Qualitative Research Practice*. Sage, London

Aronson, J. (1994). 'A Pragmatic View of Thematic Analysis'. *The Qualitative Report* 2 (1): 1–3

Aveyard, H. (2010). *Doing a Literature Review in Health and Social Care*, 2nd edn. Maidenhead, Open University Press

Banks, S. (1997). 'Professional Ethics in Social Work – What Future?'. *British Journal of Social Work* 28(2): 213–31

Banks, S. (2002). *Ethics and Values in Social Work*, 2nd edn. Basingstoke, Macmillan

Barbour, R.S., and Kitzinger, J. (eds) (1999). *Developing Focus Group Research: Politics, Theory and Practice*. London, Sage

Becker, H.S. (1986). *Writing for Social Scientists: How to Start and Finish Your Thesis Book or Article*. Chicago, Chicago University Press

Bell, J. (1987). *Doing Your Research Project*.Milton Keynes, Open University Press

Blaxter, L., Hughes, C., Tight, M. (2006). *How to Research*. Berkshire, Open University Press

Bloor, M. (1978). 'On the analysis of observational data: a discussion of the worth and uses of induction techniques and respondent validation'. *Sociology* 12(3): 545–52

Braye, S. (2000). 'Participation and Involvement in Social Care: An Overview', in Kemshall, H., and Littlechild, R. (eds). *User Involvement and Participation in Social Care: Research Informing Practice*. London, Jessica Kingsley

Brewer, J. (2000). *Ethnography*. Open University Press, Buckingham

Brewer, J. (ed.) (2003). *The A to Z of Social Research*. London, Sage

Bromley, D.B. (1986). *The case-study method in psychology and related disciplines*. Chichester: John Wiley & Sons

Bryman, A. (2004). *Social Research Methods*. Oxford University Press: Oxford

Butler, I. (2002). 'A Code of Ethics for Social Work and Social Care Research'. *British Journal of Social Work* 32: 239–48

Cancian, F.M. (1993). 'Conflicts between Activist Research and Academic Success: Participatory Research and Alternative Strategies'. *The American Sociologist* 81: 92–106

Carey, M. (2006). 'Selling Social Work by the Pound? The Pros and Cons of Agency Social Work'. *Practice* 18(1): 3–15

Carey, M. (2008). 'What Difference Does it Make? Contrast, Convergence and the Privatisation of State Social Work in England and Canada'. *International Social Work* 51(1): 83–94

Carey, M. (2009). *The Social Work Dissertation: Using Small-Scale Qualitative* Methodology. Berkshire, Open University Press

Carey, M. (2010). 'Should I Stay or Should I Go? Practical, Ethical and Political Challenges to "Service User" Participation within Social Work Research'. *Qualitative Social Work.* OnlineFirst: June 7th

Carr, E.S. (2010). 'Qualifying the Qualitative Social Work Interview: A Linguistic Anthropological Approach'. *Qualitative Social Work* 10(1) 123–43

Clifford, D. (1994). 'Critical Life Histories: Key Anti-Oppressive Research Methods and Processes', in Humphries, B., and Truman, C. (eds), *Rethinking Social Research: Anti-Discriminatory Approaches in Research Methodology,* Aldershot, Avebury

Coffey, A. (1999). *The Ethnographic Self – Fieldwork and the Representation of Data.* London, Sage

Cohen, L., Manion, L., and Morrison, K. (2007). *Research Methods in Education,* 6th edn. London, Routledge

Colaizzi, P.F. (1978). 'Psychological Research as the Phenomenologist Views it', in *Existential Phenomenological Alternatives for Psychology,* Valle, R.S., and King, M. (eds). Oxford University Press, New York

Corby, B. (2006). *Applying Research in Social Work Practice.* Maidenhead, Open University Press

Coulon, A. (1995). *Ethnomethodology.* Sage, London

Crossley, N. (2005). *Key Concepts in Critical Social Theory.* London, Sage

Crotty, M. (1998). *The Foundations of Social Research.* Sage, London

Crowe, T.V. (2003). 'Using Focus Groups to create Culturally Appropriate HIV Prevention Material for the Deaf Community'. *Qualitative Social Work* 2(3): 289–308

Daly, M. (2003). 'Methodology', in Miller, R.L., and Brewer, J.D. (eds), *The A-Z of Social Research.* Sage, London

Darlington, Y., and Scott, D. (2002). *Qualitative Research in Practice: Stories from the Field.* Open University Press, Maidenhead

Davies, C.A. (1999). *Reflexive Ethnography.* London, Routledge

Dawson, C. (2007). *A Practical Guide to Research Methods,* 3rd edn. Oxford, How To Books Limited

D'Cruz, H., and Jones, M. (2004). *Social Work Research: Ethical and Political Contexts.* London, Sage

Denscombe, M. (2007). *The Good Research Guide For Small Scale Research Projects*, 3rd edn. Maidenhead, Open University Press

Denzin, N.K. (1970). *The Research Act – A Theoretical Introduction to Sociological Methods*. Chicago, Aldine Publishing Company

Denzin, N. (2000). Aesthetics and Qualitative inquiry. *Qualitative Inquiry* 6(2), 256–65

Dey, I. (1998). *Grounding Grounded Theory: Guidelines for Qualitative Inquiry*. San Diego, Academic Press

Dillman, D.A. (1999). *Mail and Internet Surveys: The tailored design method*, 2nd edn. New York: John Wiley & Sons

Dominelli, L (2002). *Feminist Social Work Theory and Practice*. Palgrave, Basingstoke

Dominelli, L. (2004). *Social Work – Theory and Practice for a Changing Profession*. Cambridge, Polity

Dominelli, L. (2005). 'Social Work Research: Contested Knowledge for Practice', in Adams, R., Dominelli, L., and Payne, M. (eds), *Social Work Futures*. Basingstoke, Palgrave Macmillan

Douglas, J.D. (1976). *Investigative Social Research: Individual and Team Field Research*. Beverly Hills, California, Sage

Douglas, J.D. (1984). 'Introduction', in Douglas, J.D. (ed.), *The Sociology of Deviance*. London, Allyn and Bacon.

Dixon-Woods M., Bonas S., Booth A., Jones D.R., Miller T., Shaw RL., Smith J., Sutton A., Young B. (2006). 'How can systematic reviews incorporate qualitative research? A critical perspective'. *Qualitative Research* 6: 27–44

Elliott, J. (2005). *Using Narrative in Social Research*. Sage, London

Ellis, Carolyn. (2004). *The Ethnographic I: A methodological novel about autoethnography*. Walnut Creek: AltaMira Press

Emerson, R.M., Fretz, R.L., Shaw, L.L. (1995). *Writing Ethnographic Fieldnotes*. Chicago, University of Chicago Press

Fairclough, N. (2001). 'The Discourse of New Labour: Critical Discourse Analysis', in Wetherall, M., Taylor, S., Yates, S.J. (eds), *Discourse Theory and Practice: a Reader*. London, Sage

Fairclough, N. (1995). *Critical Discourse Analysis*. Longman

Fairclough, N. (2003). *Analysing Discourse: Textual Analysis for Social Research*. Oxford, Routledge

Fetterman, D, M. (1998). *Ethnography – Step by Step*. London, Sage

Fink, A. (2005). *Conducting Research Literature Reviews – From the Internet to Paper*. London, Sage

Floersch, J., Longhofer, J.L., Kranke, D., and Townsend, L. (2010). 'Integrating Thematic, Grounded Theory and Narrative Analysis: A Case Study of Adolescent Psychotropic Treatment'. *Qualitative Social Work* 9(3): 407–25

Foster, V.L. (2007). *Painting a Picture of Sure Start Parr: Exploring Participatory Arts-based Research with Working Class Women,* unpublished PhD thesis, University of Liverpool

Fraser, H. (2004), 'Doing Narrative Research: Analysing Personal Stories Line by Line'. *Qualitative Social Work* 4 (4): 179–201

Gaiser, T.J., and Schreiner, A.E. (2009). *A Guide to Conducting On-Line Research.* London, Sage

Gibson (2003). 'Grounded theory', in Miller, R.L., and Brewer, J.D., *The A to Z of Social Research.* London, Sage

Giele, J.Z., and Elder, G.H. (eds) (1998). *Methods of Life Course Research: Qualitative and Quantitative Approaches.* London, Sage

Gilgun, J.F. (1994). 'Hand into Glove: The Grounded Theory Approach and Social Work Practice Research', in Sherman, E., and Reid, W.J. (eds), *Qualitative Research in Social Work.* New York, Columbia University Press

Gillham, B. (2005). *Research Interviewing – the Range of Techniques.* Berkshire, Open University Press

Glaser, B., and Strauss, A. (1967). *The Discovery of Grounded Theory.* Chicago, Aldine

Gomm, R. (2003). *Social Research Methodology – A Critical Introduction.* New York, Palgrave Macmillan

Gomm, R., Hammersley, M., and Foster, P. (eds) (2000). *Case Study Method.* London, Sage

Greene, J., and Browne, J. (2005). 'Framing a Research Question', in *Principles of Social Research.* Berkshire, Open University Press

Grundy, S. (1990). 'Three Modes of Action Research', in Kemmis, S., and McTaggart, R. (eds), *The Action Research Reader,* 3rd edn. Victoria, Australia, Deakin University Press

Hall, C., and White, S. (2004). 'Editorial – Looking inside Professional Practice: Discourse, Narrative and Ethnographic Approaches to Social Work and Counselling'. *Qualitative Social Work* 4 (4): 379–90

Hall, D., and Hall, I. (1996). *Practical Social Research – Project Work in the Community.*Basingstoke, Macmillan

Hammersley, M., and Atkinson, P. (1995). *Ethnography – Principles in Practice.* London, Routledge

Hardwick, L., and Worsley, A. (2011). *Doing Social Work Research.* London, Sage

Harlow, E. (2005). 'Eliciting Narratives of Teenage Pregnancy in the UK'. *Qualitative Social Work* 8(2): 211–28

Hart, C. (2001). *Doing a literature search – A comprehensive guide.* London, Sage

Harvey, L. (1990). *Critical Social Research.* London, Unwin Hyman

Hek, G., and Moule, P. (2006). *Making Sense of Research: An introduction for Health and Social Care Practitioners.* London, Sage

Hekman, S. (1997). 'Truth and Method: feminist standpoint theory revisited'. *Signs* 22(21): 341–65

Helavirta, S. (2011). Home, Children and Moral Standpoints: A Case Study of Child Clients of Child Welfare .*Qualitative Social Work,* published online: 21 June

Hewson, C., Yule, P., Laurent, D., and Vogel, C. (2003). *Internet Research Methods: A Practical Guide for the Social and Behavioural Sciences.* London, Sage

Hine, C. (2005). *Virtual Methods: Issues in Social Research on the Internet.* London, Berg

Hitchcock, G., and Hughes, D. (1989). *Research and The Teacher.* London, Routledge

Hochschild, A. (1983). *The Managed Heart: Commercialisation of Human Feeling.* London, University of California Press

Holloway, I. (1997). *Basic Concepts for Qualitative Research.*Oxford, Blackwell Science

Holloway, W., and Jefferson, J. (2000). *Doing Qualitative Research Differently – Free Association, Narrative and the Interview Method.* London, Sage

Holloway, W., and Todres, L. (2003). 'The Status of Method: Flexibility, Consistency and Coherence'. *Qualitative Research* 3: 345–57

Holstein, J.A., and Gubrium, J.F. (1997). *The Active Interview.* London, Sage

Homan, R. (1991). *The Ethics of Social Research.* Harlow, Longmans

Humphries, B. (2007). 'Research mindedness', in Lymbery, M. and Postle, K. (eds), *Social Work: a Companion for Learning.* London, Sage.

Humphries, B. (2008), *Social Work Research for Social Justice.* Basingstoke, Palgrave Macmillan

Jones, C. (1983). *State Social Work and the Working Class.* Basingstoke, Macmillan

Jones, C. (2001). 'Voices from the Front-Line: State Social Workers and New Labour'. *British Journal of Social Work* 31: 547–62

Jones, P. (1993). *Studying Society – Sociological Theories and Research Practices.* London, HarperCollins

Jones, S. (1999). Doing Internet Research: Critical Issues and Methods for Examining the Net. London, Sage

Jones, S. (2009). *Critical Learning for Social Work.* Exeter, Learning Matters

Jupp, V. (1996). 'Documents and Critical Research', in Sapsford, R., and Jupp, V. (eds), *Data Collection and Analysis.* London, Sage

Jupp, V. (2006). *The Sage Dictionary of Social Research Methods.* London, Sage

Kemshall, H., and Littlechild, R. (eds) (2000). *User Involvement and Participation in Social Care: Research Informing Practice.* London, Jessica Kingsley

Krueger, R.A., and Casey, M.A. (2000). *Focus Groups: A Practical Guide for Applied Research.* London, Sage

Kumar, R. (1996). *Research Methodology: A Step-by-Step Guide for Beginners.* Melbourne, Longman

La Fontaine, J. (1985). *What is Social Anthropology?* Arnold, London

Lather, P. (1986). 'Issues of Validity in Openly Ideological Research: Between a Rock and a Soft Place'. *Interchange* 17(4): 63–84

Leach, E. (1982). *Social Anthropology* .Glasgow, Collins

Leamy, M., and Clough, R. (2006). 'How Older People Became Researchers: Training, Guidance and Practice in Action'. York, Joseph Rowntree Foundation

LeBesco, K. (2004) 'Managing Visibility, Intimacy, and Focus in Online Critical Ethnography', in Shing-Ling, S.C., and Hall, G.J. (eds) (2004), *Online Social Research – Methods, Issues and Ethics.* Oxford, Peter Lang

Levin, P. (2005). *Excellent Dissertations!* Maidenhead, Open University Press

Levi-Strauss, C. (1966). *The Savage Mind.* London, Weidenfield and Nicolson

Linhorst, D.M. (2002). 'A Review of the Use and Potential of Focus Groups in Social Work Research'. *Qualitative Social Work* 1(2): 208–28

Livingston, E. (1987). *Making Sense of Ethnomethodology.* London, Routledge and Kegan Paul

Macdonald, J. (2003). *Using Systematic Reviews to Improve Social Care,* SCIE Report Number 4. London, Social Care Institute for Excellence

Marvasti, A.B. (2004). *Qualitative Research in Sociology.* London, Sage

Mathews, B., and Ross, E. (2010). *Research Methods: A Practical Guide for the Social Sciences.* Harlow, Pearson

May, T. (ed.) (2002). 'Qualitative Research in Action'. London, Sage

McLaughlin, H. (2006). 'Involving Young Service Users as Co-Researchers: Possibilities, Benefits and Costs'. *British Journal of Social Work* 36(8): 1395–1410

McLaughlin, H. (2007). *Understanding Social Work Research.* London, Sage

McLaughlin, H. (2009). Service User Research in Health and Social Care. London, Sage

McNiff, J. (2000). *Action Research in Organisations.* London, Routledge

Menabney, N. (2003). 'Internet', in Miller, R.L., and Brewer, J.D. (eds). *The A to Z of Social Research.* London, Sage

Miles, M. (1993). 'Towards a Methodology for Feminist Research', in Hammersley, M. (ed.), *Social Research – Philosophy, Politics and Practice.* London, Sage

Miles, M.B., and Huberman, A.M. (1994). *Qualitative Data Analysis.* Thousand Oaks, CA Sage

Millar, R.L. (2000). *Researching Life Stories and Family Histories.* London, Sage

Mishler, E.G. (1986). *Research Interviewing: Context and Narrative.* Cambridge, MA; Harvard University Press

Morgan, D.L. (1997). *Focus Groups as Qualitative Research,* 2nd edn. London, Sage

Nolan, M., Hanson, E., Grant, G., and Keady, J. (eds) (2007). *User Participation in Health and Social Care: Voices, Values and Evaluation.* Maidenhead, Open University Press

O Dochartaigh, N. (2001). *The Internet Research Handbook: An Introductory Guide for the Social Sciences.* London, Sage

Padgett, D.K. (1998). *Qualitative Methods in Social Work Research – Challenges and Rewards.* London, Sage

Padgett, D.K. (2008). *Qualitative Methods in Social Work Research – Challenges and Rewards,* 2nd edn. London, Sage

Payne, G., and Payne, J. (2004), *Key Concepts in Social Research,* London, Sage Publications

Perks, R., and Thompson, A. (eds) (2006). *The Oral History Reader.* Oxford, Routledge

Pieters, H.C., and Dornig, K. (2011). 'Collaboration in Grounded Theory Analysis: Reflections and Practical Suggestions'. *Qualitative Social Work,* published Online 28 November

Pink, S. (2001). *Doing Visual Ethnography – Images, Media and Representation in Research.* Sage, London

Pithouse, A. (1987). Social *Work: The Social Organisation of an Invisible Trade.* Aldershot, Avebury

Plummer, K. (1983). *Documents of Life: An Introduction to the Problems and Literature of a Humanistic Method.* London, Allen and Unwin

Plummer, K. (2001). *Documents of Life: 2 – An Invitation to Critical Humanism.* London, Sage

Porter, S. (2003). 'Critical Theory', in Miller, R.L., and Brewer, J.D., *The A to Z of Social Research.* London, Sage

Punch, K. (2005). *Introduction to Social Research – Quantitative and Qualitative Approaches.*London, Sage

Punch, K. (2006). *Developing Effective Research Proposals,* 2nd edn. London, Sage

Quality Assurance Agency for Higher Education (QAA) (2008). *Subject Benchmark Statement – Social Work,* online at: www.qaa.ac.uk/academicinfrastructure/benchmark/statements/social work 08.asp

Radnor, H. (2002). *Researching Your Professional Practice – Doing Interpretive Research.* Buckingham, Open University Press

Ragin, C.C. (1994). *Constructing Social Research.* California, Pine Forge Press

Ramazanoglu, C., and Holland, J. (2002). *Feminist Methodology: Challenges and Choices.* Sage, London

Rapley, T. (2004). 'Interviews', in Seale, C., Gobo, G., Gubrium, J., and Silverman, D. (eds), *Qualitative Research Practice.* Sage, London

Reason, P., and Bradbury, H. (eds) (2000). *Handbook of Action Research: Participatory Inquiry and Practice.* London, Sage

Reinharz, S. (1983). 'Experiential Analysis: a Contribution to Feminist Research', in Bowles, G., and Klein, R.D. (eds), *Theories of Women's Studies.* London, Routledge and Kegan Paul

Reissman, C.K. (1993). *Narrative Analysis.* Sage, London

Reissman, C.K., and Quinney, L. (2005). 'Narrative in Social Work: A Critical Review'. *Qualitative Social Work* 4(4): 391–412

Roberts, B. (2002). *Biographical Research.* Buckingham, Open University Press

Roberts, B. (2006). *Micro Social Theory*. Basingstoke, Palgrave Macmillan

Robinson, C. (1993). *Real World Research*. Oxford, Blackwell

Robson, C. (1993). *Real World Research: A resource for Social Scientists and Practitioner-Researchers*. Oxford: Blackwell

Rogers, A., Pilgrim, D., and Lacey, R. (1993). *Experiencing Psychiatry: Users' Views of Services* .Basingstoke, Macmillan/Mind

Rosenthal, G. (1993). 'Reconstruction of Life Stories. Principle of Selection in Generating Stories for Narrative Biographical Interviews', in Josselson, R., Lieblich, A. (eds), *The Narrative Study Lives*. London, Newbury Park

Rossiter, A., Prilleltensky, I., and Walsh-Bowers, R. (2000). 'A postmodern perspective on professional ethics', in B. Fawcett, B. Featherstone, J. Fook and A. Rossiter (eds). *Practice and Research in Social Work: postmodern feminist perspectives*. London and New York: Routledge

Royse, D. (1991). *Research Methods in Social Work*. Chicago, Nelson-Hall Publishers

Sarantakos, S. (2005). *Social Research*. Basingstoke, Palgrave Macmillan

Seale, C., Gobo, G., Gubrium, J., and Silverman, D. (2004). 'Inside Qualitative Research', in Seale, C., Gobo, G., Gubrium, J., and Silverman, D. (eds), *Qualitative Research Practice*. Sage, London

Shaw, I., and Gould, N. (2001). *Qualitative Research in Social Work – Introducing Qualitative Methods*. London, Sage

Shaw, V.N. (2005). 'Research with Participants in Problem Experience: Challenges and Strategies'. *Qualitative Health Research* 15(6): 841–54

Skeggs, B. (2001). 'Feminist Ethnography', in Atkinson, P., Coffey, A., Delamont, S., Lofland, J., and Lofland, L. (eds), *Handbook of Ethnography*. Sage, London

Silverman, D. (1993). *Interpreting Qualitative Data*. London, Sage

Smith, J.A., Flowers, P., and Larkin, M. (2009). *Interpretative Phenomenological Analysis*. London, Sage

Social Care Institute for Excellence (2004). *Knowledge Review – Improving the Use of Research in Social Care Practice*. Bristol, Policy Press

Spence, G. (2001). *A Simple Guide to Internet Research*. Harlow, Prentice Hall

Stake, R.E. (1995). *The Art of Case Study Research*. Thousand Oaks, CA, Sage

Stanley, L., and Wise, S. (1983). *Breaking Out: Feminist Consciousness and Feminist Research*. London, Routledge and Kegan Paul

Stanley, L., and Wise, S. (1993). *Breaking Out Again: Feminist Ontology and Epistemology*. London, Routledge

Strauss, A., and Corbin, J. (1990). *Basics of Qualitative Research: Grounded Theory Procedures and Techniques*. Newbury Park, Sage

Stroobants, V. (2005). 'Stories about Learning in Narrative Biographical Research'. *International Journal of Qualitative Studies in Education* 18(1): 47–61

Svensson P.-G. (1995). 'Qualitative methodology in public health research'. *European Journal of Public Health* 5(2): 71–9

Tannsjo, T. (2008). *Understanding Ethics: An Introduction to Moral Theory.* Edinburgh, Edinburgh University Press

Taylor, G. (1989). *The Students Writing Guide for the Arts and Social Sciences.* Cambridge, Cambridge University Press

Taylor, S. (2002). *Ethnographic Research: A Reader.* London, Sage

Tedlock, B. (2000). 'Ethnography and ethnographic representation', in N.K. Denzin and Y.S. Lincoln (eds.),Handbook of qualitative research (2nd edn, pp. 4554–84). Thousand Oaks, CA: Sage

Walk, K (1998). *How to Write a Comparative Analysis.* Harvard University, Writing Centre

Wallace, M., and Wray, A. (2011). *Critical Reading and Writing for Post-Graduates,* 2nd edn. London, Sage

Walliman, N. (2006). *Social Research Methods.* London, Sage

Webb, S. (2001). 'Some Considerations on the Validity of Evidence-based Practice in Social Work'. *British Journal of Social Work* 31: 57–79

Wetherall, M., Taylor, S., and Yates, S.J. (eds) (2001). *Discourse as Data: A Guide for Analysis.* London, Sage

Whitmore, E. (2001). '"People Listened to What We Had to Say": Reflections on an Emancipatory Qualitative Evaluation', in Shaw, I., and Gould, N. (eds), *Qualitative Research in Social Work.* London, Sage

Whittaker, A. (2009). *Research Skills for Social Work.* Exeter, Learning Matters

Williams, F., Popay, J., and Oakley, A. (eds) (1995). *Welfare Research: A Critical Review.* London, UCL Press

Wilson, T.D. (2002). 'Alfred Schutz, phenomenology and research methodology for information behaviour research', paper delivered at *Fourth International Conference on Information Seeking in Context,* Universidade Lusiada, Lisbon, Portugal, September 11 to 13

Wolcott, H.F. (1999). *Ethnography: A Way of Seeing.* London, Sage

Yin, R.K. (1994). *Case Study Research – Design and Methods.* London, Sage

Index

259

life history research 111, 112, 163–8,
        174, 176–7, 160
    case study of 167
    criticisms of 168
Linhorst, D.M. 131
literature-based research 37, 57–60,
        57–60, 143, 198, 219
    structure of reports on 67–8, 238–9
literature review 22–3, 26, 45–54,
        190–91, 198, 225–6, 239–40
    purpose of 45–6
    stages in 46–9
Livingston, E. 75–6

McLaughlin, H. 104, 186–7, 189
magazines, professional 53
Marvasti, A.B. 6, 148–9, 155, 158, 220
Matthews, B. 242
'meaningful statements' drawn from
        research data 221
medical profession 179
methodological pluralism 94
methodology 25–6, 59, 79–80, 83–94,
        238–43, 247
    definition of 83
    as distinct from methods 79, 83, 107
micro-ethnography 154
Miles, M.B. 220
'mixed methodology' research 7, 32, 94,
        139, 148
monographs 53, 60–61

narrative analysis (NA) 173–8, 183–4,
        247
    case study of 177
    criticisms of 177
    rules for 175–6
narrative-based research 111, 164, 168
narrative interviews 84
narrative review 60–61, 247
note-taking
    in ethnographic studies 154–5, 157
    in interviews 117–18

objectives of research see aims and
        objectives
objectivity in research 74–5
O Dochartaigh, N. 198

online interviews 200–202
ontology 78–80
organisation charts 229

Padgett, D.K. 17, 90, 191, 235
participant observation 11, 37
participative research 185–95, 223, 247
    benefits and drawbacks of 187
    ethics of 194–5
Payne, G. and J. 83, 141, 165
peer review 52, 60
phenomenology 76, 85–9
philosophical perspectives on research
        78–80
Pieters, H.C. 140
Pink, S. 151
Pithouse, Andrew 11, 148
Plummer, K. 164–8
populations from which samples are
        taken 38–9, 247
Porter, S. 76
positivism 71–5, 77, 247
post-positivism 72–4
postmodernism 77–8, 152, 168–9, 177,
        178, 247
praxis 91, 247
primary data 37–8, 51, 198
probability sampling 38
probes and prompts in interviews 116
professional practice 179
publication of research reports 242
Punch, K. 128, 142
'pure' research 33, 37
purposive sampling 38–9, 42, 247

qualitative analysis 217–222
    application to social work 219
    processes followed in the course of
        220
    stages in 219–20
qualitative research 247
    benefits from 3
    core skills for 12–13
    distinctiveness of 5–7, 14, 17–18, 23,
        37, 41–2, 84
    examples of 10–11
    reasons for undertaking of 9–10
    into social work 8–9